The 12 Days of Christmas

# The 12 Days of Christmas

*The Outlaw Carol That Wouldn't Die*

HARRY RAND

McFarland & Company, Inc., Publishers
*Jefferson, North Carolina*

LIBRARY OF CONGRESS CATALOGUING-IN-PUBLICATION DATA

Names: Rand, Harry, author.
Title: The 12 days of Christmas : the outlaw carol that wouldn't die / Harry Rand.
Other titles: Twelve days of Christmas
Description: Jefferson, North Carolina : McFarland & Company, Inc., Publishers, 2023. | Includes bibliographical references and index.
Identifiers: LCCN 2022057213 | ISBN 9781476689913 (paperback : acid free paper) ∞
ISBN 9781476647661 (ebook)
Subjects: LCSH: Twelve days of Christmas (English folk song) | Carols, English—History and criticism. | Christmas music—History and criticism. | Yule (Festival)—England—History. | Bawdy songs—England—History and criticism. | BISAC: MUSIC / History & Criticism | RELIGION / Holidays / Christmas & Advent
Classification: LCC ML2881.E5 R25 2023 | DDC 782.42162/2—dc23/eng/20221214
LC record available at https://lccn.loc.gov/2022057213

BRITISH LIBRARY CATALOGUING DATA ARE AVAILABLE

**ISBN (print) 978-1-4766-8991-3**
**ISBN (ebook) 978-1-4766-4766-1**

© 2023 Harry Rand. All rights reserved

*No part of this book may be reproduced or transmitted in any form or by any means, electronic or mechanical, including photocopying or recording, or by any information storage and retrieval system, without permission in writing from the publisher.*

Front cover: Father Christmas with holly crown and wassail bowl, the bowl now being used for the delivery of children's presents, 1879

Printed in the United States of America

*McFarland & Company, Inc., Publishers*
*Box 611, Jefferson, North Carolina 28640*
*www.mcfarlandpub.com*

For Jennifer & Leah

# *Acknowledgments*

For his astounding depth of scholarship and a lasting friendship that tolerated my peppering him with questions, I owe a further debt of gratitude to Prof. Larry Silver.

My family's forbearance: patient resignation observing my solitary hunt proves their steadfast character and independence. They tolerated absences that took me from them for hours and days of curiosity's unslaked eccentricities.

The staff of Washington's Folger Library proved to be of inestimable value. Venturing into the past's foreign ways, they guided me toward noting the obscure usages of antique English, and directed me to obsolete folkways.

As ever, Maurice Varanian's good counsel escorted me out of some difficult straits that only he could pilot. His sometimes-colleague and ever-active humanitarian, Mr. Nikola Zerber once again proved a font of wisdom and knowledge. His association with Harvard University helped. And special thanks to Paula Young Lee.

For that peerless lover of books, who nurtures them to perfection, my thanks to Elizabeth Demers who this time served as a match-maker.

My thanks to Layla Milholen for her superb editorial instincts, her patience, good humor, and professional demeanor. Without her belief in this project and her expert guidance the work would not be.

And, as always, to Jennifer.

# Table of Contents

*Acknowledgments* vi

*Preface* 1

Chapter 1    7
Chapter 2    15
Chapter 3    28
Chapter 4    37
Chapter 5    45
Chapter 6    51
Chapter 7    61
Chapter 8    67
Chapter 9    71
Chapter 10   91
Chapter 11   101
Chapter 12   109
Chapter 13   125
Chapter 14   136
Chapter 15   143
Chapter 16   150
Chapter 17   154
Chapter 18   170
Chapter 19   176

*Chapter Notes* 187

*Works Cited* 217

*Index* 221

# *Preface*

In the whole body of Christmas carols sung in English, among the most famous and beloved is a song universally called *The Twelve Days of Christmas*. Its association with the holiday passes unquestioned. My objective is to fix this well-known song in its proper context. That goal is hampered by its deeply appreciated place that centers a whole cluster of poignant associations. Together those personal memories and family traditions comprise the fondest community-wide recollections of an antique holiday that, as currently celebrated, never was. How modern Christmas supplanted an earlier holiday has been well-surveyed by Stephen Nissenbaum (among others) and I will only report as much of that life-and-death contest as necessary for background. As the hostility's battle lines advanced and retreated the struggle's conditions elucidate the carol.

Undoubtedly, some readers will be displeased to learn that their favorite Christmas carol purveys something other than innocent nonsense. That's one group. Other constituencies nurture different, but equally beloved, concerns. Some considerations pose as scholarly reluctance although, for the most part, such hesitations remain highly personal. Much depends on how much each celebrant and observer invests in Christmas as it is currently celebrated.

Cherished memories are instinctively protected and become intrinsic and vital parts of a personal identity that builds up over years. Those memories are who we are. After all, it's bad enough as a child to find out that there's no Santa Claus, but much worse as an adult to learn that Christmas itself was not always celebrated as it is now—or was not revered at all but was banned by staunch Christians. Clerics in fact tried to murder the holiday, now the year's festive highpoint, and this song with it. Delivering that bulletin convincingly for the general reader poses some real problems, least of all a reluctance to re-think what Christmas must have formerly been.

# Preface

As a purely practical concern, setting out texts and usage that justify this song's re-calibration (or demotion) meant combing through an enormous mountain of material and making selections that may distort the case for some readers. Both staunch religionists and professional scholars personally invest in fixed interpretations of certain texts, hotly defended as settled renditions of meaning. Ignoring those texts as irrelevant to the present case, or explicating them innovatively, either approach will draw the ire of endowed interests. That is the nature of historical model-building: the creation of a constellation of data that will withstand intellectual probing. When we are lucky enough to have a field of surviving historical choices of documentation, information must be selected from an expanse of possibilities. Those selections are then configured to make some sort of sense, an argument, such as this book proposes. The choices of my citations seem not only reasonable but essential; others will undoubtedly find different historical extracts and records of usage that lead in other directions, but the current construction seems to adequately explain the otherwise unexplainable or, more usually, unquestioned.

Some readers will be disturbed to learn that the carol was sung for a celebration utterly unlike the festival we call Christmas—and that past holiday, with several names, hardly resembled the modern version. Dispelling comforts that succor many of us through the year's coldest dark season raises a vexing cultural problem's unavoidable, even if secondary, considerations. Disclosing evidence that appeared in pursuit of a very old song might discomfort some readers, but such irritation was never a goal.

I aimed to de-code archaic slang, which meant discovering its context in a seedy, brutal, and often hungry world. That world was also highly spiritual, with a belief-system whose roots dove deep into documented history and even pre-history. But the song's centuries-old spirituality and prevailing aesthetic is neither currently celebrated nor admired. Those gone values of a former age are not outwardly respected—except by violent sub-cultures or those of coarser sensibilities who allow public admiration of carnal exploits. But that's where the investigation inexorably led. Descending into the cultural equivalent of the unconscious, a sub-culture's sensibility and its often criminal practitioners, hide a truth from public examination and inevitable censure.

*Preface*

Pursuing this elusive suspect entailed a chase backward into the ever-fleeting past, around detours, and through barriers raised to hinder the suspect's recognition. A denizen of an underworld with outlaw associations, this subject disliked the prospect of being found and having its identity brought into the light. Now it wanders abroad in the land. The song's very ubiquity throughout the English-speaking world challenges the question of which citations best represent its authentically.

For generations it had survived by hiding from the authorities. Dragged from concealment, it masqueraded as an innocent, mingling in plain sight amid a guileless crowd of fellow celebrants. To lure it out into the open, this investigation's report had to meet its crafty suspect halfway and entice it into view using its terms of antiquated jargon, but translated into modern and highly offensive speech. Well-begun by Eric Partridge's examination of the seamy side of Shakespeare's wit, this effort needed to be extended to the less-celebrated speakers of his language, and its singers. The author somewhat regrets the unavoidable use of "colorful" language, words that may prove utterly and inexcusably offensive to some readers. But, even with propriety and the reader's sensibilities considered, such language is actually the preferable choice.

Wherever appropriate plain obscenity replaces circumlocutions or medically neutral anatomical terms, because I aim to dispel any ambiguity about our subject and restore some of its authentic off-color verve. And much of that originally slangy doublespeak—donned purposefully as protective camouflage and for fun—was meant to be shared by rollicking fellow conspirators, and not to feed the outside world's dour suspicions. For centuries, proprieties' wary defenders have garrisoned a fortress of righteousness that, if originally justified by the song and its singers' many outrages, has grown utterly illegitimate. That pious holding action has continually lost ground in clashes with psychological reality.

In the early decades of the second millennium, journalism (print and broadcast) prissily describe crimes whose severity the reader cannot guess because the term, "sexual molestation," covers everything from a snide remark, mis-understood or mis-directed gestures, to a brutal rape. Prudery, especially pretended seemliness, ill-serves precision. No such conflicts dogged this song's creators.

The carol's singers were highly specific in their bawdy references, and shameless because they did not address an audience alien to the song's ethos. They sang for their peers, leering, beery, and merry. Only

# Preface

when the song escaped its context, when overheard by unprepared and antagonistic listeners ... then the trouble began.

In its heyday the song, its associated behaviors and performance circumstances, were repugnant to a powerful sliver of society, while the unlettered majority recognized and grinned at the cascade of anatomically correct references. In Shakespeare's day, three-quarters of the English population lived on farms, but industrialization and urbanization breached the bond of singers and their agricultural world's knowledge of animal husbandry. Cities of the long pre-industrial ages were surrounded by and dependent upon nearby farmlands, usually within sight of the city walls; rural life neighbored the urban underworld. The mixture of farming's conservative outlook preserved hints of pagan folkways and impoverished petty criminals, with little to lose, merged into a common interest in the here-and-now of seasonal sensual release. For the rural folk carnality represented the reality of handling animals and recognizing their own, fully human, physical desires as sanctioned by fertility rites, while the urban underclass owned little but their, often visibly decaying, bodies that were the tools of their whoring and pick-pocketing trades. The rest of society abhorred, or pretended to scorn the pleasures that rubes or ruffians sang about when afforded leisure and strong drink.

The familiarity of such naughty terms helps us reach across the centuries to fellow human beings, people whose rough company we might not seek out yet whose humanity undeniably perdures in this song. Like other art, the carol speaks of recognizably human nature. Putting aside real or assumed prudery, we can commune with a bygone time when a slightly different jargon referred to the same terms as modern obscenities, and only by invoking current slang can the zesty verses direct us to a season of hope and satiety.

This whole exercise may seem impious. Current circumstances being particularly tender in the matter of the mid-winter holiday.

In the first decades of the twenty-first century a loathsome cabal of politicians champion resistance to a supposed "war on Christmas." Little do these cynical and opportunistic vote-thieves realize that the war has been going on for centuries. And the aggressors are their constituents who claim to be tradition's defenders. Skirmishes break out here-and-there, erupting in different places over the years but always the most ardent perpetrators fume sanctimonious and anti-sensual.

Today, led by religio-political manipulators, the contingent's ranks

*Preface*

are dominated by loud know-nothing pietists whose intuitions about Christmas rest on mis-information. Not blasphemers or atheists, but religious conservatives began the war on this festival. Their beachhead invaded the ancient holiday, aiming to impose all manner of extraneous chastity while incidentally, as collateral damage, suppressing this bawdy carol. As a result of the song's low-class origins and its powerful censors (grouchy critics infected with the worst of their distorted religion) there are, concomitantly, no illustrated verses of the subjects referred to in the song of the Twelve-Days. At least not associated with the song itself.

The under-classes hired no artists and such smut as may have been scribbled was destroyed by champions of good taste. I include images of Marcantonio Raimondi's illustrations of Aretino's papally-banned erotic poems ... to show that the upper classes knew all about this stuff, that today we would call porn. As usual, the ruling class believes it can handle, without taint or corruption, the same materials that the self-righteous believe will ruin the working classes. Funny how that prejudice endures: that power and wealth, sometimes bedecked with schooling's degrees, inure spectators to the allures (and sometimes real art) of smut.

In short, there are no old illustrations of the carol's lyrics. So, to portray some of this book's points, as much as society will circumstantially allow, other works (some quite old) depict the song's references.

To avert confusion, which I might have inadvertently fostered, Church means the institution in all its forms throughout Christendom, while church refers to a building. One more point. As a matter of personal preference, and somewhat unusually by some editorial lights, song titles are italicized. Commonplace usage packages them between quotation marks. In contrast to song titles, other artworks are routinely italicized, including paintings, operas, sculpture, books, movies, and stage plays. I have taken the opportunity to place songs on a par with other artworks. That parity was recognized when the Swedish Academy awarded Bob Dylan a Nobel Peace Prize in literature. I will do no less for our anonymous songwriters.

# Chapter 1

## Modern London

Fighting the chill I walked briskly up Regent Street, bent into the wind, coat pulled tight against my neck, mostly ignoring the shop windows blurred behind flurrying grey snow. Just ahead, a bus turning left into Oxford Street forced my halt at the corner. Compelled to stand still and look straight ahead, I stared at an otherwise seasonal commonplace: an intentionally charming outdoor performance. On the north side of the street stood a row of carolers, backs against the building, singing energetically and, hackneyed in their cheeriness, actually wearing colorful mufflers. The song, old but newly heard, baffled with lost meaning. If in the past people understood the lyrics, now, centuries later, time had rendered the verses incomprehensible. The crowds of shoppers around me knew the words by heart, as did I, verses familiar to the point of disregard. But in that moment the carolers awakened that rare feeling of novelty when a commonplace experience stands fresh. I had never before really noticed the words' extreme eccentricity.

a partridge in a pear tree
2 turtle doves
3 French hens
4 calling birds
5 golden rings
6 geese a-laying
7 swans a-swimming
8 maids a-milking
9 pipers piping
10 drummers drumming
11 lords a-leaping
12 ladies dancing

## The 12 Days of Christmas

Like you, I'd heard these phrases countless times. They're unavoidable when Christmas carols infest radio broadcasts, crowding out every other kind of music. Most of the year these few and special songs are rarely heard. Otherwise absent and hibernating, they annually wake. This song's odd phrases, verses of fondest nonsense, are carried by an attractive tune, images strung like pearls on an irresistible melody. But I'd never thought about what the words meant.

Among the most popular tunes in the English language, the carol featured on Christmas television specials beamed around the globe. This cheerful song pumped out of my car radio while driving through slush, windshield wipers an eccentric metronome, only sometimes on the beat. Representing an ideal season of the western world, the song, universally known as *The Twelve Days of Christmas*, seems gibberish that somehow attached to Christmas, and singers perform the song's nonsense catalogue—a happy roster that seems harmless enough—with a clear conscience and a sense of tradition.

Throughout the holiday I pondered its meaning, although pondered seems too serious and methodical a process, more like a curious poking at this or that odd feature. Dancing Ladies? Lords leaping? Birds in trees? Did it have to mean anything at all? The irrepressible song describes twelve gifts presented to a "true love." That itself makes the carol's relationship to the holiday puzzling as the "true love" gets equal billing with Christmas. Who was singing? Who was the lover? The quirky gifts seem unrelated to any religious celebration, especially Christmas. Anyway, love exclusively between people ignored the holiday's divine love, yet the song and Christmas seem inseparable. How many bygone lifetimes ago did families hear this song in deep winter when they understood the words? Simple questions beckoned. Finding the answer occupied unraveling many false leads because, like a treasure map's cryptic clues, the meaning seemed purposefully hidden.

Inveterate curiosity's a curse. Sensible people let little oddities slip by, reasonably gambling that life's too short to knock on every door. Unfortunately, I'm not one of them. Once some peculiarity sails into view it's hard to take my eyes or attention away; so the song sent me to

## Chapter 1

the library, that tomb of murmuring voices. Listen hard enough, pore through enough old books and surely the answer would be buried somewhere in this graveyard of ideas and emotions—once urgent, all now dusty with age. The song might float out, ghostly though contumulated with generations of former Yuletide revelers and carolers at their feasts and toasts, sneered at by dour critics of riotous Christmas. The assailants who buried the carol.

January's white sky narrowed to mazy rows of bookshelves as I pored through old volumes looking for explanations hidden in past usage. The song's meaning drifted in the cold outside, its sense unsalvageable from today's carolers because time-and-again their enthusiastic performances unspooled innocent of its message. In mild ignorance, millions of voices around the world energetically chanted its sequence of numbered verses.

Books were, at first, only so helpful, and repeatedly crashing against the past's printed barricades opened only a slim breach in opaque history. Progress in the library dragged on and the old pages resisted yielding up any sense, until—like any magic password's Open Sesame—through a small gap I peered into the lost past. Not that the library effort was wasted, but the key appeared bobbing in the air, like Macbeth's dagger.

## 3700 Miles Away

In the darkened theatre I was enjoying Michael Kahn's direction of the 1613–14 play by John Webster (1580–1634?) *The Duchess of Malfi*. Kelly McGillis starred as the Duchess; the character called Ferdnando, played by Donald Carrier, uttered a line that uncorked the Christmas carol of the 12 Days. Abruptly, as I wasn't expecting it, the impenetrable past opened a panorama of thoroughly un-modern joyful human depravity. The song's invisible meaning stepped into plain sight.

Eleven lords a-leaping refers to sexually mounting. That's how the King James Bible (1611) uses the word, and there's no more decorous source than Holy Scripture. Only a few years after that sacred book appeared, Ferdnando in *The Duchess of Malfi* angrily barks:

FERDNANDO: Till I know who leaps my sister, I'll not stir. (II:5)

## The 12 Days of Christmas

Webster chose an ancient sense of the word which usually refers to the mounting of animals for copulation. Specifically, the male leaps (the female). If a modern author wanted a similarly enraged character to roar he would not politely inquire "I'll not exit until I find out who is having intimate relations with my sibling"; neither would Webster's line translate as "I'm going to stand here until I discover the name of the person engaging in mutually enjoyable intercourse with my sister." Never averse to writing the utmost indelicate vernacular Webster put into the furious brother's snarling mouth a direct and unmistakable obscenity. Ferdinand fumes. Seething, he glares about and (translated in modern English) bluntly screams "I want to know who's fucking my sister!"[1] That's what the carol's Lords are doing.

That seems impossible. How could a Christmas carol include such indecency? Maybe Webster's word-choice represents a fluke. If Webster proved the rare writer who employed the word this way, the citation could be ignored. One off-beat usage doesn't define how people really talked. But Webster was not alone.

Only two years later, Ben Jonson (1572–1637) cites the affront, in his work of 1616, *The Devil Is an Ass*, "could you ha' Beene satisfied with a leape o' your Host's daughter" (III), which became the punchline of every subsequent joke about traveling salesman making a call down on the farm. Jonson reaffirmed Shakespeare's *Henry V*, 1599: "If I could win a lady … by vaulting into my saddle…. I should quickly leap into a wife" (V:2); leap here means to copulate, with the added joke about riding and saddle.[2] And Jasper Mayne's *The Citye Match, a Comœdye*, 1639 records the knee-slapper: "Why what are you? you will not leap me, Sir, Pray know your distance" (II:3).

Shakespeare lived before the fanatical Puritan cleansing that, in a humorless plod, remodeled English society. Repellant to his rambunctious acting company friends, the so-called cleansing proved costly when Puritans repressed theatrical amusements. Not total dolts or pointless kill-joys, the Puritans had their reasons. Rather than pretended refinements, Shakespeare's lusty public obscenity allowed staggering variety of vulgarity to soak common speech and even upper-class entertainments. Today's theatrical productions often suppress or ignore Shakespeare's ribaldry that—if sponsored by Elizabethan nobility and occasionally performed for the crown, with all their original smut—made real money at the box office when played for a ragtag afternoon's outing by law clerks and trolling doxies. Few moderns imagine how

## Chapter 1

lewd were entertainments now considered impeccable. His jokes conspired with an audience that knew his puns and were amused to hear their own off-color speech on the stage. And apparently sang earthy lyrics at Christmas.

Shakespeare's bawdy public and the groundling's tastes sprouted from the same loam as the carol's singers who mingled in the crowd attending his plays. They gathered at mid-winter to sing a song with at least one lusty image that, somehow, has come down to us cleansed of naughty associations.

If the men in this song were leaping, screwing, what were the women doing? Fornication is not performed solo. The carol could have been an all-male jest but it likely would have died out if it failed to entertain everybody.

The song represents an equal opportunity rollick. The cliché has always been that when women lapse into reckless behavior they tend toward sexual license, squandering a good name and reputation by dissipating their chastity—a theme consistent with the rest of the song as its meanings re-emerged. The carol alludes to these lapses with then-current slang, but such cant was not generally recognized in proper society. Hardly coy about its references, polite company renounced such language and therefore, rarely documented, now such slang has totally lapsed. As old as language itself, as a kind of speech parallel to overt meaning, winking at hinted vulgarities wasn't usage just reserved for gutter talk. The luxury of indulging in everyday slang can recede with time, becoming remote, because language has fashions too, and obeys deep and irresistible tides that sweep out old words for new. Criminal cant preferred concealed meanings to hide intentions from eavesdroppers and cops, but so do hifalutin texts indulge their professional jargon, impenetrable to civilians. The tradition is ancient.

The Gospel of "John was written to be obscure, arcane, even offensive. Composed for insiders, it was equally written *against* outsiders.... Crucial to such anti-language is that it makes no sense to the rest of the world."[3] Sometimes called a sociolect, these languages of in-groups are spoken without a grammar and are intended to be unintelligible to outsiders—perhaps like the odd pile-up of phrases sung in the carol of the Twelve Days.

Subcultures—religious, business, scientific, sports, or criminal—

## The 12 Days of Christmas

change their self-identifying vocabulary as descriptive terms evolve and their characteristic phrases, used knowingly like passwords that bestow credibility, allow entrance to a conversation or society. But even non-standard vocabularies change for reasons of style and aptness, as does conventional speech. Slang, such as the carol's apparent payload, evolves adjacent to standard language. A sub-group's word-stock, its vocabulary choices, describe situations and conditions while concealing the group's meaning from others: outsiders to be cheated or suspected and therefore purposefully misled. To be useful to the sub-group, denotation must differ from the normal speech of everyday speakers and clearly in the carol of the Twelve Days now out-dated cant informs the song and its meaning, secreted in slang and jargon of outlandish imagery.

A facade of capricious nonsense (non-denotation) has long obscured this carol's meaning but once noted as antique slang, that veiled mode of expression clarifies the whole.[4] Yet the carol, drenched in formerly-current slang, enjoyed slang's exclusivity, as spoken for and by a sub-group wishing to remain a self-contained social unit. And, in that slang, the song's vernacular quite specifically describes lusty women as eager as the Leaping Lords.

As today, bird imagery (which permeates the song) referred to women, specifically, sexually-available girls, still called "chicks" in America or "birds" in British English. Such allusions confirm how the song contained more than just one out-of-context bit of gendered jargon.

A goose was routinely understood as an Elizabethan prostitute. In *Loves Labors Lost* a nobleman (as debauched as a leaping lord) esteems "A green goose a goddess: pure, pure, idolatry" (IV:3) where, "a green goose seems to be a fresh, young whore."[5] Today the term goose more innocently features in the endearing, "you silly goose" while the verb "to goose" means to poke the buttocks—instances gentle enough for everyday speech. Bygone carol singers who invoked leaping lords intended no such propriety because the word goose formerly steeped in off-color sexual associations.

Goose once meant a venereal disorder in general, syphilis in particular. A swelling of the groin caused by such a disease was called a "Winchester" goose referring to Southwark prostitutes.[6] When this carol was

12

## Chapter 1

young, alluding to a Winchester Goose, or a goose, introduced a wry anti-clerical critique of London's greatest whoremaster, a Bishop of the Roman Catholic Church. He exemplified a queue of splendidly gowned holy Churchmen whose income flowed into heavy wooden coffers overflowing with gold. That money stream near the Thames issued from no

Remains of Winchester Palace, 12th century construction mostly destroyed by fire in 1814. Southwark Borough, London. Sitting atop Roman ruins, the palace served as the city home of the Bishop of Winchester. All that survives of his vast sprawling residence is a single large wall, pierced by the tracery of a now glass-less 13 foot rose window. The wall occupied the western end of a great hall, and this remnant hints at the palace's opulence. The three openings, now floating high on the wall above the excavated street level, are not windows but doors that led to a buttery, pantry, and adjacent kitchen. The palace complex grew to include a brewery, gardens, a court for lawn bowling, tennis court, and its own jail. The jail started as a single cell and over many centuries ballooned into a large prison called the Clink, a term that now colloquially refers to all prisons. Like the rest of the palace, the ruined prison is no more but the palace's skeletal remains rise on Clink Street (photograph by the author).

### The 12 Days of Christmas

pure fountain but from a miserable sewer of whoredom. And the entertainments—of the inns, brothels, gambling dens, theaters, and arenas for the cruel "sports" of bear, bull, or badger baiting—included lewd drinking songs, carols caterwauled at that most ribald mid-winter season. At least one such song survived, face freshly scrubbed and glowing innocently as a robed Christmas chorister.

Why would singers of Christmas carols want to sing a frankly obscene song, or a song with smutty lyrics? The answer depends on understanding what a Christmas carol was for, who sang them, and why. One thing stands clear: the song celebrated a version of Christmas Norman Rockwell never painted.

No song with even one obscene or suggestive lyric would center a family's wholesome holiday amusements. And terms rich with winking double-entendres (or formerly less ambiguous words like "leap") would not be sung with children present. What parent or grand-parent would instruct the kiddies in a dirty joke? If the carolers, or a more pious audience, understood even a single lewd verse's meaning—or granted that even one verse *might* sound lewd to others—the song would be unwelcome at a family-friendly gathering, much less serve as a seasonal religious diversion.

Banished from the home, revelers bellowed the carol in seedier settings, places and company that welcomed the song's catalogued off-color references. That is key. Because if moderns hesitate to concede the song's many indecencies even one smutty verse impugned the whole carol. You can't plant one dirty joke in a song meant to charm Yuletide-gathered generations. This song was never meant for youngsters' ears. But carolers were not family-centered; they merrily invented and enjoyed harshly amusing imagery that suited rough times and lives.

# Chapter 2

## Caroling

First of all: what is a carol? There wouldn't be any carolers without knowing why people were singing these songs in mid-winter. As the linchpin of every murder-mystery: If you know the motive, an action's intent appears. But the incentive for going about caroling has changed considerably.

Carols are songs of religious gladness generally associated with a season. Their year-round vitality dwindled over time as carol singing retreated from all but one phase of the year. Now they are mainly sung at mid-winter and concern Christmas.

In another aberration from past practice, today carols reflect only the most innocently honeyed worldview, a virtuousness that would have astounded early carolers. A roster of today's most popular carols shows them as uniformly dainty, and such purity locates the gap once occupied by the antique carols, the songs extirpated by Puritan purges. In olden days a very wide range of emotions could appear in a carol. Moreover, contrary to popular perception, most currently sung carols are not ancient. The really old carols were swept away in the bowdlerizing of Christmas and, being truly old, *The Twelve Days of Christmas* survives as an anomaly bearing a cargo of anachronistic meanings.

Modern carols filled the breach left by the exit of naughty songs. The words to *It Came Upon a Midnight Clear*, were written in 1849, by Edward Hamilton Sears, a Unitarian minister in Wayland, Massachusetts and in 1850 it was set to music by Richard Storrs Wills, of New York. In 1856, a Unitarian clergyman of Boston, the Rev. John Pierpont, wrote *Jingle Bells* as a secular celebration of the Christmas season. *We Three Kings of Orient Are* was composed around 1857 by John Henry Hopkins, Jr., rector of Christ's Church, Williamsport,

### The 12 Days of Christmas

Pennsylvania. Henry Wadsworth Longfellow (1807–1882) wrote, *I Heard the Bells on Christmas Day,* subsequently set to music. *O Little Town of Bethlehem,* written in 1865 by Phillips Brooks, an Episcopal rector, was set to music three years later by his organist. *Away in a Manger* was first published in 1885.[1] Famously, *Silent Night* was authored within recent history. And that's probably the only modern carol heard more often than the carol of the Twelve Days. Many prize their ability to sing all 12 verses of one nonsensical carol but, aside from the opening lines and chorus, most folks can't sing *Silent Night* all the way through.

America's most popular contribution to caroling was a nineteenth-century composition that revived an old Welsh melody (a drinking song, whose tune was used by Mozart), set to new words as *Deck the Halls*. This song hardly mentions Christmas. It extols the pagan holly and encourages singing or trolling "the ancient Yuletide carol." These references to the Yule and the "gay apparel" indicate the song was composed just before the complete Victorian reinvention of a sanitized Christmas that finally erased the record of early caroling. Caroling's history had been purposefully wiped out and the new carols, not themselves ersatz, were dupes, "useful idiots" or body-snatchers, set to annihilate the old by taking their place.

## Old-Time Caroling

The meaning of the Twelve Days carol, and the subsequent attack on the song's message, gains clarity with distance in time and space. As for so many things: we have to step back to see the whole silhouette, be it a mountain or a love affair.

Back in America the library's lights, suspended a few feet over a heavy oak table, dispensed somebody's idea of ideal brightness, a flat glow without character. The light lacked noticeable color, seasonal associations, or time-of-day. Such smooth illumination's unlikely to foster inspiration as does starlight, fading evening, or even winter's feeble sun. Down the lengthy and almost deserted room, tall windows sieved weary daylight that collapsed exhausted on academic volumes. Despite artificial light's evident failure to mimic the outdoors for inspiration, reading opened mental space that unfolded, reaching back in time, through kingdoms and well past today's ideas of proper conduct. Imagination

## Chapter 2

released backward in time, and across a black wintry ocean to enter surprising yesterdays where carols were risqué music. Astonishment yielded to a strange story.

Far from chaste entertainment enjoyed by the devout, carols were among the most doubtful aspects of the Christmas holiday, itself a frightful festival to pious Christians. And the formerly controversial holiday of Christmas flaunted no aspect more dubious than its carols. Supervised by diligent teachers, today's Christmas pageants with crèches and paper beards resemble nothing that existed in the past. Worse, ignorant of the holiday's lewd promise to earlier celebrants, in broadcasting the carol of the Twelve Days mass media innocently pumps out a cesspit of language, thinking it was always, and traditionally, inoffensive.

The "worst" Christmas carols never changed their offending words, but their offenses were lost and long-forgotten. Christmas carols, originated in pagan round dances, which became popular as occasional entertainments throughout Europe well before 1050. For centuries, authorities of the Catholic Church issued a succession of fiery condemnations and prohibitions against caroling. In London, as elsewhere, from early as the thirteenth century and continuing into the eighteenth, Christmastime saw street hawkers selling sheets of carols to shoppers—tabloid entertainment for the holiday crowds of the growing post–Medieval cities.

## Jailed for Singing Carols

Nourished by worldwide trade, London grew densely populous with the influx of workers who made the English Renaissance bloom its vivid forms.[2] Every sector of society was changed. The relatively quiet and tolerated Medieval community-run brothels transformed; some, infused with outside capital, "privatized," others went public because medieval towns operated brothels as a community service. Whenever the business cycle turns upward public services are privatized and when the economy ails the tide moves in reverse. In the dawn of modern Capitalism bordellos were state-run. By the Renaissance, streetwalkers were controlled by law and propriety, the businesses no longer owned by the citizenry but out-sourced. This raised a question about the flip-side of the business, what to do with violators who were not publicly regulated?

# The 12 Days of Christmas

Jails could not correct strumpets from their trade so a few special hospitals were assigned the job of penitentiaries; these were every bit as effective in their day as modern prisons at curbing drug use or prostitution: Nil. The unfortunates who were caught were, nevertheless, jailed (probably because they or their pimps failed to suitably bribe local authorities or offended, or cheated, the wrong person).

Contemporary annals of the public-to-private conversion prove scarce. The few records from the ministries running the brothel business (as opposed to private bordello records) provide an eye-opening tale: "On 26 February 1575, Jane Robinson was delivered to Bridewell [Hospital] for correction, not only for being 'a common harlot', but also for 'having ribald songs and filthy talk'...which disturbed the peace."[3] That should bring us up abruptly.

Let's consider this woman's legally-sanctioned detention in terms of our carol. A whore was not arrested solely or principally for plying her trade but for singing lewd songs—one of which we may know. Foul-mouthed Jane wasn't alone. Other parishes and shires chronicled similar misdemeanors. They issued reprimands for singing dirty carols while observing the Yule day because singing these lewd songs represented an indictable offense. These "geese" were a-laying, because a "lay" is a song, among other things. Presumably, Jane's incarceration in Bridewell's prison-hospital proved as helpful as similar penitentiary confinements today and, bereft of other remunerative work, she was probably soon back on the street retailing her wares.

The previous year, 1574, the Records of the Aberdeen, Scotland, Kirk Session, notes that "Fourteen women were charged for plaing, dansin and singin off fylthe carrolles on Yeull Day, at evin, and on Sunday, at even thairefter."[4] It couldn't be more plain: the authorities would arrest women for singing carols on Yule/Christmas day, filthy carols.

Four-and-a half hundred years later I strolled up Regent street, also arrested, not by constables but momentarily halted by the sight and sound of earnestly joyful carol singers.

Today's carolers understand not a word of what they were caroling, and if they had they'd have disbanded in shame. But, stopped in my tracks by the time-defying marvel of their singing, a growing inquiry led to the centuries-old incarceration of women for singing carols, very likely including (or especially) the very one I heard. The old-time singers' carols, customarily associated with the season, were not intended to evoke the easy nostalgia of an imagined family-centered Christmas

## Chapter 2

past; instead, they summoned a deep tradition and a worldview unfamiliar to moderns. Invoking good-will toward men, as commonly hoped today, seems the principal goal of modern singers who just enjoy the, gosh, good clean fun of the group activity. As seasonal background music, radio broadcasts of the same songs cheers the air of an office or a street-corner. Today's singers would be abashed to insist their singing argued for lurid personal behavior, or an outlook inflaming social rebellion, or to advertise their sexual availability through suggestive music. And, when I heard the song, as if for the first time, no such associations flooded the corner of Oxford Street as a red bus turned the corner.

Though at first sung about any subject, by the early fourteenth-century carols became popular religious songs. A handful of carol tunes and about 500 texts survive from the Medieval period. Mainly known by scholars, nobody sings these carols on street corners, radio, or television. There's a good reason.

Although some reconstructed performances have been tried, all too little is known of secular, let alone popular, music of the time. Part of this deficiency results from the outlook of the original scribal musicians. They were the first to be trained in the new arcana of notational transcription and, as highly disciplined academic scribes, they consciously avoided off-color stuff. Little survives from a conjectured trove of unsophisticated plebeian music as likely existed, however popular at the time. Concerning "the most famous musical manuscript of the fifteenth century" (a document acquired by the Bodleian Library by 1817, though first noticed in 1895) its cataloguer, David Fallows, remarked that the "most important, of its 245 hitherto unknown works most were secular songs, a genre scarcely found in the early fifteenth-century sources available."[5] The rarity is understandable.

It would be wonderful to discover a wealth of ancient carols because adding their contemporary supporting and explanatory context material could decipher the naughty parts of the *Twelve Days* carol. A sufficient number of surviving carols and ancient songs, ditties, or rowdy puns, would cross-check how questionable vocabulary was used. Unfortunately, few of these old songs outlasted hostile centuries when they were hunted like outlaws, which they were. After all, in 1575 the whore Jane Robinson was jailed for singing her "ribald songs," music that nobody likely wrote down. So, the carol of *The*

# The 12 Days of Christmas

*Twelve Days of Christmas* must suffice to exemplify much destroyed or lost material. It lingers on, the surviving ambassador of a phantom musical race.

The song endures, continuing to serve as those long-gone singers' envoy, a message-in-a-bottle from a world forcefully driven underground by prejudice, a world annihilated in a cultural purge. Because we are dealing with a cultural liquidation as madly fervent as the present era's cultural/ethnic cleansings, few such lively songs outlived their dour persecutors' wrath. The carol of the *Twelve Days* must represent many vanished brethren perished in an annihilation by no foreign invasion: a people wounded itself.

Although we only know Jane Robinson's name, but not the fourteen other women charged for performing filthy Yuletide carols, even on Sunday, we seem to recognize them and hear them. They're tipsy with booze and giddy with their own transgressions against the good folks woken from righteous sleep by hollered lurid songs. There's a bit of revenge in the women's singing—these outcasts from proper society taking musical retribution for their pariah status. In the faint retaliation of the powerless they find themselves out on the street while the offended parties, snug under featherbeds and duvets, may be the very clients the singing ladies so recently serviced.

The last embers of the night's banked fires wink out in cooling bedrooms while, outdoors, the women sing an old song. They're angry at fate that put them on the street, when not in a brothel. They're slightly inebriated, if they can afford the drinks otherwise furnished by their over-charged bordello clients. They're resentful in their sisterhood railed at for a function required by a society that turns against them and their songs. We know these women. We know their male cohorts. We know their humorless antagonists. All parties to the dispute still walk among us, grappling about propriety and seemliness, the haves and have-nots.

Most old carols associated with Christmas; some are Passiontide or Easter carols. Many of the oldest carols refer to the Virgin Mary, the Christ child, or the saints whose feast days follow Christmas. Some songs counsel moral behavior but others are amorous, satirical, sorrowfully repentant, or topical—pretty much the same mix of subjects as in modern folk music. Some carols were rowdy secular songs, and a few

## Chapter 2

astonishingly lewd songs endured long enough to be recorded in the earliest compilations. The idea of lewd carols may seem an oxymoron. But a great inversion turned a world upside-down. Songs caught up in that revolution, the naughtiest became the most beloved, sanitized by their proximity to Christmas. In that turmoil the carol—an activity and a kind of song—changed character.

The medieval English word carol and *carole* (French and Anglo-Norman) refers to a popular dance song with pagan associations definitely not limited to Church-sanctioned celebrations.[6] Pre-Christians relished caroling and Christians continued to enjoy the heathenish dance right into the high noon of Christendom's great spiritual age, the time of the cathedral-builders. Stonemasons carving soaring architectural wonders sang carols with about as much spiritual purity as today's laborers who sing as distraction from drudgery. Perched in lofty spires, beyond earshot of sullen ecclesiastics far below on the ground, stonemasons chipped away to shape fantastic Gothic buildings, their songs timed to their mallets' pounding; the air carried away the words of dirty carols they sang to one another ... when the clergy weren't around inspecting construction progress.

Then, as now, leisure-time entertainment or worksongs on the jobsite lighten grinding labor or boredom. Wherever it occurred—in fields prepared for planting behind stolid teams of huffing oxen, by the forge's wheezing bellows beside the foundry's hammering, carpenters who timed the two-man saw's shuttle, the farriers, or the stonemasons—this entertainment displeased the Church. Less pious workers dredged up fond recollections of good old pagan days. For many families in parts of Northern Europe idolatry was still a recent condition and cherished memory.

Craftsmen and laborers enjoyed singing bawdy carols and on lordly estates each rung on the social ladder sang different phrases to their carols, borrowing other classes' favorites for parody (just as today's pop music grows from deep roots in the underclass). Not only rude laborers sang them winking to each other as they colluded in chanting shared insinuations, carols also accompanied the aristocracy's amusements at court balls when carols were sung as dance songs, only with different words from what the peasants sang. A medieval French poem observes how enviously poor women ogled the aristocracy's extravagant dresses and cautioned the young against emulating the professional prostitutes who attended fancy parties:

## The 12 Days of Christmas

> Girls, when you are doing the *carolle*,
> Dance nicely with the beat,
> For when a girl acts out of measure
> Anyone seeing her thinks her wild.[7]

Do not, in trying to emulate lower class dancers' dirty dancing, stress the back-beat. Cole Porter warned about emotions apt to flare "When they Begin the Beguine" (1935), but "When they Commenced the *Carolle*"(caroling), this irresistible dance incited high emotions and indecent behavior. Not all caroles were family entertainment. Especially if the holiday hijinx involved trolling call-girls brought in to liven up the office Christmas party. By singing and dancing to carols.

In different forms, carols featured in the celebrations of all social classes. Professional musicians sang them at court while commandeered variants of high-class songs were sung in simplified versions for laymen's church-sponsored events. They were roared out in popular festivals, even holidays associated with religious events. The problem being that carols were modified for either Christian or pagan celebration, the latter a distinct problem for clergy who didn't regard the two faith-systems as compatible or interchangeable. The evidence for this was scant, but undeniable.

At the time when carols came into disrepute, a jovial scene depicted in a medieval illumination shows that in an outward show of (feigned) piety nobles did not "join hands in a carole or other dance, which were much disapproved at the time," and another old story recounts "sacrilegious carollers who were doomed to dance for a year after they disturbed a priest, significantly during his performance of a Christmas mass."[8] Times have changed since then. In yesteryear, Carols clashed with the Church.

In olden days carols did not sweetly augment Christmas's religiosity. They challenged the Mass for the celebrants' attentions and loyalty. The singers tempted listeners away from the Mass when caroler's drowned out the sound of the priest's celebration of the eucharist. Village-wide raucous dancing and singing enticed with a rare treat (along with drink and food) while services in the church droned on and attracted only the most fearfully loyal parishioners. Church and caroling competed, as two worldviews. Yet malefactors were not punished with excommunication or lesser religious penitence from within Christendom but, magically, they were fated to dance for a year. Dual forces battled, both magical; one contender represented by the carols

## *Chapter 2*

and the other championed establishment Christianity. No wonder from the Church's perspective singing carols imparted disgrace: they confuted what the Church wanted to instill. It turned out that everything about carols was opposed by clergy, including their performance on Christmas. Odd. For us religious carols inseparably fuse with Christmas, which was not always the case. Separating churched religion from Christmas unties the knot.

Vehemently opposed the popular celebration of the Christmas season it inherited, the Church suppressed every manifestation of pagan caroling and other demonstrations that mingled the old pagan holiday with the Christian. The mid-winter celebration was supposed to belong to the Church, exclusively.

You can't blame the Christian priesthood for trying to extirpate pagan songs and dances that entreated nature, not God, to perform as people bid. The old holiday's accompanying songs recounted heathen celebrations' distinctly carnal pleasures:

> Without acquitting all medieval clergy of narrow-mindedness or hostility to the idea of young people enjoying themselves in their own way, we must yet recognize an aspect of the song-accompanied ring-dance [the carol] ... its supposed association with actual witchcraft. It is not necessary to commit oneself to any particular view of what history records as witchcraft to understand how this association would impair the moral standing of any and all *caroles* in a time and place of concern about witches' activities. It is quite clear that the usual dance of the witches was the *carole*.[9]

The song that accompanied witches who danced the *carole* hailed from society's lowest and least reputable reaches. There humanity's spirit darkened into keeping the company of animals possessed by Satan or spirits sent as his emissaries. Shady and suspect types sullied the carole or, the other way 'round, singing a carol proved one's disreputable character. Today these scary folks at the community's borderlands, if not fashionably labeled Bohemians or the avant-garde, prowl as the "other," distinguished from reputable society. Naturally, for those regarding themselves as adventurous, then as now, the demi-monde summoned alluringly. The dance and the song tempted to dark deeds that awarded shadowy power to the powerless. Always an attraction.

Dangerous behavior may beguile, whether a nightclub-hopper's

## The 12 Days of Christmas

imbibing the underworld's latest drug, drinking questionable alcohol during prohibition, going slumming, reading banned books, or dancing like a witch. Sampling the lower classes' supposedly creepy, but definitely exotic, life colors the singing witches' tunes with risk-taking's unmistakable appeal: misbehavior whose allure remains recognizable across generations and centuries. Fashion operated then as now as dances from the lower classes percolate upward, becoming more respectable as straitlaced society tries the risqué. Examples are everywhere.

Although its origins date to the sixteenth century, the once suggestively racy waltz erupted onto the nineteenth-century scene as the first (initially only marginally acceptable) social dance that allowed couples' full-length touching—no light fingertip proximity. Begun long ago, that evolutionary trend continues to bubble upward from peasant dance to high society. Today, dances and their music born in America's Latino or Black communities gain worldwide acceptance just as earthy caroling began in the social netherworld. Also, street-wise slang drenched in sexual innuendo or gangsta code loses its specificity when pop music circulates to oblivious singers outside the ghetto. Middle-class celebrants rarely ponder the words' original meaning, phrases that accompany dirty dancing; in the past, cultural elevations from the underclasses were equally commonplace. And also tended to stretch the limits of propriety.

Old-time carols could be considerably coarser than anything sung in a Christian religious context or in a proper home setting but, testing our ideas of old time domestic gentility, they were immensely popular. Their original singers would have been astonished to learn that today they seem as wholesome, commendable, and cultured as a waltz.

But something happened, and we do not know what, because at the threshold of the Elizabethan age, around the year 1550, the carol appeared "to have lost its great popularity with some suddenness." At that time musical innovations, mainly European imports, "caused the medieval carole to become the amusement almost entirely of children and rustics. As a consequence the term 'carol' lost its, already weakened, medieval meaning of 'dance-song' and became the vague synonym for 'song in general' which remains in common usage today." A cultural earthquake inverted the carol's function.

The time and place of the carol's identity-loss might be pinned down but, as a result of this upheaval, few today have any inkling of

## Chapter 2

the naughtiness of caroling. After the work of instilling cultural forgetfulness was completed, most people today believe carols are songs of high-minded and purest innocence. The songs have been thoroughly laundered and only by casting back into a gone era can their mischievous vitality be retrieved.

Before the Elizabethan age the carol thrived as a definite form, widely-recognized, and well-understood as a type of musical ring-dance. It named the song with which the dancers supplied their own accompanying vocal music, especially the lusty Christmastide carol. But what next happened to the carol must be seen in context of an epoch driven by its own dynamics, as are all eras.

The first Elizabeth's dazzling reign marked the rise of English Protestantism, and the new religion's triumph correlated with the old song's demotion. Why did one have to die for the other to live? The Roman Catholic hierarchy and the common priesthood were already united in loathing the carol and everything it stood for as "both melody and monstrosity were associated in people's minds and the long tradition that linked music and lubricity."[10] Of all the murderous differences that unsheathed swords between the old and new Christianity, one target held steady; both Catholic clerics and Protestant preachers hated caroling.

When the English church transformed itself the dislike of carols remained as "Protestant reformers ... regarded carols as lingering remnants of Papistry [and] found them no less difficult to put down than had the older Church.... The association, real or feared, of the *carole* and its song with sexual misbehavior appears to have been as strong in the new order of things as in the old."[11] Although English Catholics tried to suppress caroling that the Church regarded as pagan, the song-and-dance nevertheless heartily survived the Church's best efforts (because the verses promised inextinguishable sexual enticements unavailable through the Church).[12] Protestants worked to silence caroling that for them recalled Catholicism.

Granted, carols' erotica was shunned, but if we learn what specific offenses today's archetypical carol gave to devout listeners, the *Twelve Days of Christmas* may preserve otherwise hidden affronts to good taste. One off-color verse and bird-girl suggestions only point the way. After the old Roman Catholic Church ardently tried and evidently failed to extirpate the songs—and caroling staunchly remained much beloved in the hearts of common folk—the reformed churches in their Protestant zeal doubly indicted caroling as filthy heathen songs tainted by Catholicism; if not logical, this proved an effective argument, like accusing Jews of being Capitalists and Communists at the same time. Impossible, but useful in a practical propagandistic way.

Despite the appropriately quaint dusting of seasonal snow swirling around them, the handsomely dressed carolers I'd heard entertaining holiday shopping crowds on Oxford Circus would have been hooted from the street corner if their words were properly understood. And if correctly understood they'd probably slink away rather than be caught singing such smutty words in public. The problem, a gap in the transmitted meaning, evidenced a mass amnesia induced by all the forces of propriety convened.

Modern seemliness mounted its moral edifice atop still-vital Medieval life without the ancient one's permission. The corpse wasn't dead, yet the mourners eagerly tried to bury the protesting culture. Naturally, modernity proved a bad fit for olden ways. However opaque the curtain that Christianity lowered across the stage of folkloric life, gaps peeked through here and there. The veiled usurpation of a still vivacious lord of the winter was aided by forces that used the festive season's distractions like a magician's stealthy misdirects to divert attention from its smut.

# Ordained Amnesia

The carol's origins were successfully eradicated along with a civilization whose memory remained buried for centuries. But who forced its oblivion? Why rob old words of their youthful vigor when they served robustly and faithfully? The story of this cultural murder emerges from the fight for mid-winter's celebration, a festival of the cold season known by many names throughout the world. To re-take that festival a counter-revolution fought back against modern Christmas. Not a nebulous intellectual movement, a *zeitgeist* without a manifesto, the insurgents were real people who risked life, property, reputation, and limbs in their struggle against the Church and Christian propriety. The struggle

*Chapter 2*

knew no surrender but continued, a quiet and little-noticed guerrilla insurrection executed as cleverly as the defiance practiced by any cultural minority. This carol was one of Yule's weapons, a grenade mistaken for a cuckoo's egg (innocent-looking, but lethal) planted among the Christmas goodies.

# Chapter 3

## A Word About Yule

We use the term so casually now that the great mid-winter festival of Yule has lost the deeply religious meaning it held for ancient Germanic peoples. Originally a cold weather pilgrimage festival to pagan temples, at Yule farmers and herdsmen offered sacrifices from their livestock, feasted of their sacrifices, and drank the new ale.[1] They journeyed to sacred sites with sufficient provisions to sustain them throughout the festival—as did pilgrims to Jerusalem for Passover or Mecca for the Haj, although in cash societies money, rather than barter, could tide you over (and like theme parks, towns contested to host pilgrimage sites for their ancillary businesses). The festival named the season: the Yule-tide period between mid–November and early January.

An English Benedictine monk, Bede (672/3–735) observed how the Anglo-Saxon calendar's month *geola* coincided with modern December and January. That is, the "cold season" corresponded to modern words like gelid (even becoming "jelly" via French), meaning icy cold, frigid, as in "congeal" or the slightly related, glacial. While Yuletide is attested from around 1475, the noun yule (or juul), being of pagan usage, came late to written English, being recorded only in 1630 as derived from Latin noun *gelu*, meaning "frost" or "cold."

Usurping then re-shaping what it commandeered, the Church morphed the ancient 12-day festival into "Christmastide" a season (sometimes called Twelvetide) lasting from Christmas, 25 December, until the evening of 5 January. The Christian holiday, that overlay and supposedly eclipsed the Yule, tried to strangle its forebear. But in Nordic countries even the Christianized version of Yule preserves family pagan rituals and practices of the mid-winter holiday. As northern Europeans and speakers of a Germanic language, English still occasionally refers to the mid-winter holiday by its bygone name with bygone customs: the Yule log, toasting the wassail with ale or mulled wine, feasting on meat, etc.[2]

Probably the only reference to the Yule that the average English-speaker still encounters is the Yule Log. Originally the Yule log was lit to relieve the season's cold and to bring light into deepest mid-winter night (a festival of lights akin to Hanukkah or Diwali). This custom dates back to late antique Rome. The pagan metropolis nurtured an enduring love for renewing the sacred calend (New Year's) fires, which were a scandal to Christians. A monk who had served in Exeter and Nursling, St. Boniface knew these customs well, having been born in Friesland (and christened with the good-old Anglo-Saxon name of Wynfrith); he had the attendant customs abolished by Pope Zachary (d. 752). That should have put an end to the Yule log but the Church's invalidation of the old holiday's outward signs availed naught against the public's great affection for the Yule, whose celebration continued, notably in the Yule fires. Only in 1577 the Yule log again became a licit public ceremony in England.

The Yule log enjoyed great popularity especially in Provence, while in Tuscany, Christmas is simply called *ceppo* (block, log). In England, a tenant had the right to feed at his lord's expense as long as a "round" of wood given by him ("a wheel"), would burn; accordingly, attempts have been made to conflate Yule with wheel. Landlords gave tenants a load of wood on the birth of a child; the German Kindsfuß was a present given to children on the birth of a brother or sister. And gifts, their nature and number associated with the Yule, abide at the heart of one carol.

## Sometimes a Cigar Is Not a Cigar

The song's gifts only seem a disconnected jumble, but each contributes some peculiar attribute or quality: not just lords, but leaping lords, not just ladies, but dancing ladies, etc. When superficially considered the preferences that color every listed gift don't seem to point at an underlying or essential purpose. But a pattern emerges on close inspection.

Although each gift carefully qualified its condition by number and modifier, the song's words hint at nothing sensible in aggregate. No true love gives a large potted plant with a singing bird in it, twelve times over; after a few days, seeing another one coming the lover would bar

### The 12 Days of Christmas

the door against such unwelcome deliveries—a nuisance gift dispatched from the florist's hothouse to fill even a large home with a mess of twittering partridges. The song was not literal. Nobody sings about craving more greenery. A pear tree needs watering and pruning. Who would want all these trees and birds? Is the "true love" giving desired, or even desirable, gifts? A house full of lords leaping about, coy maids milking, pipers loudly piping, etc: surely the song cannot list what people actually coveted. The situation seems hopeless if taken literally. Or the pear tree and partridge carry an alternate meaning associated with a true love. The key of insinuation unlocks lost implication.

The carol's primary image required no knowledge of botany and very little about birds. But looking at the song's overall context—within religious, social, and the historical framework—suggests why this chorus repeats an enthusiastic, almost manic, fondness for trees and birds, but we have to understand the whole song to understand the astonishing chorus. If, to modern ears, the lyrics' plain meaning makes no literal sense, the carol's authentic intention rises from playful imagery that functioned on more than one level, all centered around celebrating the Yule.

## Old-Time Christmas

> "the work of the harvest is hard and urgent and there
> is no time for orgies"[3]
>     ... But afterward?

Pious folk in pre-modern times suspected everything associated with the popular celebration of Christmas. Devout Christians dreaded the season—the festival's dubious origins and its deeply pagan celebration. With harvested crops stored and next spring's seeds resting unplanted, when cattle lowed snug in the barn, the mid-winter season afforded a year-end break: the common folk's boisterous Saturnalia.

Named for a Roman god of agriculture (but called by different names in northern Europe) Saturn's festival flourished, the merriest of the year. This multi-day party erupted as wildly as a college student's spring break, but in mid-winter. Saturnalia was celebrated in December when gifts (especially candles, little boxes, and dolls) were exchanged and slaves were treated as their masters' equals.[4] A mock king presided

## Chapter 3

over all this joyful misbehavior as the lord of misrule. And misrule meant up-ended social conventions when the wealthy hosted open houses and cheerful guests wandered into their neighbors,' paying calls and bearing gifts and libations. Food and drink were offered for the poor and a topsy-turvy inversion of rank had to be tolerated ... temporarily. Modern imaginations may fail to conceive the festival's full uproar based on hundreds of years of creative ingenuity invested in devising how to cut-up, unleash disorder, overturn decency, and generally install commotion as the norm. Small wonder pious Christians loathed it, because Saturnalia's customs survived even when the old religion dimmed to a pale memory as spreading Christendom infiltrated north and west.

When the classical world was overrun and Rome's European empire faded in the West, mid-winter's rites remained so beloved that they lived on, and pagan customs were attached to Christmas. Not coincidentally the two holidays fell on the same days of the calendar and were easy to confuse, sometimes purposefully.

The Roman celebrations around 1 January were harshly denounced by the Church-father Tertullian in the third century. In the early fifth century Maximus of Turin added his disapproval—as did other angry Catholics through the middle ages. Nevertheless, the Roman practices they abhorred survived as Christmas gifts, cards, and chests. If those early Christians could only see how ineffective their rebukes were—what a shopping street looks like at holiday time. Against the admonition of the Church Fathers carolers still sing surrounded by a home's stacked holiday presents, or in stores where those gifts are for sale. Since the Church was obviously losing the battle of Christmas shopping, to decrease the offending customs' influence, theologians created an escape clause. Mid-winter gift-giving was retroactively conscripted as honoring the offerings brought by the nativity story's Three Kings (who supposedly arrived on 5 January, the last of Yule's old-time Twelve Days festival), thereby substituting a religious model for feudal aristocracy's Yuletide largesse. This subterfuge fooled nobody.

In a series of take-overs and mergers, by the fourth-century mid-winter solstice celebrations were associated with New Year, then combined with Christmas, which itself combined with the Northern European holiday of Yule. The song of twelve days of gifts partook of a gone world and what now seems like outright nonsense meant something in that mid-winter universe of pagan merriment because, during

## The 12 Days of Christmas

the centuries when Europe underwent Christianizing, many who first sang Christmas carols were born as pagans or their grandparents still fondly revered the old time religion. Perhaps their parents remained avidly heathen. The old ways were affectionately remembered, just as we cherish our childhood's holidays and want to re-create them for our own children.

New Christians missed their pagan calendar mumming when the remarkably lewd *Modranicht*—the "Mother Night"—highlighted mid-winter festivities. Memories of the Celtic goddesses of fertility, called Matres, mingled with Christmas eve. Unsurprisingly when the holidays blended, Modranicht eventually combined fertility rites with Christian observance and the result celebrated virgin birth along with the regular kind. It's easy to see which was the more believable. Also one offered better partying.

As the Celtic Earth-goddess and a lord of the dead, Mother Earth received the dead whom she had nourished with vegetation, symbolized by evergreen shrubs such as the mistletoe. (These evergreens, recycled as Christmas ornament, represent eternal life and their associations evolved to symbolize resurrection-in-the-flesh. She was also worshipped with a sheaf of corn from the last harvest, akin to Ash Wednesday's re-used palms.) Her celebration flaunted all manner of delights. Every one of them irked the Christian clergy.

To no avail in 743 the Church condemned the mid-winter Tabulæ Fortunæ (food and drink offered to obtain increase) but the practice lives on: people still leave cookies and milk, hot cocoa or sandwiches, for a mysterious benefactor, the large elf Santa Claus, even if they have forgotten that the snacks were an investment with precedents in cultic fertility.[5] Tell anybody that on Christmas eve they likely re-enact a vegetable sacrifice for fertility and few would nod approval, but that's the case. Surviving customs, however unconsciously staged, preserve real clues to the twelve-day song's meaning.

Gift-giving—especially from an enigmatic, elfin or saintly, donor—now intrinsically marks the celebration of Christmas. Nothing about the Christian holiday's scriptural origin sponsors a potlatch but the festival's spectral pagan ancestors looked on approvingly as moderns annually re-create the old holiday season's earliest customs. To Romans the Saturnalia was a time of merrymaking and exchange of gifts so, at first, the Church opposed very idea of gift-giving as a hold-over from the pagan holidays that predated Christmas. Mid-winter gift-giving reeked

## Chapter 3

of paganism and the song's "true love" ignored Church preferences by honoring each day of Christmastide with a gift that was definitely not a donation to the parish. And gift-giving wasn't even the worst of it, just a typical part. The Saturnalia's attending Mardi-Gras atmosphere simmered considerably raunchier than anything that goes on publicly in New Orleans. Rio, maybe. What was the old-time holiday like?

Tenth-century English penitentials "prescribe three years' penance for 'anyone on January 1st going about dressed as a stag or a calf, identifying himself with the nature of beasts.'"[6] This street-festival was observed community-wide, gaiety against which sober authority mounted useless opposition to people who identified "with the nature of beasts." Though under severe Church sanction, parishioners still chose to rollick at mid-winter dressed as animals, and behaving as such. Shucking off civilization's restraints allowed for open-air rutting, rough combat, and unrestrained slaking of every appetite. People craved this festival and would not abandon it; centuries later, edicts promulgated in London in 1334 still forbade the wearing of false beards, painting faces, mumming, taking part in plays or interludes, or wearing masks or other disguises during Christmas.[7] Leaving the Middle Ages behind, the old ways continued up to the threshold of the Renaissance and the era when we like to think modernity appeared. But, even then, the Yule's venerable claim to the mid-winter season defied yielding to Christmas; Yule enjoyed primacy in the people's hearts.

The great and ancient festival of Yule, when all work was put aside, lasted from Christmas till the 12th night and all manner of amusements were undertaken in its honor, but today Yule is gone from every calendar. The Church's triumphant imposition of Christmas proved so complete that the vacancy in the yearly cycle passes rarely noticed. Nobody sends Yule cards. There are no Yule specials on radio or television, no CD-compilations of Yule favorites … although some of the songs live on, repackaged. Yule is history. A dead brand name lingers on the shelf with other curious old trademarks. The side-effects of that forced retirement grew apparent in the unintended consequences of incidental cultural sabotage.

Christianity's victory over Yule rendered songs of Yule unintelligible. Yet, Yule endured for its faithful celebrants who partied on, even after the occasion was wiped from the year; songs of the Yuletide festival became nonsense to those not in the know. Over time, most of the Yule's carnival atmosphere was suppressed but a little of it remained in

### The 12 Days of Christmas

circulation, unnoticed—a ticking time bomb of pagan joy in the Christmas season.

Steam rose a lazy trail from a mug of tea. Winter layered me in a beautiful sweater my wife had knit. I sat alone. Books scattered over my desk, others heaped on the floor nearby, open books atop others. From these piles a ghostly picture began to emerge: devout Christians, who in Autumn shuddered contemplating the coming holiday, were neither self-righteous nor sanctimonious hypocrites. Regular pious folk were genuinely fearful of the unbridled ribaldly of Christmas as it was formerly observed and especially as it was celebrated in the song of *The Twelve Days*. Degeneration continued into fairly modern times.

At St. Andrews, Scotland, Archbishop Hamilton railed against "carreling and wanton synging in the kirk, and all uther vice," as recently as 1552.[8] Singing carols, especially in Church, was wicked: how times change. Archbishop Hamilton did not address melodious carolers on a snowy corner cheerfully raising money for charity while entertaining shoppers. Apparently caroling was then utter vice, condemned outright as wickedness. What was vice became virtue.

## Down and Dirty

To gather some sense of who the ancient carolers were and how their favorite song-and-dance was dismissed as a "vice," regard the admonition of the Rev. Henry Bourne of Newcastle, England, who in 1725 specified that caroling was an especially alarming activity since it was "generally done, in the midst of Rioting and Chambering and Wantonness." Let us be clear: "'Chambering' was a common euphemism for fornication."[9] This needs a bit of explanation.

Despite its similar sound and acquired meaning, the "forn" in fornication has nothing to do with the "porn" in pornography (from the Greek *pornos*, whore, and *graphein*, writing, hence writing about prostitutes). The prefix "forn" refers to the mean underground vaulted rooms occupied by the lowest class of Roman whores. Hence the Reverend Bourne fastidiously substituted an English word, chamber, for a late Latin phrase meaning subterranean cells—a replacement only the classically educated would get. The Reverend was riffing on the King James

*Chapter 3*

Version of *Romans* (13:13), "Let us walk honestly, as in the day; not in rioting and drunkenness, not in chambering and wantonness, not in strife and envying." Therefore, into the early eighteenth century, a time more readily imagined than Rome—when America and France were being peopled with newborns who would one day wield muskets in a North American revolution or pull the guillotine's lanyard—even so recently, caroling was deemed obnoxious and associated with whoring. By 1607 the word chambering already meant simply "to indulge in lewdness" and by 1613 of a specifically sexual debauchery. Even stunted imaginations can conjure what the proper musical accompaniment might have been to parties of men going "chambering."

Carols supplied the musical relish then, and today's songs for the same occasion would be equally out-of-place in a church, or around the family's Christmas dinner. Yet, those rascals eternally parked at the far ends of social norms think otherwise: given the chance, deviant characters probe propriety's limits for the pure joy of testing what people will tolerate. Nothing seems more fun than rioting with buddies, drunkenness as a goal, chambering for its obvious pleasures, and wantonness with all the allure of outlaw culture. Unruly when indulging and trying our patience, but to their peers miscreants joyously recount their exploits or, deeply melancholy in drink or the confessional, temporarily repent, until the next opportunity.

Some families endure one relative who tries everyone's tolerance when after one or several drinks too many begins to caterwaul an off-color song such as a gang of drunken buddies sing on the way to a brothel, chambering. If such tipsy relatives represent breaches in modern decorum, try to imagine an entire society composed of people who think it's a good idea to carry on this way and that their favorite songs are carols. Imagine that these bawling drunkards think the very best and most appropriate season for such behavior occurs during the holiday some called Christmas, others Yule.[10] We probably wouldn't like these people. They recall a mass of drunken football hooligans but—not outliers scorned as abhorrent boors, their detestable conduct ignored by average sports fans or policed by authorities—the mob was sanctioned by their community. To the degree that we find such behavior repellant, the enemies of old-style caroling have won.

We—you dear reader and I—have become adversaries of that old ethos. We value personal space (and not having to step around puddles of vomit or avoid random violence). We have built a society that esteems

## The 12 Days of Christmas

decorum and sexual identity undisturbed by unruly violations of person. Yet, these people, from whom I would move away if encountered in a public space, even in a bar, represent this story's heroes as they champion an unbridled, perhaps candid, appraisal of human wants and appetites. They are authentic in a way their adversaries are not.

On one side range the misbehaving louts, albeit sincere and pent-up with a once-a-year chance to expressively liberate their desires, while their opposition implores them to trust an invisible god who wants them to desist in the name of a future personal redemption and resurrection to a spiritual life without either beer, combat, or sex—so unlike some lusty pagan versions of the afterlife. I don't much admire either party in this debate but honest immediacy vests with the carol-singing side.

The song of the twelve days fossilized behavior that's no longer publicly sanctioned, or is squeamishly approved only within limits both geographic (the naughty parts of town) and sequestered to certain times of year, and by certain people, mainly young and hence dismissible. Today, rowdy community-wide gaiety breaks out only occasionally, followed by subsequent hangovers and (feigned or real) regret for sexual infidelities and their consequences. Such jubilant carnivals remain joyous but can become unpredictably nasty, even deadly, as in the past.

# Chapter 4

## A Season of Release

A clear picture of early caroling sweeps away sweet Victorian images—of rosy-cheeked roaming singers gathered beneath the soft flickering glow of gas streetlamps—and replaces such treacle with a decidedly more colorful picture of boisterous crowds of youth "in the midst of Rioting and Chambering," perhaps dressed as animals. Past and present collide in the alcoholic haze wreathing the original *Twelve Days* carol. Disorderly gangs' off-color songs are probably no different today than ages ago; the old carols celebrated the same things as lewd songs nowadays. Those long-gone chants and songs resembled the sound track of sailors' shore leave and such crude vocal entertainments abstained from praising gallantry's manners and tender code of faithfulness. Brothel-visits and drunken clamoring have not changed, probably never will change, and a Yule carol pairing booze and sex exhibits a certain logic.

The reason the perennial duo, sex and drinking, accompanied Christmas was simple: in December "the year's supply of beer or wine was ready to drink. And for farmers this period marked the start of the season of leisure. Little wonder that it was a time of celebratory excess.... Christmas 'misrule' meant that not only hunger but also anger and lust could be expressed in public," fueled by abundant strong drink.[1] Since agriculture's Stone Age the yearly rhythm remained the same: harvest took place in autumn, meat was slaughtered and began curing in November, and fermented beverages appeared in early- to mid-wintertime. The holiday combined alcohol, feasting, respite from toil, and recreational sex. The primordial mid-winter festival arose from nature's own pulse. The very world seemed to condone Yule.

The cold season's respite from fieldwork liberated the peasants'

## The 12 Days of Christmas

pent-up creativity. Their ingenuity had simmered during the previous months of sexual deprivation when every ounce of strength went to the urgent labor of nurturing and gathering crops, then preparing the harvest for storage. In the months before the much-anticipated moment when strong drink was ready, everybody strained, too tired to perform sexually. Then the lid came off. Peasants could express their longings in a much-awaited release of inventive hedonism. This natural annual rhythm wove into national legends and myths of every agricultural society.

To anybody living before the modern era this would have seemed obvious when over 90 percent of the population engaged in some sort of farming or husbandry. Only our latest generations lost touch with an annual cadence established twenty thousand years ago and regularized in post-glacial Neolithic settlements. Francis J. Child's authoritative, *The English and Scottish Popular Ballad,* presents a text (No. 149a) collected in 1716 but probably much older, "Robin Hood's Birth, Breeding, Valor and Marriage." This was a penalty-song, typical of a game called forfeits that can become a reward-song, a kind of beer-pong. Rewarded singers were given strong drink:

> But not a man here shall taste my March beer[2]
>   Till a Christmas carrol he sing:
> Then all clapt their hands, and they shouted and sung
> Till the hall and the parlour did ring. (stanza 16)

Sing a Christmas carol, win a mug of beer. Sounds merry, until things inevitably get out-of-hand in any tavern with a drinking game in progress.

Today, excessive drinking seems either a personal failure, perhaps a moral lapse, or a disease of chemical imbalance, but not usually a community-wide

**Robin Hood on Horseback, c. 1475, artist unknown. As an outlaw hero who preyed on the wealthy, Robin Hood served as the early carol singers' admired natural ally. He rides a horse and carries his characteristic bow.**

## Chapter 4

goal. Except that neither abstinence nor moderation prevailed at old-fashioned Christmas when, months after the vintage was barreled or brewing began, drinks were finally available and rollicking drinking contests played unexceptional features of a season of mis-rule. How these mid-winter festivals were formerly celebrated, with violence and lewdness, is today unimaginable. "Holidays were the safety valve of the medieval system. All except May Day and New Year's Day celebrated religious feasts.... In any town there were certain holidays, usually lasting several days, which were celebrated with particular zest.... They were occasions for miracle plays, football matches, horseraces, tournaments, animal baitings, fireworks, clowns, jugglers, processions, and banquets." And old-time Christmas, being neither May Day nor New Year's Day, was celebrated like other pagan festivals. Why not? Christmas was not in the Bible.

Yet, the Christian god fit so well into the existing pattern because his putative birthday was already being celebrated as a season of fecundity. Authorization for the newer holiday was sketchy at best and wholly unbiblical, but hypocritically embraced for the opportunity of licit rioting.

Then, as now, some Christians more than others rely on the Bible to justify and explain their faith. "The Puritans were well aware that their ultimate authority, the Bible, did not indicate whether the nativity of Christ had occurred sometime around the winter solstice or on the fourth of July. They recognized it for an assimilated pagan holiday, and they were therefore opposed, partly because it represented the corruptions of popery, partly because of the pagan saturnalia that still accompanied it."[3] For Protestants, Christmas embodied corrupt papist doctrines redolent of the pagan past, and not just in Rome.

Even five hundred years ago, on the very threshold of modern times and with the rise of Protestantism, still thriving and well-beloved Yule posed a real competitor for people's affections. The old pagan holiday refused to succumb to centuries of Catholicism's energetic Christianizing. Clearly, a day of prayer and penitent fasting at the wonder of the Messiah's birth is not to be compared to a universal drunken orgy, with music.

Nobody but the Church could think of a good reason to stop celebrating the Yule. Stern pronouncements from gorgeously-gowned and bejeweled Catholic clergy to keep Christ in Christmas struck strict Protestants as unpersuasive defenses of the Christmas holiday they

### The 12 Days of Christmas

wanted to spurn entirely. Neither Catholic nor Protestant ministry's arguments swayed the debate's third party: the huge mass of people who, excluding pious Christian neighbors, rioted in the streets supposedly, or conveniently, on the occasion of the Lord's birth, while actually practicing a tradition older than the nativity. Sermons from both parties of Christendom failed to wheedle grubby peasants from enjoying the Church's lusty competition.

## A Reasonable Dread

The wretched Christmas holiday appears wholly unlovely judging from the reaction of people who actually had to face this tidal wave of brawling, street dancing, and loud singing. Good citizens tried, somehow, to control it.

The institutional response from the civic-minded, like many blunt government reactions, floundered like the Prohibition on alcohol or the War on Drugs: both excessive and useless.

Christmas was forbidden by Act of the English Parliament in 1644. I know, I know, it's hard for Americans to imagine: England without Christmas. England represents the imagination's very home of the modern Christmas, its style and traditions are best envisioned in Victorian London or at warm gatherings in an English Country House. Yet, just as the idea of this modern holiday was forming the government outlawed it, which suggests how objectionable was old-time Christmas. Parliament decreed that the day was to be marked by a universal fast and was to be a market day. Shops were compelled to be open and business to proceed as usual.[4] Plum puddings and mince pies were condemned as heathen because they were associated with pagan Christmas—and the ban on their consumption, along with turkey and Christmas ale, was only rescinded in 1660. The conservatives (who, in this case, were anything but puritanical) resisted Parliament because the traditionalists were not arguing for restraint but for the older, livelier and menacing, unrestrained variety of Christmas.

At Canterbury blood was shed when the two versions of Christmas were contested. The factions abandoned words for fists and weapons. An uncivil war broke out about how to celebrate Christmas, neighbor clubbing neighbor. America wasn't immune. The fight came to the New World, along with the songs.

## Chapter 4

Among the earliest of the Puritans' decrees, Christmas was outlawed so that this heathenish holiday would not spread its sickness to the New World. America offered a pure Garden of Eden where each colonist's and explorer's footfall tread a pristine earth not yet doused with the old world's sins. For the first religious settlers and subsequent homesteaders, importing to uncontaminated shores the worst of the old European Church's degenerate religion threatened the most revolting possible failure since Eve's conversation with the serpent. All the shabby festivities associated with the olden Church were unseemly and the long-serving Governor of the Massachusetts Bay Colony, William Bradford (1590–1657) took pains to see that his people worked in the fields on 25 December to express their contempt for what he called, "with a rare flash of Puritan wit, the Fool's Tide instead of the Yuletide."[5] As might be expected, Puritans weren't all that amusing; Bradford's reference intended no kind of joke but endorsed a well-founded observation.

Robert Graves relates that "at the conclusion of [the mid-winter Saturnalia] ... the ass-eared god, later the Christmas Fool, was killed by his rival."[6] Against stern Church sanction, men cavorted in the street dressed as animals and dramatized an archaic contest; the Christmas Fool continued a really ancient, a prehistoric, tradition. If a colonial American governor could cite this neolithic custom as objectionable, it yet lived in the hearts of the people.

The practices of Yule continued to seep into Christmas celebrations until Christmas became so offensive to the commonweal that in 1652, the English Parliament was presented with a *Remonstrance Against Christmas* and once again Parliament decreed that 25 December should come and go without being commemorated in any way, being a day like any other. In protest, London shopkeepers shuttered their businesses and markets, ignoring Parliament's new rules, while "dampened festivities undoubtedly took place in private. By 1660 Christmas had already been restored."[7] Even after the 1660 Restoration, Dissenters continued to brand Yuletide "Fooltide," recalling its pagan ancestry. Great Yule's disciples resisted having their renowned feast so easily expunged and only at this time is it possible to obtain a clear written account of the ribaldry of the reinstated Christmas, descriptions before that date being scarce.

Perhaps Yule reigned even bawdier in former times but earlier records had to survive withering criticism and purging by literate clerics. The very people most opposed to the songs of old Christmas wielded the censor's stamp, and few documents escaped the torch or

## The 12 Days of Christmas

scissors. But among medieval folksong and carol collections the bawdy Christmas songs exist in unlikely disguises. Their concealment can be exposed by recognizing the most likely literary camouflage the malefactors donned to hide their subjects. Faint clues give up the game.

For nominal Christians, peasants and freedmen, the holiday's attractions included, but was not limited to: masking that allowed public sinning without an acknowledged detection (although all knew each others' identities), only slightly more wholesale mummery, robberies in the street (mugging) and home burglaries, whoredom by professionals and amateurs, murder (both pent-up revenge or opportunistic), extraordinarily vigorous and innovative "amorous" expressions in public without the bonds of marriage, satirical and/or heretical miming, Bacchanalian excesses of every sort brazenly carried on within sight of clergy who dared not protest for fear of life, voluptuous mixings of genders and even species with the greatest possible anatomical inventiveness, un–Christian pagan dancing, drinking to excess, roaring at all hours the most vile obscenities, savagely idolatrous toasting with copious wassail, dicing and card playing with the inevitable violence that gambling entails, cursing and clamoring blasphemy, and singing carols. This is a holiday we would not recognize. Testimony comes from Shakespeare's young contemporary, perhaps the paramount Jacobean dramatist—compared to Shakespeare's quintessential Elizabethanism—Ben Jonson (1573–1637).[8] A character in Jonson's *The Alchemist,* 1610, one Ananias (a Deacon and colleague to a Pastor of Amsterdam, Tribulation Wholesome, probably an Anabaptist) approaches Subtle, the charlatan alchemist, for help in minting money to advance Puritanism in Britain.[9] To please his knowing audience Jonson's character (III:2) reflected the pious abhorrence of the mid-winter holiday in this shocked remonstrance:

> SUBTLE: And then the turning of this lawyer's pewter to plate at Christmas....
> ANANIAS: Christ-tide, I pray you.

The street-smart Subtle uses the equivalent of slang, or at least the laity's vulgar term for a vulgar holiday, while the self-righteous Ananias finds any mention of "Christmas" odious. The playwright understood theater-goers' affections. Jonson lambasted the ostentatiously righteous, the suppressers of Christmas revels.

## Chapter 4

The conflict between Anglo-American Puritan culture and its subversive opponents who sang the *Twelve Days* carol, could not have been more pronounced; on either side of the Atlantic survive reminders of the mysterious disappearance of old Christmas and its songs.

○ ○ ○

For twenty years after the unseating of the Dominion of New England in 1689 we know little about Christmas celebrations in America, but in 1721 the Rev. Cotton Mather of Boston (whose spiritualist theories undergirded prosecution and execution of the Salem Witches) entered into his diary for 30 December: "I hear of a number of young people of both sexes, belonging, many of them, to my flock, who have had on Christmas-night, this last week, a Frolick, a revelling feast, and Ball [dance]"; and ruminating on these abominations, Mather wrote a sermon for next Christmas that he published as *Grace Defended* in which he accused infiltrators of early Christianity of having introduced promiscuity into the Church, of, "giving themselves over to fornication [and] ungodly men turning the Grace of God into wantonness."[10] Christmas was still associated with fornication.

Despite his thundering admonition things did not change immediately, or soon, or at all. Momentum had been building for some time. Cotton's father, the staunch Puritan preacher and zealous foe of intoxication, Increase Mather had already decried in 1712 that "The Feast of Christ's Nativity is spent in Reveling, Dicing, Carding, Masking, and in all Licentious Liberty ... by Mad Mirth, by long Eating, by hard Drinking, by lewd Gaming, by rude Reveling."[11] Since Mather specifically cites "Dicing [and] Carding," something else was meant by "lewd

Cotton Mather, Mezzotint, c. 1700, Peter Pelham (ca. 1695–1751), an American limner and engraver, was born in England.

43

## The 12 Days of Christmas

Gaming," which turns out to be the indecent pastimes catalogued in *The Twelve Days*. Before getting to a description of the song and a list of its sex-drenched lyrics, accretions of modern decency should be peeled away.

The mid-winter festivities mingled sex with survival, and no countervening orders by the Church would displace time-tested superstition mixed with common sense about the cycles of nature: "Caroling was often among the activities confessed by accused persons in the witchcraft persecutions of Scotland in the sixteenth and seventeenth centuries."[12] The nature-cults practiced by accused witches (outright psychotics, or innocents succumbing to torture, or conservative but misunderstood nature-worshippers) deferred to, and tried to tap, the world's undomesticated forces.[13] Both its practitioners and spectators knew the carol's song-and-dance as accompaniments to magic; caroling's darker side utterly disregarded the proprieties of the Christian life. *The Twelve Days of Christmas* arrives into our present from mid-winter fertility celebrations and this song may represent one of the last outcroppings of primeval culture left in our midst. An archaic survivor, the song may be some version of a pre–Christian artifact, not to be judged by current social standards.[14]

Except for scholars of Church history, most of us forget just how recent was Christianity's final usurpation of mid-winter. Recall that "The first royal broadcast, made by George V at Christmas 1932, associated royalty with *an annual festival of growing importance*" [stress added].[15] Just so recently did modern Christmas ascend to its primary spot in the calendar: its current style of celebration was not established until well into the age of radio.

Old-time Christmas and lingering memories of gusto-filled caroling must be imagined since nobody now living experienced them. Mostly, its foes chronicled Old Christmas and their objections and admonitions persist as the primary tool to unearth the carol's past. Yet, to give its critics their due, if published today the carol of *The Twelve Days of Christmas* would be assigned an "X" rating. But, then again, so would Christmas. To see why it was suppressed, and how it survived, necessitates re-creating the context in which carolers first belted out the tune. Yearly, the English-speaking world marinates in a song whose meaning generations were taught to ignore.

# Chapter 5

## The Song

When delayed in crossing a street I freshly noticed a song that, like countless others awash in mass communications, I'd heard innumerable times. Every year that tune perfuses the two months preceding Christmas, now a season with its own aural "weather." The air fills with sounds as distinctive as Spring's birdsong, Winter's quietly sifting snow, or rustling leaves in Autumn—because Christmas commands a complete season, almost separate from the other four. Recorded carols play in public spaces and live musicians ring handbells, mixing pop songs with holiday wishes. And humanity actually strives to be joyful, forgiving, and generous. Christmas-themed movies promote love and tenderness, however cynically expressed for comedic effect.

Once I appreciated the song's strangeness, all the times I'd heard the carol became a "before," then a page turned and each subsequent hearing joined an "after" confirming that this alien song had fully infiltrated our world, a foreigner wandering from the past. The carol had outlived successive censorings of the mid-winter festival following the great purging of Christmas begun in the seventeenth century. Then it survived the Victorian era's even more insidious expropriation when it was confiscated and re-issued as a guileless ditty. That decontamination created the holiday's innocuous modern version.[1]

Under the double onslaught of Catholics and then Puritans, caroling almost died out, "causing Englishman William Hone to predict in 1822 that in a few years caroling would be heard no more."[2]. To keep alive that custom, when Charles Dickens published his short story "Christmas Festivities" in December 1835, he evoked the holiday's exemplary family celebration[3] and Dickens appealed to the reader's notion of the perfect gathering, all gaiety and good-will with grudges

## The 12 Days of Christmas

forgotten, when participants "fill the glass and send round the song." That is, the entire family throws off the year's stuffy reserve, along with any lingering personal slights, to enjoy their reunion and, amid the season's blessings, belts out a song of rounds before they "fill another, and troll off the old ditty." Dickens' imagined family sings merrily in a manner now only recalled from the words of *Deck the Halls (with Boughs of Holly)* that advises we "troll the ancient Yuletide carol."[4] Carol-singing remained essential to the conception of Christmas, even with its original purposes mostly forgotten. Yet, in the twentieth-century carols were heading toward extinction and once lost to a living performance tradition reconstructing their sound would be about as successful as conjuring the gait of a dodo. Luckily, some carols fared better than the dodo or passenger pigeon.

Besides possessing a catchy melody featuring unforgettably thumping rhythms and glittering alliterations, the *Twelve Days* endured because, almost alone of rowdy Medieval tunes, its zany content was re-packaged in a mild wrapper.

Despite some idiosyncratic quirks, *The Twelve Days of Christmas* well represents the form of a chain-number song, many of which feature religious or pastoral content. In particular, a sub-group enumerates its verses in the manner of a cumulative song. Each verse repeats all foregoing lines so the new verse with a new gift is always a line longer than its predecessor. Dating from no later than the fifteenth century, this group includes *Twelve Apostles, Green Grow the Rushes O* (whose misunderstood words gave Mexicans the name for the US soldiers who sang it: Gringos), *Seven Joys of Mary,* and all of them perhaps derived from the Hebrew *Echod mi Yodea* (Who Knows One?), a song Jesus probably sang at his family's Passover seder.[5] Identifying the song-type to which song our carol belongs raises a central dilemma. The German, Spanish, Hebrew, Austrian, Northern French and Langeudoc, versions of these chain-number songs all enumerate sacred objects grouped by number. Each of these songs are religious allegories, but *The Twelve Days of Christmas* is not. There is not a single religious image in the *Twelve Days*.

Attempts to assign holy references to the 12 verses have been miserably dishonest failures: miserable because of the insidiously pious motives to appropriate the song which require lapses of consistency and

## Chapter 5

reasoning. Nevertheless, efforts to inject religiosity into the carol and seize it for Christianity remain appealing to do-gooders; publicity usually peals a warm welcome whenever a dishonest theorist announces they've attached religiosity to the song as a kind of catechism. Journalists sigh contently, happy to make tasteful what would be, if understood at all, devoutly lauding the season's sensual pleasures and not the least bit sacred.

Moderns have trouble memorizing the verses; scarcely anybody gets them right the first time because we do not recognize the circle of allusions the words originally intended, yet it remains widely sung. The form of *The Twelve Days of Christmas* is indisputably old. An authoritative source states that *The Twelve Days of Christmas* is: "An English cumulative carol belonging to the category of the number-chain formula, enumerating the gifts sent by a lover to his lady on each of the twelve days from Christmas to Epiphany. First published in Husk's *Songs of the Nativity*, in 1868, it was there noted as having been printed in broadside during the preceding 150 years."[6] Already we encounter some problems. Why assume that the gift-giver is male ("gifts sent by a lover to his lady")? Why assume that the recipient is female? The reverse could be true, gifts from a woman to a man. There's also that blank century-and-a-half; the song may be considerably older. The carol's initial appearances in the literature was marked by highly prejudicial readings.

The carol's first collector, William Henry Husk thought that despite a broadside's claims for its antiquity "the song could not reasonably be an Old English Carol" as it seemed to him, "rather fitted for use in playing the game of 'Forfeits', to which purpose it was commonly applied in the metropolis [London]."[7] Husk presumed that the combination game-and-song began only a bit earlier than some forty years before he wrote. But his description falters if we visualize the party game he recalled.[8]

## Playing and Singing Forfeits

The players of forfeits sat in a row; each sang one sequential verse of some tune or a line of a nonsense chant until someone made a mistake, misnamed a gift, or flubbed the melody, and that player paid a forfeit or penalty for the mistake. The song continued until a number of forfeits were accumulated by players who then had to redeem them by performing some task. This game would not survive as a TV game show, but there were raunchy versions of it.[9] While primarily a children's game adults played it as well, just as some children's games are still revived at parties but with adult rules. At one time the forfeits were paid in cash but by the early nineteenth century a kiss was substituted in a daring challenge to propriety; such audacity thrilled players at the time. The penalties, depending on the company and the players' whim, varied from sedate to lewd. That is the key. Understanding *where* and by whom the song was sung changes every sugar-plum notion of the carol's origins into a tale for which the children must be ushered out of the room.

Forfeit songs were often drinking songs sung by alcohol-fueled groups partying. Consequently, arguing that *The Twelve Days* had become "only" a forfeits song does not render it wholesome and harmless. Likely sung as part of a tavern game it should be visualized in that raucous setting and—once re-contextualized from the sedate mid–Victorian parlor—the song's lost meaning rouses from history's sleep. Some form of forfeits long preceded the mid-nineteenth-century rage for this party amusement. Although well-fitted to the game, the song was much older.

In Charles Dickens' 1843 *A Christmas Carol,* Ebenezer Scrooge visits his nephew's home and marvels that the assembled guests "didn't devote the whole evening to music. After a while they played forfeits; for it is good to be children sometimes."[10] By which Dickens teaches several points.

He featured the game in his story specifically because it was boisterous and not usually played by adults in that era. Scrooge remembers the game as a childhood amusement of decades past, which sounded quaint by the mid-nineteenth century. Additionally, Scrooge's nephew and his guests have to abandon their music-making to begin playing forfeits; the two, quite separate, activities were perhaps incompatible (which may not have been the case in the past). No song or instrumental performance accompanies the game, as virtually any game with penalties could be called forfeits. We can trust his narrative's particulars because Dickens' recitation of this scene's details had to ring true to his contemporary readers. Also, it's telling to consider what details he omits.

## Chapter 5

The game of forfeits sounds decorous today, but according to a book about Christmas traditions published in 1852, it was "too romping and noisy an amusement for the chilling atmosphere" that developed in later Victorian drawing rooms.[11] It was easy to fall into Husk's erroneous assumption that *The Twelve Days* must have been composed to accompany the game. The song traveled with the game—a cultural parasite thriving on its host's catchy melody—but also the song flourished without the game of Forfeits, and traveled far.[12]

Old England's song of *The Twelve Days* took root in America, at first east of the Appalachian mountains in communities founded by English settlers, then it seeped into the general imagination as an essential part of Christmas cheer. The carol was sung everywhere in America and throughout the English-speaking world, usually with the same or similar lyrics, although their order is sometimes jumbled:

  1 partridge in a pear tree
  2 turtle doves
  3 French hens
  4 calling birds
  5 golden rings
  6 geese a-laying
  7 swans a-swimming
  8 maids a-milking
  9 pipers piping
  10 drummers drumming
  11 lords a-leaping
  12 ladies dancing

There is really only a single form of this song.[13] Such uniformity seems oddly anti–Darwinian; in all its long life the carol hadn't taken on wildly different forms in different places.

There was a reason why the street-singers on snow-swirled Oxford Circus and farmers in the Ozark Mountains, why everyone, sang basically the same version. If the song was meaningless, a senseless cumulative chain, its form would not have remained stable for so long. Tra-la-la's and other sonic graffiti would have blighted it. Local references would have worked their way in. The gifts would have up-dated to more currently desirable swag. But it remained clean of such doodlings. A hidden structure holds the whole thing together and this

## The 12 Days of Christmas

arrangement, even if only sensed unconsciously, proved sufficiently powerful to inhibit messing up the numbered verses or the gifts. That concealed pattern stood against improvised changes, organic cultural evolution, and suppressions dictated by authoritarian attempts to deflect folklife's vigorous mid-winter liberation.[14]

Yet, the explanation for the song's intact preservation hid in plain sight. Somebody desired these gifts in prodigious quantities or, at least, wanted to sing about them. The carol must have referred to something people were glad to sing about. And what the carolers were glad to sing about is what people everywhere have always craved, which is why the song never changed.

On the twelfth night all the preceding verses had been sung on previous evenings (even if those "evenings" did not exist outside the song that was sung at one go). The last verse capped a list and summed the lot: an amazingly lewd catalogue. On the twelfth and last night each gift was mentioned in the order we will examine them.

## Chapter 6

## Twelfth Night

By the song's finale everybody knew the joke before the dancing ladies came on stage. The ending's simplicity marks the song's concluding "day" whose culmination makes sense once the colorful preceding images introduce it. Twelve ladies dancing sounds innocent—if we enter the song backwards, from the last verse, however bygone carolers belting out this tune had already established the song's moral context. Her ears burning with shame and cheeks flushed, Modesty had fled, many verses previous.

A vision of dancing ladies summons recollections of cheery Christmases, which seems reasonable for a holiday now celebrated with outings to Tchaikovsky's *Nut Cracker* ballet; long-ago, carols were the sung lyrics for a dance. Yet an activity's meaning can radically change with time, and dance, like prayer, alters drastically from place-to-place and in different times. Not today's recreational dances performed almost solo, often in a nearly dark but blindingly loud club as moving points of light play over a fevered scene's party-goers. Nor were garlanded springtime maidens safely giggling in mutual delight amid a landscape all green with bright promise against which they moved in bleached shifts. And certainly not the ritual dances captured stiffly on temple walls from Egypt to Angkor Wat where distant chanting hallowed the performers' steps and cadenced meaningful gestures.

When we dance we mean, we create meaning, even if completely non-discursive—and dance remains the artform about which we can say the least as its content evades words and makes ballet the ideal respite for a generation of information-workers weary from a day of reading and moving symbols on screens. But none of that was on the mind of the carol dancers.

## The 12 Days of Christmas

Despite the modern acceptance and universal admiration for everything associated with Christmas, the Twelve Ladies who danced the carol displeased some spectators. Dancing was not a Church-sanctioned aspect of the often licentious Christmas celebrations. The sour critics had a point.

Long before twerking, dancing's exertions mimicked sex. Or, social dancing sponsors the flirtatious size-up of a possible consort. We attend dances to meet potential partners, or as romantic foreplay with current partners. The phrase in zoology "mating dance" approaches redundancy among humans.

At dances the sexes meet and examine one another for bodily fitness and physical charm, or to reenforce bonds of attraction. Dances provide the occasion for courting, and a great place to show off the body's suppleness. These displays overwhelm Christmas's occasion because, if the dancing is lively and sincere, few except Dervishes consider high theological problems while dancing. Almost meditational, dance can, and perhaps should, drive every other idea from our heads, which is one reason to dance.

Dancing would be hard work, if it weren't fun. If dance did not promise alluring and seductive release, tired workers would seek a full sabbath from toil and just kick back but, given a bit of respite, field and factory laborers everywhere enjoy dance's stimulation. Dancing's rewards must be considerable to entice laborers into new exertions; upper class dances require less effort. Measured and refined, court dancing demanded little genuine exertion or real physical contact (usually no more than finger-touches). There were exceptions like the exhilarating court dance *Lavolta*, a favorite of Queen Elizabeth I. During that dance the male partner, throwing his left arm around his lady's back, placed his whole right hand, palm-up, under his female partner's crotch, repeatedly lifting her into the air, to mutual delight. Who could make this up? This raunchy dance was cited in *Henry V* (III:5) when Shakespeare's despairing French aristocracy consider eugenics to improve their breed:

> DAUPHINE: By faith and honour,
> Our madams mock at us, and plainly say
> Our mettle is bred out and they will give
> Their bodies to the lust of English youth
> To new-store France with bastard warriors.
> BOURBON: They bid us to the English dancing-schools,
> And teach lavoltas high and swift corantos;[1]

## Chapter 6

La Volta, c. 1580. This painting, often thought to depict Queen Elizabeth I dancing Lavolta with Robert Dudley, Earl of Leicester, is actually French, of the Valois School (possibly painted by Marcus Gheeraerts). The dancers' identities are not known. Penhurst Place, Kent.

From the Italian, *volta*—meaning both leap or vault and "the time"—the lavolta (called *la volte* in French) was a wildly popular Renaissance dance in western Europe's royal courts. In the sixteenth-century lavolta was danced in fast triple time and performed to the same music as a galliard.[2] A series of leaps distinguished lavolta as the woman's partner raised her off the ground, turning either to the right or to the left.

Dance and breeding, dancing and sex. The higher the lavolta, the better, Shakespeare seems to advise.

A personal point: invoking William Shakespeare is not intended to impress the reader with literary high-mindedness. He's here to prove that the carol's language thrived vital in its time because Shakespeare's plays supplied popular entertainments. If too obscure for his clientele the playwright's vocabulary would vacate theater seats and empty

# The 12 Days of Christmas

his purse. Theater patrons knew what he was talking about and Shakespeare's usage provides a touchstone for decoding the *Twelve Days of Christmas* because his vernacular confirms the carol's language.

The forthright and unsuspicious verse of twelve ladies dancing seems modest enough, until we learn that in archaic jargon "dancing, as with one's heels, was also used of women as they lay on their back in bed."[3] Dancing not only implied being sexy or provocative: dancing meant sex. The two were interchangeable in slang. To leave 'em laughing, Shakespeare, that consummate showman, ends *Much Ado About Nothing,* with a double-entendre:

> BENEDICK: Come, come, we are friends, let's have a dance ere we are married, that we may lighten our own hearts, and our wives heels.

To dance with one's heels was "to beat the bed with one's heels during the rhythmic motions of the sexual act."[4] With the woman almost always beneath the man (and formerly that was the Church's preferred moral position) the woman performed the heel-dance. The phrase represents a highly graphic description of hip-grinding, earnest and climactic, screwing. No far-fetched reading, the word dance featured in pre-modern slang to describe the 12th verse's women who we find dancing and claim to be ladies—and those two traits are all we know about them.

Relatively new to northern Europe, the Church's version of organized religion came off badly in comparison to indigenous culture. Counterpoising the presence of the Virgin, as the Lady who banishes every pagan spiritual mistress, the word "lady" also referred to fairies or a nymph, thereby soliciting a reverse magic to Christianity's. (To those who heard Christianity's master narrative for the first time, the most credible part of that story had God impregnating Mary.) If even a whiff of witchcraft accompanied a circle dance the carol lost any claim to innocence. That association helps explain why the zealous Church tried to expunge these songs, although today nobody singing the song thinks they are thereby flirting with or committing witchcraft.

Some wizarding phrases went underground, wore the mask of innocence and thereby survived into modern times. When mistress

## Chapter 6

*bona fortuna* attended a game of chance (shooting craps, in earlier times called dicing) Frank Loesser and Abe Burrows summoned her to Broadway's *Guys and Dolls* in a song called *Luck Be a Lady Tonight*—the well-behaved and merciful lady frequented a floating craps game. The word "lady" sounds so proper today but her presence hardly guaranteed the entire song was a decorous carol for, as slang, dancing ranged from picturing wanton release to real indecency. Everything depended on context.

One of the principal meanings of "lady" was a kept mistress, as in a "lady of pleasure," which refers to a courtesan, a whore. The carol's ladies are not merely ladies who happen to be dancing but ladies who are known by their dancing, their occupation. A wry mirror-image of social elevation peeks from "ladies dancing"—after recognizing dancing's lusty connotations. Everything depended on the ladies' attached attribute.

To our ears, the decorous word *lady* is so steeped in propriety that today some women scorn it, with its insinuation of automatic deference used as a screen for subjugation. There's some of that sexual politics capering in this verse's background. Contrary to modern associations, from the seventeenth century the word formerly carried untoward associations: "Ladies fever" meant syphilis; a "Lady of the Lake" was a kept mistress; "Lady-feats" referred to "a bout of venery": what you did with dancing ladies[5] When you went out drinking and chambering. And bawling out obscene carols.

Not only did dance mean to fornicate but, especially, it meant submission. To dance attendance (or to wait upon a person) showed constant attention and obsequiousness. The word originally implied that somebody stood waiting for somebody else while "kicking one's heels," usually in an antechamber. With ever-diminishing force this meaning lived on through the nineteenth century. John Skelton's *Why come ye nat to courte* (1522) contains the line: "And Syr ye must daunce attendance, And take patient sufferaunce, For my Lords Grace, Hath now no time or space, To speke with you as yet." Skelton was known for his wry, sometimes uncouth, humor whose words would have been dipped from the same lexical hopper of condiments as the carol's vocabulary.

Shakespeare's, *Henry VIII*, c.1613, features the same usage: "To suffer A man of Place.... To dance attendance on their Lordships

## The 12 Days of Christmas

pleasures" (V:2).[6] The dancing ladies were not only sexually active, they were compliant, ready and just waiting to perform and please. These affiliated definitions carry two related, but not ambiguously cloudy, inferences. Each sense strengthens the other to merge into a single intensified hybrid as the word's slightly different meanings form an amalgam.

Dance can figuratively mean to lead a person in a wearying, perplexing, or disappointing course. Such a diversionary treatment is still called a "song-and-dance," a verbal delaying or distracting tactic that forces the victim to endure an extended digression with no adequate result. Anybody who has purchased an automobile has been given the song-and-dance when the salesman passes the customer off to a manager who can deliver bonus value—for more money. The name for this stratagem has a long history that can be dated no later than the first quarter of the sixteenth century when perennially sarcastic John Skelton complained that Fortune "toke me by the hand and led me a daunce." This connotation has not diminished with time. Together the three meanings of dance conjure a manipulative, sexually active, coquettish though (seemingly) submissive, mistress—times twelve, the veritable stable of a well-stocked brothel. What's a whorehouse doing in a carol? As a type, a Christmas carol would seemingly forbid such a reference, but this preposterously lewd image grows more plausible when integrated into the rest of the song. In any case, excluding such references reveals modern prejudice; we have to remember what Christmas used to be and why the Church hated it, a festival that offered an excuse and occasion to go whoring and drinking.

Saved for the last day of the twelve-day celebration, this verse may blaze a particularly outrageous image. A "lady" designates not just any woman, but the mistress of a household. ("Is the lady of the house at home?") This ancient rank of preferment and elevation arrives into the present from distant Old English.

From the fifteenth to the sixteenth century, The (or My) Lady was prefixed to the Christian name of a female member of the royal family, as Princess is now. Accordingly, in 1594 Shakespeare in *Richard III*, could issue a stage direction: "Enter the Coarse [corpse] of Henrie the sixt…. Lady Anne being the Mourner" (I:2). Social inferiors, especially servants or slaves, used the phrase "my lady" in speaking to a women of high social rank.

The final indignity would be the invasion of the lady/mistress's

## Chapter 6

pretentious detachment by imagining her screwing. That was precisely the point because, when this carol was first sung, there were no Fleet Street tabloids to broadcast invasions of privacy. There were no celebrity magazines at the grocery check-out, and no check-out counter. During Christmas the social ladder was thrown away, for a little while anyway. While the Renaissance developed its intellectual-artistic refinements and invented Progress that looked to the future for perfection—instead of seeking teachings from a past Golden Age—on social levels deep below the aristocrats' bloodthirsty scheming and statesmanship, peasants maintained their ancient tried-and-true superstitious beliefs. Their age-old convictions (perhaps reactionary in view of gradual European awakening to classical liberalism) about fertility and seasonal cycles synchronized their Yuletide escapades. With society divided into an upper history, with its dynastic ways of warfare and etiquette that fill our textbooks, a lower and largely unrecorded world of scabrous lower classes conjured an image of the lady's carnality, scorning all chaste propaganda about class differences. What could be more deliciously raffish. Peasants imagined their "betters" acting on a lust that churned no different from their own stews.[7]

In taverns, brothels, or during the debauched Christmas festival, lowly drunkards bawled the *Twelve Days'* lewd imagery of the female head of household in her sexual situation—horizontal resignation in the "missionary" position. For certain women (and some men) heterosexual intercourse always involves abjection, a fall from grace and dignity into the missionary posture yet, while this carol accepts lust as perfectly human, the song bristles at social submission. Sex was not being ridiculed but the social charade that certain pretentious ladies don't do "it." Yet, obviously, the upper classes evidently reproduced through procreation, like everybody else. The carol's madcap anarchy ridicules those upper-class women called ladies—bodily no different from the singers, although presenting themselves as extravagantly genteel creatures of artificial manners taken to extremes. Aristocrats engaged in exorbitant habits of dress and convoluted circumlocutions to express sentiment, which the singers' frank expression refuted with self-consciously bawdy abandon aimed at so-called refinements of society's higher ranks. And, thereby, something of the singers' identity is revealed.

Obviously boisterous and likely drunken, the carol singers were freed from decent manners; their targets for ridicule suggest the carolers' lineage. The carolers' ranks drew from a permanent underclass,

## The 12 Days of Christmas

"Saint Paul the Hermit Sees a Christian Tempted" from the Saints Paul and Anthony Cycle in the *Belles Heures of Jean de France*, duc de Berry, 1405–1408/9. Herman, Paul, and Jean de Limbourg (Franco-Netherlandish brothers, active in France by 1399–1416), ink, tempera, and gold leaf on vellum, 9⅜ × 6⅝ in. (23.8 × 16.8 cm). Made in Paris (The Metropolitan Museum of Art, The Cloisters Collection, 1954 [54.1.1] fol. 191r.).

An example of upper-class hypocrisy. Jean de France, duc de Berry (1340–1416), commissioned the era's most gifted artists, the Limbourg brothers to create a private devotional book, produced between 1405 and 1408/09, likely in Paris. One gorgeously illuminated scene depicts an episode in the story of Saint Paul the Hermit (c. 347). An Egyptian peasant considered the first Christian hermit, having fled into the wilderness to escape his unfaithful wife and the persecutions imposed by the Emperor Decius (c. 201–251).The Saint harbored decidedly unworldly notions of fleshly desires whose abhorrence recommended his solitary, and celibate, life in a cave. This illustration shows the moment when Paul witnesses an incident that confirms his decision to flee into desert.

A stylishly dressed young woman of the upper class tries to seduce an elegant young man.

## Chapter 6

a rural peasantry and, eventually, an emerging working class. These groups experienced fixed congenital status, some attached to feudal lands and others to a trade.

Social class, inherited and immutable, determined the carol's concerns because only once a year were such class constraints lifted during the mid-winter festival and, accordingly, the song addressed topics pertinent to the singers' identity. (Professional minstrels or master poets sang of different matters, or of the same desires but in veiled and lofty terms.) The verses' satirical targets suggest a community. Some singers lived at society's legal fringes. Others were normally solid working-class tradesmen or the agricultural peasants whose crops enriched their local lords. These commoners joined the madcap romp's opportunistically heady liberation.

There is no way to construe the casual singing about Dancing Ladies to have been anything other than a breach of etiquette, indeed, coming from the mouths of drunken commoners, a grave insult ... at best. Was this the verse's only meaning? No. But one among a cluster of social-sexual associations (not unlike the Leaping Lords). This verse delivered a tight constellation of implications, as the song's related insinuations scintillated with lewd suggestions, each happily glinting in its own wit. Each verse's image abetted the other images by strengthening their clever ambiguity about the shameless lewdness that typified the ancient holiday. The rest of the carol's lyrics make clear that dancing's mere face-value was never intended, except as the set-up for a joke.

The dancing ladies are not merely lustily fucking—a universally recognized pleasure, though sanctimonious types pretend to ignore that every life begins in such a congress. Just by being sexually active a dozen ladies raze the pretention's edifice because "dancing" ladies shatter a fiction that has crippled many an emotional life: the masochistic myth of courtly love.

The object of chivalrous devotion a "lady-love" was the impossibly chaste female, the verse's target—the cool unreactive female who refrains from sex or finds the idea disgusting. But, as one of the leading scholars of carols bluntly put it, "The carol is not an aristocratic genre, however, and the conventions of courtly love touch it hardly at all."[8] Actually, such carols rebut courtly love, its absurd assumptions of longing and self-loathing in search of a sadistic particularity. Rarely sung in the castle, farmers knew this song, and they knew the earth as intimately as the body of a lover. Farmers' interests in fertility proceeded,

## The 12 Days of Christmas

based on generations of experience that was incongruent with scholastic theologians' airy paragons. The agrarian ideal avoided chastity and favored coupling while an increasingly triumphant Church forced underground fertility's cultic awe and its celebrations.

With similar interests, the aristocracy the Church coveted an orderly citizenry. Even as they struggled against each other, these two senior estates would inevitably lose in any redistribution of society's privileged goodies. Considering that feudal wealth only trickled up, like early pornography—that began as a critique of unbridled, mostly imaginary, monkish passions and nun's presumed lusts—this song contained more than a hint of social comment.

When(ever) society breaks down, amid a cessation of work and consumption of the drug-of-choice, waves of sex and revenge-murder erupt.[9] The ruckus might occur once in a generation, or more often whenever social inequalities forcefully re-balance rather unexpectedly in revolutionary liberation. Or a release valve could be scheduled each mid-winter. In the transitions that heralded Modernity, that release seemed worth a season of chaos. it seems more tolerable than the modern consumerist reality that leaves the season's celebrants with remorse for excess purchases and unaffordable debt rather than bodily bruises, unwise sex, and intemperate drinking. A merrily anticipated temporary liberation curbed the peasants political horizons. Then as now.

The dancing ladies conclude a cycle that, with the other verses, emphasize a society inverted. Untangling the carol's enigmatic phrases relates the next verse's meaning to the whole arrangement.

# *Chapter 7*

## A Lordly Eleventh Night

> And it came to pass at the time that the cattle conceived, that I lifted up mine eyes, and saw in a dream, and, behold, the rams which leaped upon the cattle were ringstreaked, speckled, and grisled. (*Genesis* 31:10)—King James Version,[1] published 1611

> the lusty Moor
> Hath leap'd into my seat—*Othello* (II:1)

The twelve dancing ladies radiate all sorts of unanticipated, because now obsolete, associations. Taken together those connotations insinuate an unwelcome lascivious tone for a now-beloved carol. Such carols offended upright citizens' sense of mid-winter piety, and the song's staunchest devotees intended effrontery. Sung as a bleak season's anthem, the carol offered its singers the promise of sated desire, a welcome pledge of sensual release from cold and dark.

Despite its sequence of appealing farmyard animals, the carol was never intended for the kiddies.[2] Sung in its original context—far from snug family hearths and more likely in taverns or bordellos, or chanted while dancing the carolle—rectitude effects no last-minute save of the carol's dignity. The song never delivers a virtuous moral. Despite the next verse's sober-sounding rank of "lord," because this song challenged stateliness and decorum official propriety wandered away, truant from every verse. The carol teaches neither how to obey "betters" nor to know one's "place" and behave accordingly.

## The 12 Days of Christmas

From very early use, the term "lord" distinguished a man of exalted position in a kingdom or commonwealth. There are no lords in a lawless anarchy and the mention of nobility or aristocracy evokes social order, usually imposed from above. The word "lord" recollects a structured world with a top and a bottom, which implies all manner of associational relationships and obligations. So, how does a "true love" *give* a lord, or eleven of them?

The ancient festival inverted social situations. Public celebrations of pre-modern Christmas *temporarily* overturned social-sexual mores when the bonds of lordship and duties to husbands could be scorned, even taunted. For a fleeting time at the mid-winter season any behavior was possible; at Yuletide lords became servants, or at least felt compelled to indulge in exaggerated (perhaps even sincere) hospitality, while servants played masters when the Lord of Misrule governed.

Although Dissenters continued to scorn Yuletide as "Fooltide," after the Restoration Christmas incorporated some of Yule's artifice. The highborn were caricatured as low; the normally forbidden was not only permitted but abounded rampant. Anarchy contravened every normal social standard because during the rest of the year it was usually neither smart nor safe to mock the lord who ruled a large or small domain but at Yule, and later Christmas, all was allowed.

In this uproarious atmosphere, both highborn and low knew what the song's words meant.

The carol's lords could be the twelve dancing ladies' husbands, or any husbands that the song cares to mock. Not surprisingly, husband's would be leaping, because sexual access defined their distinctive kind of lordship. The great myth holds that the lord of his domains may assert sexual prerogatives, the lordly privilege of defloration.[3] The mention of a leaping lord's, albeit often mythical, sexual depravity suggested the need for social reform.

In the carol, lordly fucking ensues 121 times (eleven lords × 11 days) which suggests a "leaping-house," as a brothel was called. Shakespeare's 1598 *I Henry IV* has the Prince of Wales upbraid a minor noble, Sir John Falstaff: "What the devil hast thou to do with the time of the day? unless hours were cups of sack [dry sherry wine], and minutes capons, and clocks the tongues of bawds, and dials the signs of leaping houses" (I:2). The song's lords bound forth with all the eagerness of the sexually hungry—just as drunken carolers went "chambering" to their favorite leaping house.

*Chapter 7*

"The Feast of Fools," a bass-de-page illustration in *The Romance of Alexander*, the episode of Alexander and Dindimus 1344. Jehan de Grise and his workshop, 1338–44, Bruges or Tournai (with folios, added in England after 1400, that contain Marco Polo's *Li Livres du Graunt Caam*, The Books of the Great Khan) (Bodleian MS 264 fol. 21 v, Catalogue of Western Medieval Manuscripts MS. Bodl. 264, Bodleian Libraries, University of Oxford Libraries Catalogue Identifier: SC: 2464). A literary novel type, written from the third century BCE onward, *The Romance of Alexander* is here given a sumptuous treatment where the manuscript's marginal curiosities presented vivid scenes of everyday life. The Feast of Fools shows cavorting celebrants, some in animal costume.

The lords doing the leaping announce themselves of questionable character, but this song was not created for the peerage's amusement but by commoners who had no great love of their rulers.

After mortifying their ladies, reciting the character defects peasants saw in their betters continued and, although the language used to describe these failings has aged, the jokes haven't. The lords described as *leaping* may resemble a leap day, intermittently injected into a year to standardize its length. We recognize that usage even if we no longer taste that word's intended off-flavor that comes around but every four years.

A leap day occurs as no ordinary day and leap lords are not customary lords, but sub-standard. This sense of deficiency survives in leap days or leap years that appear as irregular, extraordinary, events inserted into the orderly running of the clock and calendar, which would otherwise work imperfectly. The lords compare to a modern leap second implanted into or omitted from time-reckoning to bring the clock into correspondence with another scale of time-keeping. This sense of

## The 12 Days of Christmas

**Interior of London Brothel, a leaping house.**

deficiency or flaw carried over to the jargon of other trades. The most inferior quality of tin ore was leap-ore.[4] And leap peas are parched-peas. There were also "leap-Christians," of which the witty John Trapp (1601–69) complained in 1647: "Leap-Christians are not so much to be liked, that all on the sudden, of notorious profane become extremely precise and scrupulous."[5] They are defective Christians. Things that are "leap" satisfy basic requirements in a pinch to keep the system going, and the carol's lords are leap.

They are not just sexually depraved but are leap-lords. The song infers that leap-lords in the scheme of creation represent a social necessity to keep the world in order but the nobility should not be taken too seriously or more solemnly than needed to maintain things in equilibrium. The lords are merely, and unendearingly, a peculiar part of nature that must be tolerated, as a leap-skip refers to the crooked knight's move in chess, a game which, like life, occasionally requires some odd moves. Clever carol singers smirked at their own wry sense of social justice: that their mid-winter improprieties hurt no one, but real-life lords cause actual pain and harm.

These leapers might be lords with defective titles, new nobility, or ersatz nobility, born like the rest of common mortals and undistinguished but for a title and the power to enforce their will. They are not intrinsically better, the carol implies. There are, after all,

## Chapter 7

situations in which lordliness is no compliment, but indicates inherent degeneracy.

As early as 1690, underclass slang mockingly used the term Lord for "a very crooked, deformed, or ill-shaped Person."[6] Right-thinking peasants carried a grudge, expressed in the image of a mangled nobleman, such as *Richard III*. The toiling and often hungry lower classes also seethed with a justified indignation at their overlords' conspicuous consumption. To live like a lord is to fare luxuriously, squandering ostentatiously, a condition of perennial excess that the poor might envy or disdain because their labor represented the ultimate source of aristocracy's wealth.

To treat someone like a lord entertains them sumptuously and with profound deference, often under compulsion. The inconvenienced or coerced commoner forced to render involuntary hospitality reserved pent-up derision for an appropriate moment—and sang their mockery when allowed by the holiday of social inversion. Caroled displeasure erupted in public when Yuletide granted harassed peasantry the freedom to express the year's, or a lifetime's, accumulated misery with their own leaping lord or with the whole pyramid of nobility carried on the backs of the aching peasantry. Other sins needed to be accounted.

To be drunk as a lord is to be completely intoxicated, and from late medieval times it was understood that to drink like a lord did not mean to drink in moderation. By the middle of the seventeenth century John Evelyn's insightful account of England under the Commonwealth, *A Character of England* (1651, published in London, 1659) could refer back to a well-established understanding: "The Gentlemen are most of them very intemperate, yet the Proverb goes, 'As drunk as a Lord.'" In Evelyn's day the lords' intemperance, already proverbial, eclipsed decent behavior. If the aristocracy had been notorious only for drunkenness but remained jolly and affable while inebriated, no one would care or sing derisively about it, but aphorisms coined by those who knew them best portrayed the lords as foul-mouthed braggarts.

Sir Thomas Elyot's influential work *The Governour* (1531) was written by an eyewitness embedded in the court's aristocracy who discoursed on the nobility's defects: "For they wyll say he that swereth depe, swereth like a lorde." The printer Edward Cave (b. 1692) initiated the first periodical called a magazine and in it, *The Gentlemens Magazine* amplified this character flaw in 1770: "As drunk as a Lord Similarly,

# The 12 Days of Christmas

to swear like a lord." So much for any residual dignity that, resistantly and against evidence, adheres to the carol's lords.

The song's leaping lords are not commended; they are not merry flush-faced celebrants of Christmas,[7] but drunk and swearing specters of grim sexual depravity ravishing their toll of peasant maidenheads and keeping harlots busy, when not attending to the legitimate procreation of their own class. This sense arises from the distinct pejoration connoted by the word leap, just as fucking is not all joy but can be invoked as a vulgar expletive to mean a faulty, disagreeable, or a substandard situation (other motorists, sports umpires, etc.).[8]

The verse's noun and verb are connected in more ways than one. An early intransitive sense associates leap to the family of words related to "lope, to run." So that leap might mean to go hastily or with violence, to rush about or to "throw oneself forth" in the obsolete sense of "to escape." Leaping lords are recreants, too, cowards. Branding "leaping lords" an inferior kind of "leap" aristocracy, slurred the social chaos that prevailed during, and cast a long shadow after, the Wars of the Roses (1455–87). The whole upper-class mess were flawed leap lords; when needed for mutual aid, they scattered for self-preservation, or fled to rebellion—false to one another and contrary to their oaths of fealty.

Leaping lords were not nice guys; they leaped to break out in an illegal or disorderly way.[9] They were rowdies. They caricatured sexual monsters with whom everyone else had to live while tolerating upper-class lust as the price of survival. In modern terms, yelling "You Leaping Lord!" might be accompanied by an equally uncouth gesture. Everything depended on the situation, the tone of the season, and the gathering. On Christmas the nobles' unchecked carnal appetites (even if mythical) and cowardice could be mocked, as long as that ridicule hid in plain sight as part of a general inventory of sexual misadventures and escapade. If the criticism had been overt and believed sincere, rather than a passing Christmas revel, the carol's mockers of their lords' sexual parasitism would not have lived to sing the next verse.

## Chapter 8

## Tenth Night

Hailing from the merriment of a suppressed Saturnalia, *The Twelve Days of Christmas* survived by trading on its ambiguous appearance, a song that appeared benign to the uninitiated and had been outrageous to the knowledgeable. And fun to sing. Camouflage, looking like one thing while being another, allowed it to outlive very real attempts to kill everything it stood for. With the memory of its original situation suppressed and eventually forgotten, the clergy felt no need to harass this song into oblivion. If they hadn't forgotten about it, perhaps clerics sensed it was naughty but like the rest of society they had no idea what it was about. It's hard to persecute something that you're not sure is guilty of anything. Authorities couldn't censure it unreasonably when they had no clue what the song described. So, the song survived.

Why ten drummers? Not seven or eight? Amid an inexorable numerical chain, does this tenth verse fall into a meaningful position within the cycle? Despite some recorded variations in the verses' positions and numbers the people who invented and sang this song may have been bawdy, illiterate, and often drunk, but they weren't stupid. Folk-wisdom observed structural niceties, albeit to sometimes describe gross indelicacy.

The tenth day brought rhythm's pulse, introduced here for good reason: unrelenting drumming can be highly erotic. Maurice Ravel understood the allure of insistent strokes when composing his seductively repetitive *Bolero*, 1928. That piece begins with a flute and snare drum in a symbolic duet of shapes and sounds whose recognition would

# The 12 Days of Christmas

delight a caroler. Dwellers in a Freudian universe may reflexively find a duo of tubular and splayed forms allusive, but earlier observers came to the same recognition. Out-of-context this might seem improbable, but the Twelve Days song's framework supplies meaning in both the riotous conditions when it was sung and the cumulative spirit of the surrounding verses. Context promotes what would otherwise seem a strained reading of a Christmas carol's improbably irreligious payload. Neither impertinence nor squeamishness should avert our glance.

The ten drummers play upon a matrix, the drumhead's surface. It's ill-advised to beat too hard as breaking (or penetrating) that plane ruins the drum. But, except as metaphor, the carol's singers couldn't have cared less about orchestrations, specifically percussion with musical instruments. The carolers contemplated sex.

Their alcohol-fueled erotic rumination unfolded as a flood of clever puns, metaphors in then-current slang, double-entendres, metonymy, and simile—all terms unknown to illiterate early carolers although such rhetoric subsequently featured in a Viennese medical doctor's description of sexual innuendo. Inexorable rhythmic contact without penetration resembles the motions of female masturbation. The singers solicited folk wisdom's keenest metaphors about repeatedly stroking, rapping, or tapping the drum's top skin with bolero-tempo rubbing and massaging of the vulva.

The drumming may be auto-erotic, or practiced by another (man or woman) on a pleased female recipient and, while this would seem a strained reading if the carol of the *Twelve Days* were the only song to make this allusion, with this very image other folk-songs celebrate rising excitement. Finding such parallels heightens the probability of the carol's covert, winking, meaning.

Centuries later, the same witty substitution occurs in the double-entendre-ed song *I've Been Working on the Railroad:* "Some one's in the kitchen with Dinah/ strumming on the old banjo." The song's dirty joke crucially depends on visualizing old-style banjo technique. This "railroad" song pre-dates the claw-finger style of banjo plucking common today when each finger, including the thumb, strikes a different string in sequence; in olden days banjos were strummed. Visualizing the thrummed banjo as a stroked skin-headed instrument, the singer recounts that somebody else (not the innocent singer who pretends, or confesses, to being a voyeur) entertains Dinah, idly masturbating her, "strumming on the old banjo."[1] American railroad workers who sang

## Chapter 8

this tune were, apparently, concocting nothing new. Their folk-song only re-invented a staple of art.

For a very long time musical instruments, especially plucked strings, appeared in paintings as surrogates for the female body. From Carravaggio to Vermeer, paintings that depicted one activity (a couple playing music together, music-making in a group, or music lessons) actually signaled sex or seduction. Railroad workers made the same point without the painters' fantastic theoboros, courtly lutes, or the arcane ancient Greek bandorla which supposedly gave its name to the banjo, though Southern slaves never beheld such a thing and called their instrument the banjar. The pear- or almond-shaped bodies of stringed musical instruments supplied stand-ins for women and an instrument covered in skin improved the analogy.

Centuries before railroaders or fine art painters, mid-winter revelers advertised their pleasure in a carol that solicited the same association. The drumming in an old English Christmas carol intended the same salacious significance as banjo-like thrumming.

Usually a solo activity, female masturbation may be part of mutual arousal, or foreplay, but is suggested by the ten drummers—the ten fingers. The image *had* to occur at verse ten to match the hands' digits. This is hardly a small consideration. *The Twelve Days* recognizes women's pleasures. That sounds like a modern viewpoint, and it is (with the implicit self-congratulations that we, males and females, finally accept sexual equality). But before moderns could liberate female sexuality women's obvious erotic enjoyments were theologically and medically suppressed. How extraordinarily proto-modern the carol is: its verses do not discriminate between the sexes. Indeed the verses take turns celebrating gender differences with a liberality that became a problem.

Accounting female erotic interests equivalent to men's, the carol's women are not exploited as un-reciprocated sexual objects. Not all merely submit to husbands in order to bear children. Surprisingly—to the modern sensibility that views the past as an endless spectacle of either female compliance/abuse or, from Eve onward, as *femmes fatales* apt to lapse into bawdy sinning that degrades men—in many verses of the carol's revelry women appear as full sexual partners. The song portrayed females as happy participants in a pre–Christian ethos that neither condemned their sex for the Fall nor attributed to women inherent and insidious moral weakness. Nor assumed they were passively sexless.

The above may sound like an implausibly strained reading of this

## The 12 Days of Christmas

verse, but for two looming constraints. If we dislike what we discover about bygone slang we are not free to dismiss it as merely distasteful, however bizarre or unpalatable. Alternatively, if the verses individually, and the carol in total, mean nothing, we're stranded in incomprehension, just as we started. Yet, some verses quite clearly refer to, and employ, known usage for lewdness. True, some of the verses are more obvious and accessible, but this is not one of them. Yet, the surrounding framework buoys the song's overall connotation and does not preclude the present reading of ten drumming fingers. In the song's context, other verses of *The Twelve Days* characterize women as men's complete erotic equals.

As confederates in mid-winter ribaldry, at Christmas "My true love" gave her something she wanted.

# Chapter 9

## A Night of Piping

If this were a modern song we'd expect what happens next.

Recent centuries bequeathed mainstream society a growing tendency to prefer public decency of a particular sort. Inherited norms of propriety condition how we encounter the carol. But long-gone social settings and the identity and likely inebriation of the carol's probable singers, should change expectations about the carol's subjects. Gradually, verse by verse, the song's presumed innocent and cheerful holiday themes are replaced by the scurrilous. Finally the song bulges rife with offensive language that challenges defenders of a more dainty accounting of this Christmas carol.

Christmastide's expected music conjures a playlist of pure and family-oriented songs. These vocals preach the virtues of generosity and patience, are spiritually up-lifting and nominally serious about religious Christmas. Such music suggests their performance context: settings furnished with clean linens, the gathering of family and friends wearing hand-knit sweaters indoors, in rooms that do not reek of spilled drink and sweat. Less reputable situations were the carol's more likely settings, rife with curling chimney smoke, the odor of gin slops, stale beer and, without plumbing, worse smells. Shadowy deeds fringed naughty music with the ruffians' mildest transgressions snubbed by decent folk as "dansin and singin off fylthe carrolles on Yeull Day."

It's easy to assume that "dirty" songs were mainly sung by men, at work or play. Without much regard to women's feelings about male appetites, they presumably sang about desire for home, lovers, honor, adventure, family and longing for women—less gallantly called lust. That presumption, that "dirty" songs flourished in stag parties, saloons, or brothels, is unimaginative. This song's lusty place featured in the

## The 12 Days of Christmas

melee of old-time Christmas. It's a hard mental adjustment but the more thoroughly assumptions derived from the modern holiday are erased, the more the carol's original intent emerges.

Well-lubricated by new ale, the song had formerly detonated under mid-winter's wan daylight. It was heard in smokey rushlight or in the glow of flickering candles that barely illumined some questionable company. Because women lived amid outlaws and scofflaws (yesteryear's biker gangs) their hearty, beer-fueled, voices also sang the carol in fireplace-lit taverns, and full-throated women heartily joined in because *The Twelve Days* balanced male lust with a fair rendition of women's arousal. Its mirror-imaged gendering avouches the song's generosity of spirit.

Featuring multi-orgasmic consummations, the carol's sexual saturation sidesteps some same-sex erotic preferences whose inclusion would, wholly anachronistically, award the song a post-modern notion of fairness. It's not that the past suffered from limited erotic inventiveness or preferences, but introducing untimely modernisms cannot help to restore the carol's vitality. Some desires are left out, though few. Those omissions rendered no tacit moral judgements but only recognize a limit imposed by twelve verses. Priority dictated the roster of imagery, not propriety.

Verse ten's female stimulation follows, and is soon matched by, verse nine's distinctly male foreplay. The carol's generous equivalences never presume one form of sexual expression superior to any other. This carol's view of the genders celebrates equal-opportunity gratification.

## Music

The sound of the pipes carried a ardent associations, some romantic. (In India the sound of the oboe-like shennai is associated with weddings, and Coleridge had something similar in mind when his Ancient Mariner hastens to a wedding proclaimed by a "loud bassoon." Formerly, double-reed instruments recalled nuptials.) Music conjures solemnity, joy, patriotism, heroism (as the bugle summons martial associations), longing, devotion, or eroticism. The orchestral harp or celesta seem all ethereal spirituality. Just listen to Benedick (not Benedict, meaning "good speech," a blessing, but *Benedick*, a good dick) rail:

## Chapter 9

> BENEDICK: I do much wonder that one man, seeing how much
> another man is a fool when he dedicates his
> behaviors to love, will, after he hath laughed at
> such shallow follies in others, become the argument
> of his own scorn by falling in love.... I have known when
> there was no music
> with him but the drum and the fife; and now had he rather hear the
> tabour and the pipe
> (*Much Ado About Nothing*, II:3)

The soldier Benedick admires the shrill "drum and the fife" whose blaring martial music stirs his soul, while the "tabour[ine] and the pipe" accompany love-making, dancing, and wooing. The "tambour" ambiguously refers either to a shallow or bass drum or a tambourine, the latter likely to pair with a pipe. These pipes may be bagpipes, pipes-of-pan, or flutes, but one thing is clear: For coupling, summon the pipers! Plain meaning supposes these pipers are bagpipers. So stipulated, the song's sense is conveyed, not in arcane symbols or oblique references, but in words whose obsolete meanings can be hauled up from a murky past, if fishing in the right libraries.

The nine pipers are strolling musicians; their presence underscores the song's unassuming origins because this instrument "is the sole property of no nation but the common property of the European peasantry."[1] The song's pipers confirm peasants' preferences, an earthy proletarian worldview and not an upper-class tribute to hard-working provincials. Pipes were used as "background music," a precursor to Muzak "piped" into factories and other workplaces. Henry Best noted, in his *Rural Economy in Yorkshire in 1641*, "There is 6d. allowed to a piper for playing to the clippers [sheep-shearers] all the day." The workers who listened to, and those who played, the pipes cherished many hopes for leisure, a recess that was antithetical to the aristocracy's interests. When the carol evoked the pipes, it signaled a political and social station in life.

Shakespeare mentioned the pipes in 1599 to usher informal merriment when, at last converted to love, Benedick shouts: "Let's have a dance.... Strike up Pipers" (*Much Ado About Nothing* V:4). He's consistent.

Accompanying dancing, pipes heralded carousing. The instrument's loud skirling summoned participants to gather for merrymaking,

## The 12 Days of Christmas

and pipes accompanied the dance that, too often for proper society's approval, was the carol(e). There's added cleverness in the 12-Days song. This verse conjures a visual pun that complements entreating pipers to the dance.

Playing an instrument was minstrelry, usually performed by professional entertainers. Minstrels were not vocalists. Since carols' singers regaled themselves vocalizing, minstrels played the pipes while carolers continued their dance-song.

Peter Brueghel (the elder) c.1525/30–1569, *Peasant Dance*, c. 1568, oil paint on oak panel, 114 × 164 cm (Kunsthistorisches Museum, Vienna, Inv.-Nr. GG_1059). The Netherlandish Renaissance artist Pieter Brueghel the Elder (1525/30–1569) brings all the carol's associations to bear in the image into his *Peasant Dance* 1567–69. Animated by the piper's loud music, peasants dance in a circle on the nominally religious occasion of their village's patron Saint's Day (the 3rd–4th century martyr St. George, whose feast day is 23 April) but in their merriment they steadfastly ignore an effigy of the Virgin hanging nearby on a tree. Instead of attending sacred Christian devotions, on the left peasants sit in front of the inn at a table stocked with food and beer; on the right, highly animated dancers crudely caper, graceless but energetic.

## Chapter 9

Detail of *Peasant Dance*. On the left an amorous couple kiss ardently and heedless of public scrutiny. Like the dancers in the foreground the artist depicts these peasants monumentally with an Italian-influenced attitude toward representing figures—a manner usually suitable for majestically portraying the nobility. In the foreground, a highly annoyed piper plays with puffed out cheeks. Surrounded by ample drink, the musician is pestered by an oblivious drunkard who, in tipsy obtuseness, may be requesting a tune or trying to force the piper to drink. Clearly, the piper cannot stop playing to quaff from the proffered jug. In the background a flag associated with St. George celebrates the day, but also marks an inn that, to enhance its income, serves as a brothel, because beneath the saint's ensign a potential customer is being dragged into the establishment by the proprietress: the sacred and profane in a contest of wills.

After rowdy peasants quaffed enough strong ale or cider between dances, it must have perennially occurred to the brightly inebriated that the bagpipe's shape resembles male organs. This conspicuous association proved indelible once noted. It appeared in a rollicking song, *The Rolling Blossom* as sung by a wily whore who cheats a would-be client, then chortles: "I left the youth to stretch his pipe," meaning to masturbate.[2]

Once bagpipes are visualized as an anatomically correct representation, piping pipers invokes oral-phallic play. (Though fellatio derives from Latin, to suck, it is universally called a "blow job," with its verb-forms: "s/he blew him/me," with further associations to piping.) We might try to disregard the sexual connotation because, as the old joke attributed to Freud goes, "sometimes a cigar is only a cigar."[3] But sometimes it isn't, when the sight of a piper ignites a sex-searching drunk in the throes of mid-winter revels.

Christmas copulation invited the pipers to the party and the instrument especially conjured sexual indecency, related to the marriage bed or not. The nine pipers attending the carol of *The Twelve Days* implied the song's lewdness, and the accompanying dance itself circled rife with associations, few of them wholesome.

Today such material as the carol flaunts is reserved for pornography or "transgressive" stand-up comics. With sometimes repulsively explicit language about anatomical functions in excretion or love-making, comics work "blue" to delight a tiresome audience self-consciously proud of its own supposed transgressiveness. But, before avant-garde awareness degraded and tediously democratized some of the past's revered and canniest comic artists (who now count among the pantheon of that high art) were long-ago foreshadowed when sucking a penis became a joke about blowing an instrument; this carol repeated the old trope. In *Henry IV part 2*, just such explicit banter erupts in a disreputable tavern in Eastcheap (II:4), exactly the sort of place that heard the carol bellowed.

Mistress Quickly, the proprietress, shares company with Doll Tearsheet—a whore's nickname referring to "dancing with her heels" in energetic bed-destroying sex:

> PISTOL: God save you, Sir John!
> FALSTAFF: Welcome, Ancient Pistol. Here, Pistol, I charge you with a cup of sack: do you discharge upon mine hostess.
> PISTOL: I will discharge upon her, Sir John, with two bullets.
> FALSTAFF: She is Pistol-proof, sir; you shall hardly offend her.
> MISTRESS QUICKLY: Come, I'll drink no proofs nor no bullets: I'll drink no more than will do me good, for no man's pleasure, I.

The character named Pistol (which meant "pipe," hence the character carries the pejorative name of penis, a prick), will be charged/loaded,

*Chapter 9*

Holland's Leaguer (Wellcome Library, London. Wellcome Images). **In the early years of the 17th century this high-class Southwark Brothel, Holland's Leaguer, prospered in Old Paris Garden. It supplied a fashionable hangout generally secure from intrusion by the law, debt collectors, or otherwise unwanted visitors who might disturb the clientele. The Bankside location, in the Liberty of the Clink, sat outside the authority of the London civil authorities and, operating in the shadow of the palace of the Bishop of Winchester, the tony name, Paris Garden, may have been a witty corruption of parish garden.**

not with gunpowder, but fortified wine. As for ordinance: the two bullets are not cannon balls but his testicles; their discharge, semen. When Mistress Quickly stoutly announces that she'll drink no bullets, she means that she does not "swallow..." "for no man's pleasure." Oral sex was fair-play as repartee for a popular playwright parading crude wit about a shamelessly clever underclass. And their gathering-place was exactly the sort of low-life (and sometimes high class) tavern where the

# The 12 Days of Christmas

Hieronymous Bosch, *Garden of Earthly Delights* triptych (Museo nacional del Prado, Madrid). Prominently, in the middle of the right wing of his great triptych, *The Garden of Earthly Delights*, Hieronymous Bosch (c.1450–1516) placed a pink bagpipe situated like an offering upon an altar. The painter visually compared the musical instrument to male organs and his phantasmagoria exalted the penis-scrotum. Around the huge pink bagpipe an assorted group, including a bishop, prance or perform a circle dance. Centrally positioned, the bagpipe-as-penis is venerated as the great (mis)leader or generative force. Europe never so glorified the penis as in India, where the linga-phallus stands for the god Shiva, but Bosch's work suggests that visual culture once accepted comparisons now relegated to academic reference.

"Bagpipe as Penis," *Book of Hours*, Use of Rome (the "Hours of Joanna I of Castile" or the "Hours of Joanna the Mad"), 1486–1506 (British Library add MS 18852 fol. 299r). At about the same time as Bosch worked on his immense *The Garden of Earthly Delight* another artist, painting on the much more modest scale of a hand-held book, used the same visual joke, which was apparently well-known.

## Chapter 9

drinking song of the *Twelve Days* would be right at home. The theater audience well knew of such hangouts, just steps from the Globe in the very territory patrolled by Winchester Geese.

Shakespeare's stage strutted an un-shame-able underclass who share some of the upper classes' loose morals, but without aristocracy's kingdom-robbing ambition. Those characters' contrition awaited a later play, *Henry IV part 2* but, before their penance, these ruffians acted the abysmal morals of Christmas revelers: theft, drinking to excess, lassitude, whoring, fighting, lying. Depicting crude plebeians amused the upper classes paying audience and regaled working-class commoners who could afford to attend. Audiences still crave seeing themselves portrayed. Four hundred years fresh, Shakespeare's joke continues to draw laughs from uninhibited modern audiences.

The holiday offered respite for muscle-weary carolers to recover from physical exhaustion. In mid-winter recess peasants could savor the few delights life offered the illiterate and, by most standards, impoverished. Oral sex tempted an attractive alternative to work. If this seems too explicit—like the discomfort of imagining parents in sexual congress, let along great-great-grandparents—the holiday's community-wide festival of ingenious sexual couplings wasn't invented recently. The idea that the past loved chastely while we explore and dare the marvelously kinky and sexually inventive just unfurls the pennant of another generational self-aggrandizing notion. With little commercial entertainment, few times a year afforded an intermission from drudgery. Only during these much-anticipated interludes home-made merriment ruled. Not everybody went to the theater.

Contemplated without a romantic haze, peasants' lives knew scarce sensuality to light a drear existence. Jean Anouilh (1910–87) poignantly evoked this reality in his play *Becket* (1959) when the king learns the facts-of-peasant-life from his Chancellor, Thomas à Becket:

> At twenty he has lost his teeth and taken on that indeterminate age the common people have. That man may have been handsome. He may have had one night of love, one minute when he too was a King, and shed his fear. Afterward, his pauper's life went on, eternally, the same. And he and his wife no doubt forgot it all. But the seed was sown.

If Anouilh's art does not suffice, earnest scholarship pronounced essentially the same verdict, that for medieval peasants, "Their main

## The 12 Days of Christmas

solaces in life were getting drunk once a year at the village feast and taking their pleasure at night with their wives," or somebody else's.[4] That "once a year" consolation, Christmas/Yule relieved sexual deprivation, somewhat. The festival sated hunger in feasting and ale. With scant work in winter's dormant and fallow frozen fields, plentiful strong drink helped suspend civility's every normal limit.

At Christmas carefree license prevailed. In fullest irresponsibility the underclasses regaled in the illusion of freedom and the reality of debauchery. The Church feared this annual religion-canceling event that clergy were forced to witness: the sight of their own parishioners practicing as connoisseurs of most of the deadly sins.

This carol's catalogue of sins describes an actuality whose approach good citizens shuddered at; the Church and the upright laity dreaded the immorality and property destruction while, after the festival, the carousers wistfully recollected personal highpoints with satisfaction. As the festival receded, some celebrants regretted hangovers, a newly acquired venereal disease, ruptured marriages, bruises and broken bones, and money lost to gambling. If memory of that traditional mid-winter orgy faded, there's a reason. Physical pleasure is not sufficiently accounted as part of the folk tradition because successive crusades of (the specifically Christian idea of) moral rectitude systematically erased erotic considerations from the official record.

Campaigns of eradication issued from those charged with record-keeping: academics and clerics set the censorious tone of recollection. Not surprisingly, generations of academics overlooked the carol's network of lewd secondary meanings which, taken together, produce overwhelming evidence of lusty peasant culture—then and now.[5] With prejudices about each genre's proper content, aestheticians, who were also the song's inheritors, found such carols' highly objectionable subject-matter improbable.

Academic editors tending toward fustiness ("good taste" as defined by an imagined mass-audience) ensured that few folktales feature both requited lust and a happy ending, unless the hero could be portrayed as a trickster. To be acceptably included in a tale sex could only be slyly stolen by men or women. Gratified lust (as legitimate an appetite as any other) just seems an unsatisfactory reward for a genie's wish. Nobody answers the genie's age-old offer with: "having been stranded on this island, for my first wish I want to get laid." Yet, that seems an entirely reasonable request, if beyond the bounds of folklore's filter.[6] After the usual fairytale's arduous quest the pay-off is never sex for the Handsome/Charming Prince (or Princess/heroine), which seems uncharacteristic compared to what really motivates people.

Mythic love-stories do not end in a blissful session of love-making when that is why the lovers wanted to be together in the first place. No folk-hero goes off in search of the perfect fuck while, in reality, that is just what every new generation seeks. Forget "Sex in the City," the primordial quest found itself replaced; instead of sex other desires predominate in expurgated folklore and the edited folksong catalogue.

Folktales feature wanderers who happen into ghostly abandoned banquets piled with quantities of hearty food and high cuisine's most exquisite refinements. Peasants never saw such variety of victuals, except when espied through the window of the manner house or once a year at the gentry's laden Yule table. Culinary longing, more than caloric fuel for sustenance—the gustatory and aesthetic delights of texture, aroma, and taste—proved an acceptable theme to middle-class folklorists and an easily imagined yearning for often hungry peasants. Other desires fared poorly.

Amid the peasants' battle with scarcity and hunger, one festival's arrival heralded adequate food, drink, and release from work's endless cycle. A well-fed lull ushered lust to the forefront, as "December was the season—the only season—for fresh meat."[7] Feasting and drinking commenced just when an oasis of leisure granted opportunities to act on other cravings. Given the song's witty language-antics, an unsurprising meaning of piping involves food.

Fresh victuals, alcohol, respite from endless field chores, and sex were all briefly available at the same time of year, a season formerly consecrated to gods of fecundity ... and the Church wondered why it was having a hard time selling a holiday dedicated to virgin birth? The Church tried to suppress gift-giving, feasting, sex, drinking, and caroling about these seasonally-occurring pleasures. Good luck with that.[8]

## Feasting

Regarding the pleasant conjunction of food and sex (relief and stress-reduction off-loaded to the autonomic nervous system that regulates involuntary functions): several uses of piping mean to transfer liquid—whiskey, ale, wine, beer, etc.—into a pipe or cask. That seems

## The 12 Days of Christmas

germane to the time-of-year when strong drink first became available. Accordingly, this punning phrase associates instrumentalists with decanting or piping liquor into smaller containers for serving and drinking, a lively prospect.

The verse can mean that musicians are busily siphoning cider, wine, or ale from casks, because the carol fails to mention *what* they are piping, purposefully keeping the image ambiguous. They can be playing music or pouring liquor. (Give the piper a wee dram and let the piper reciprocate by offering you a mug: true Christmas spirit. Popular folksongs still urge giving the fiddler a dram.) Some verses that seem straightforward turn out to be vaguely suggestive while other verses that appear silly or unintelligible emerge as quite explicit. The song's ambiguities depend on obsolete slang carted into the present. After the past delivers its consignment to the present, what the carol lacks proves as important as what it describes.

Stirring my cup and absent-mindedly looking outside, the afternoon's chilly rain seemed as dreary as the prospects of accurately and fully imagining this obsolete holiday. The practitioners of old-style Christmas in England rarely involved either wealthy gentry, landowners. or rich merchants who could afford to hire painters to record the festival. British artists chiefly captured their patrons' self-consciously refined and mannered antics, stiff lordly poses in front of ancestral lands, or concocted military scenes of valor. Surviving images of peasant merrymaking are much scarcer than the upper-classes' self-aggrandizing confections.

Like scientific progress, artistic evolution does not advance in lockstep across media or coordinate with nationalities. Sometimes poetry takes the intellectual lead, or music makes great strides, or painting, and those arts' competencies unevenly distribute among peoples and eras. Because Renaissance England was not nearly as visually evolved as continental Europe (unlike England's writers) the surviving artistic records of peasant festivals come mainly from the hands of Flemish-Dutch artists.[9] Likewise, until the Romantic period, literature shunned considering the lives of common laborers, tradesmen, or agricultural serfs.

Literature (perhaps rightly, given the dramatic possibilities) considered the powerful few who—having purchase to shape their own lives and their kingdoms—molded grand history while serfs droned on in the background, eating the same daily diet and toiling endlessly anonymous. Even later literature that romanticized common field laborers,

*Chapter 9*

as salt of the earth invested with folksy righteousness, rarely deigned to chronicle peasants' rites. The learned rebuked uneducated commoners for acts the carol registered with glee. And sometimes those same acts, when brought to the attention of prevailing legal authorities, who could use the literate state's coercive power, arrested for questioning, jailed or fined, and punished carol singers. Practitioners of pagan mid-winter rites of social and sexual abandonment may have fared worse if they exceeded even the community's temporarily dilated standards.[10]

Images of Yule were always scarce and (like pornography) successive generations of heirs guiltily destroyed their unwanted endowments

"Cannibals" (detail of a page with a border of foliage, flowers, leaves; including drawings of cannibals, a walled town, and exotic animals with a giraffe, lion, camel, and elephant), c. 1330–1340, with the full page paintings attributed to the "Master of the Cocharelli Codex" (active in Genoa) with contributions by at least two artists, one may have been the Genoese Monk of Hyres (active c. 1370) (British Library add Manuscript 28841 fol. 3).

Leaves from a prose treatise on the Seven Vices, written in two columns on parchment, and a verse on events from the history of Sicily in the time of Frederick II (1298–1337) (ff. 2–7). The current sequence of pages re-shuffles the original order, and the work, re-bound by the British Museum (only a fraction of the original survives) is now scattered in several collections in London, Florence, and Cleveland.

Parchment leaves (with a page size of 170 × 110mm with a text space of 125 × 80 mm) mounted on paper guards bound together in an album of 7 leaves with miniatures and historiated borders in colors and gold, of human figures, insects, birds, animals and sea-shells.

## The 12 Days of Christmas

of smutty pictures. Then, as now, the poor controlled meager artistic means and until quite recently neither museums nor fine homes regularly preserved folkart. In any case, folkart's practitioners produced images that, though still highly suggestive, were too crudely worked to capture the carnival's fine details. Without visual evidence, the lower-classes' rowdy past evaporated like the rising wisps above my coffee mug.

The cost of employing an artist to draw or paint Yuletide fun loomed prohibitive, as unthinkable for the poor as retaining a courtly poet for panegyric's elaborate flattery, but pipers could be hired on a peasant's budget. Few artists lauded the peasants' winter gusto, mischief, and misrule. But, if art preserved such images I knew who to call.

Pieter van der Borcht (c. 1535–1608/11), *Peasant Fair on a Festival Day* (Boerenkermis), 1559, etching/engraving on paper, height: 29.7 cm (11.6 in); Width: 46.9 cm (18.4 in) (The Metropolitan Museum of Art, Purchase, A. Hyatt Mayor Purchase Fund, Marjorie Phelps Starr Bequest, Barbara and Howard Fox Gift, and Charles Z. Offin Fund, 2000). A Flemish painter, draughtsman and etcher, Pieter (or Peter) van der Borcht (c. 1530–1608) produced numerous drawings, engravings, etchings, and woodcuts that appeared in illustrated books. His exceptional productivity has suggested that his name actually represents an entire workshop of assistants and disciples who produced work under his name. Mainly his works, like this raucous village scene (after Pieter Brueghel the Elder, (1526/1530–1569), portrayed so-called genre subjects on historical (nominally) religious topics.

## Chapter 9

**Pieter van der Borcht, Detail: Circle Dance with pipe, drum, and drink. Here is an example of Benedick's complaint (*Much Ado About Nothing*, II:3) about a fellow who formerly relished the martial sound of "the drum and the fife" but now prefers the less bellicose "tabour and the pipe." In this scene of village revelry van der Borcht's one-man band, indicates that the townsfolk cannot afford more musicians because they spend their money on the two-fisted barmaid's proffered flagons.**

The phone sat on the desk before me, a spoon's length from the coffee: caffeine being the drug-of-choice for such forays. Professor Larry Silver, one of the world's leading experts on art answered my call. He listened to my frustrated questions and, as hoped, pointed out similar customs that art did record.

Like the Scottish Kerk-mass, a Flemish village's *kermis* hosted a once-a-year saint's day. (The celebration resembled modern St. Patrick's day in America, where the patron saint of Ireland furnishes the excuse for tavern visits and raucous gratifications.) That morning entailed attending church—and sometimes taking in a miracle or morality play performed outdoors—before the rest of the day and night broke loose in celebratory activity, especially wild dancing, fighting, covert whoring, gambling and drinking. Like the Yule, kermis day permitted a kind of liberation, whose over-indulgence and excess prompted a Flemish proverb that cautioned general sobriety, "'tis not a kermis every day." All those other days of the year bound the community in thrifty altruism and measured fellowship, a benevolence sorely tested when

# The 12 Days of Christmas

Pieter van der Borcht, Detail: open air fornicating.

Pieter van der Borcht, Detail: peeing and defecating with a piper in the middle ground.

## Chapter 9

Pieter van der Borcht, Detail: riotous fighting.

Pieter van der Borcht, Detail: the pious on their way to prayer, the day's nominal religious occasion. The faithful make their way toward the church, before which hang the banners of St. George. On the left a raised stage mounts a scene in which, contrasting with the shuffling queued worshippers, a pilgrim bursts upon a couple in the same poses as fornicators in Fig. 19. This detail may present an open-air consummation so dreaded by the religious but popular with unlettered peasantry.

drunken fights broke out. But when sobriety returned those relationships repaired … or, following serious harm, grudges were carried as multi-generational feuds (truly, the spirit of Christmas year-round).

The great Flemish artist, Pieter Bruegel (1525/30–1569) showed animated taverns, dancing to bagpipes, and flirtations. Bruegel inscribed his satirical print of *Kermis at Hoboken* with the tag, "The

# The 12 Days of Christmas

peasants delight in such festivals: to dance, jump, and drink themselves drunk as beasts. They insist on holding their kermises." And Prof. Silver, drawing on his vast erudition as effortlessly as a magician extracts a rabbit from the hat, recalled that Bruegel's contemporary, Pieter van der Borcht (c. 1535–1608/11) had produced a similar print with a similar inscription: "The drunkards delight in such festivals: fighting and brawling and drinking themselves drunk like beasts." Yule was even wilder but, because of cultural difference between the Netherlands and England regarding the proper role of visual arts, we have pictures of kermis. Those images prominently depict the centrality of beer, ale, and cider consumption—in conjunction with musical piping. We have no real pictures of Yule, but carols preserve the festival's behavioral instructions.

Though the song hints at the role of the strong drink that suffused the festival, completely missing is any sign of tea, chocolate, coffee, or tobacco—all products of the age of exploration. Water, being a beverage of dubious merits and likely to cause illness, was scarcely imbibed. Children drank weak beer and adults saved higher alcohol beers for festivals. Queen Elizabeth I drank a quart of strong beer with her breakfast. In England, tea drinking only replaced beer drinking at breakfast in the eighteenth century. (One does not *pipe* water into a "drawing room," there one *draws* water for coffee or tea. The room's functional name disregards drafting with a pencil.) Absent commodities suggest that the song formed before the seventeenth century when these imported goods came into general use ... but not for all classes simultaneously. Although coffee houses grew plentiful in London and tobacco was smoked as a genteel indulgence, these luxuries only gradually trickled down to the peasantry.

While liquor may be suggestively piped, tobacco smoking goes unmentioned because the carol's pipers do not puff on clay tobacco pipes. Among the working classes, only sailors on fifteenth–sixteenth-century missions of exploration came into contact with such wondrous commodities. In the first generations after tobacco's introduction to Europeans the rare product was available only to aristocrats before gaining widespread acceptance as a valuable cash crop. If the carol of *The Twelve Days of Christmas* circulated by the middle of the fourteenth century, it probably achieved its recognizable form by the end of the

## Chapter 9

seventeenth century—without mentioning tobacco, and other exotic goods. No tea, coffee, chocolate, or even distilled whiskey, but coarser, more medieval beverages are being piped. Or, somebody may be draining, piping, the fluids of the true love, if the penis is regarded as a conduit, a pipe to be piped. That's Shakespeare's joke about a character named "Pistol."

The "pipers" mouthing the pipes may be female, but were probably males—hence this verse extends a complex jest, possibly of homoerotic images and wordplay. But until recently sexual preferences neither clearly demarcated either taboo gender segregation nor their conjoining. Beginning in antiquity and continuing into pre-modern life, each maturing male's preferences were expected to roam through gendered sexual possibilities. Varied companions offered different experiences.[11] Each was suitable to successive developmental ages: like trying different foods, not necessarily a moral choice but a matter of preferences and not necessarily life-long partialities. Sexual predispositions expressed, usually aristocratic, knowledge about prevailing taste or manners.

In antiquity and through the early middle ages appropriate partners and sex acts changed in their acceptability but these shifting individual preferences were rarely elevated to public memory. Chronicles of sex usually cached personal annals—confessional, boastful, or soppy with contrition (if pompously filigreed with intimate details), or inferred from the record of partialities (a king's male favorites). But, when narrated with foaming outrage from the seat of authority, the establishment's official morals shunned Yuletide's unsophisticated peasant transgressions as sinful, wasteful, and dangerous to the Establishment. Lordly transgressions rampaged with less rebuke from the pulpit. Leaping Lords, indeed.

The collective memory starved, lacking nourishment from the bureaucratic register of scandal and indignity. So we never learn *exactly* what poor Jane Robinson sang, locked up in Bridewell Hospital after disturbing the peace with "ribald songs," because transcribing her repertoire would have breached the very decorousness she violated. (Clumsy exceptions have registered in official annals. The otherwise dull US government printing office in 1986 issued the Meese Report [Final Report of the Attorney General's Commission on Pornography], which became a best-seller because it entered into evidence, and therefore reproduced,

## The 12 Days of Christmas

the otherwise illicit naughty goods.[12]) This song, conveniently or discretely overlooked because it was never filed and catalogued as an administrative document, preserves a catalogue of imagery that tests assumptions about Christmas and caroling. In the song we encounter a tally of the scorned, banned, and sometimes criminalized.

Carved in stone to last the ages, bombastic proclamations fade and are forgotten but this song survived by selective forgetting. The official record omitted the carol's inventory and, chameleon-like, the carol aped an innocent ditty and thereby its content gained virtual invisibility. Eventually beneath notice, the carol endured long after olden Christmas was outlawed. When the winter festival re-appeared so did the song, but without the key to its lyrics.

This carol celebrated the mid-winter's holiday that blossomed a pan-sexual release. It tolerated or encouraged almost every excess. The Church, meanwhile, was burning the song's sodomites and non-clerical pederasts.

At Christmas the community celebrated having successfully negotiated another year, with hopes to fortunately traverse the coming deep cold and collectively arrive at bright Spring. The harvest in, together the singers crossed the year's darkest, most mysterious, nights. The festival offered fresh meat downed with new beer, fighting, and games, with lusty songs to accompany drunken chambering. There's not much left of such unbridled enthusiasm, let alone orgiastic release in thoroughly sanctioned community-wide events.

Both food and sex combine in the phrase "piping hot," which may characterize the pipers. It's the only phrase we still use that carries any of the gusto of this verse's original language.

## *Chapter 10*

### Milk, an Animal Truth

Today this song of the *Twelve Days* features centrally when conjuring an exemplary Christmas. According to the rare ideal, the family gathers intact, cordial and loving, smiling at a pyramid of colorfully wrapped packages under a decorated tree near the fireplace's burning blaze. Despite the scarcity of such warm gatherings, the season's songs infiltrated the whole fabric of modern life. Everybody knows the words and, regardless of how we celebrate the mid-winter with lights and feasting, these verses return to center stage from the periphery of mere anthropological or historical interest.[1]

In the days when carolers fully understood the lyrics, the people who sang this song were no smarter than we. The carol concealed no erudite game of hide-and-seek with secret clues hidden away, because the original singers already knew the slangy references. Illiterates, they couldn't have mastered anagrams anyway, or explored historical texts. The carol's sly verses were generally understood by the people who laughed when Shakespeare floated the same smutty jokes across the Globe's stage. For those familiar with its jargon, the carol of *The Twelve Days* required no arcane cipher to break its riddles and yet, across the borders of time and space, no art travels with a universal passport. Each art requires introduction to its conventions.

Once, centuries past, the song bawled out commonly understood situations. The phrases cradled a widespread kind of speech that subsequently seemed cryptic or silly yet, when its first singers flourished, the verses' colloquialisms conveyed real desires. No one, then or now, truly wants the actual list of gifts.

The verses' exquisitely creative morsels of demotic language were savored by low-lives and peasants, bar flies in taverns or, after drinking

## The 12 Days of Christmas

their fill, men on their way to and from chambering, and petty criminals. Their delectation pleased farmers on a once-a-year bender who, otherwise shackled to a relentless wheel of daily chores, enjoyed self-consciously breaking the bounds of civility and, among other misdemeanors, caterwauling these naughty phrases. Apparently among the singers were sex-workers and their customers in legal or illegal stews, who regularly, regardless of the calendar or festival day, shattered propriety's every constraint (and were sometimes arrested for drunkenly, and more or less tunefully, bellowiing obscenities). The carol singers did not mask their carnal hunger. In contrast, today's popular music, which aims to shock, seems pretty circumspect when crooning about "romance" that actually means lust,[2] or when performers theatrically shout about angry sexual frustration or political impotence ... without naming specific wants.

A pornocopia, *The Twelve Days* celebrates both the male and female notions of satisfactory and abundant sex, though female lust was less well understood than men's. In that matter the carolers' old-time confusion should not elicit condescension. Whatever the activity's ancillary fun, sex was for procreation, as the Church taught. Until recently nobody understood what the anatomical, psycho-sexual, and operational gender differences meant.

The field's path-finding scholar mused that "Female orgasm and the means of producing it were and are anomalous.... Its lack of correlation with fertility and conception remains counterintuitive.... In both the recent and the distant past, it seemed only reasonable to assume a priori that men and women would be sexually gratified by the same act of penetration to male orgasm that made conception possible."[3] (As late as the nineteenth-century medical specialists and scientists were "uncertain about the existence and strength of the sexual instinct in women" and that "Woman's instinctive motherliness did not ... presuppose an instinctive sexuality."[4]) Such notions represented the best and wisest thinking for a very long time. It still represents the ideas of many men and some women about what their own desires should be. But the carol presents another viewpoint, an older idea based on experience uncontaminated by the Church's theorizing or early psychology. And the carol's attitude toward the sexes might lead us to wonder who composed the lyrics that so wisely accounted for female lust?

## Chapter 10

Sexually active women can subscribe to the carol's inventory of gratifications, especially the verse that features eight maids a-milking. They appear as the song unreels a list rather than a developing series of conjunctive elements where each following item gains its sense from what directly preceded it. Mainly, alliteration and a few key numerical landmarks anchor the verses in place. The carol promotes no coherent thesis but celebrates male and female wants.

Amid a pan-erotic festival of Dionysian release for every passion, the carol resists the common-sensical view of male-dominated sex as the default assumption. Women can, unconditionally and joyfully, join in this song, even those who argue that heterosexual sex must be inherently patriarchic, besides being phallocentric. For militants, intercourse remains the expression of domineering males and mostly compliant females, the former exploiting the latter dupes (who are recompensed in one or another manner). The outlook of *The Twelve Days* is more nuanced, although recognizing human frailty. Parts of the carol deal with exclusively female pleasures.

Though an old song, the carol's women should not be visualized as modern fantasies of slender pale-skinned Victorian aristocrats dressed up as rurals: a hard template to crack if romanticizing the countryside doused with a treacly unreality. Those seductively fraudulent images carry profound political implications. (This mirage spans social class and includes Jane Austen's gentry amid a benignly fecund countryside and Marie Antoinette's fantasy of herself as a rustic and uncomplicated milkmaid escaping the royal court's harrowing.) Sturdy rural girls had appetites to match. As Germaine Greer described them, seventeenth-century "[m]ilkmaids were stout and straight, strong enough to carry two bulky wooden pails suspended from a yoke across their shoulders, and sure-footed enough not to slop the precious milk out of the pail as they travelled over the uneven ground. Spilt milk was a disaster, and milkmaids wept piteously over it, afraid of being beaten." (Greer directs our attention to *All's Well That Ends Well*, "he weeps like a wench that had shed her milk" [IV:3].) Such girls' cravings matched their robust living; their trade implied a skill translatable to other circumstances. If it were not saturated with Yuletide's social inversions, this verse alone tints the song with a distinctly anti-establishment viewpoint.

## The 12 Days of Christmas

Simple phrases, virtually free of latinates, suggest *The Twelve Days* began life before the beginning of the sixteenth century or perhaps a century earlier. Milk is an ancient word and the dearth of neologisms accentuates the carol's age (bolstered by the absence of exploration's bounty, like tobacco). A noun, "milk" can operate as a transitive verb that means to extract milk by handling from the teats (of a cow, goat, ewe, etc.). Only mammals yield milk. Initially, this usage seems irrelevant, but the ancient carolers' singing came through smirking lips. They didn't care about academic grammar, although syntax nevertheless colors their meaning.

As an obsolete verb, it meant to give or yield milk, mainly of livestock and usually cattle, but even of women.[5] (Conversely, to milk the ram or the bull was figuratively to engage in an enterprise doomed to failure.) Also the word meant to cause (milk) to flow and to stream out of, while an even older and outmoded sense meant to eject milk. Those who milked were, from daily practice, specialists although virtually everybody on a farm could milk livestock and most people lived on farms. While anybody could milk an animal, only some practitioners were sung about.

Milkmaids describe dairy farming's most commonplace occupation

**Milkmaids, 1916, Shakespeare Tricentenary (courtesy Archives and Rare Books Library, University of Cincinnati).**

## Chapter 10

and also damsels who are yielding milk (and hence not virgins)—perhaps wet nurses (nurse-maids). These maids may be suckling their own children or others.' Once a commonplace of womanhood, two inexorable tides converged and yanked Occidental women from engaging this age-old skill of nursing. That disjunction severed multi-generational households' knowledge of the craft of lactation. To enhance industrial output, the model two-income family was foisted on the middle and working classes, a pattern that had, heretofore, imposed drudgery on the truly poor—or rural couples who maintained dual occupations, but preserved their specialized oversight zones on the same farmstead's home and fields. The change ripped families from multi-generational households during the factory's workday, and the mechanized schedule created a new ignorance about the body. With the spread of industrialization, inexperience about lactation was widely exported, with disastrous results. For lack of money infant formulas were watered, which starved the child nutritionally and robbed its mother of lactation's physical and psychological benefits. Modernization, that freed women for the industrialized workforce, and consumerism's global power to promote bottle-feeding and commercial infant formulas—both vectors combined to reduce traditional and healthy suckling. The carol-singers knew no milk banks, bottle-feeding of factory concocted baby formulas, or an office's lactation booths.

Wet-nursing furnished a commonplace sight of everyday life. (In a parallel structure analogous to blood relationships, wet-nurses—even today, in Islam—often hold a status akin to actual motherhood, allowing that Milking Maids may be twice maternal. In this re-doubling, blood relations resemble milk relations.[6]) The maids may be lactating after having given birth or they may be milking other creatures. In either case, they know a frankly hands-on relationship to living creatures that have had sexual experience and subsequently given birth, which insinuates the milkmaids as potential erotic playmates—the classic farmer's daughter. There is no milking of any animal without its first giving birth and no birth without sex. These maids know warm bodies that have known sex, their own or others. This natural connection stood foremost in the un-prudish minds of agricultural workers who represented the population's overwhelming majority before the Industrial Revolution dwindled the ratio of farmers to city workers in increasingly urbanized manufacture-based economies.

Modern metropolites self-aggrandize their hipness; in earthy

## The 12 Days of Christmas

matters the countryside lives immediate to carnal reality.

Swathes of Renaissance London's urbanites were never far removed from, and were constantly reminded of, animal facts-of-life as keepers or riders of horses; chickens and geese pecked in urban dooryards and hogs roamed city lanes. Unhappy underfed cows tenanted city yards, but yielded fresh milk, however watery and low in butterfat. Until very recently everyone lived close enough to animals to know that milk did not spontaneously arise in sterile containers at the shop.

Maid A-Milking (courtesy Emily Lowell, The Milk Maids of Mobile, Alabama).

The recently industrialized world forgot agricultural experience as ever fewer farmers fed ever more people with foods that—manipulated after passing through substance-altering factories—yielded ever more calories. The first-hand experience of milking receded from the familiar everyday event it used to be and nursing mothers are less common a sight than in centuries past. That absence partly resulted from a growing middle-class daintiness about women who milk; breasts were to be hidden precisely because they are sexual attractors. Eventually Victorian niceties and circumlocutions imposed an indignity where this verse infers none.

Though unmentioned in the song, milking implies breasts and if the milkmaids yield milk, they are not virgins, hence they were sexually active and may be currently available. And eager.

Anything pertaining to human breasts strongly evokes sex. To argue that breasts should not be visual sexual signals picks a fight with zoology. Human breasts developed their size and prominence high on the torso to draw attention and evoke interest, and their pronounced display (compared to other mammals) signals sexual anticipation. They are a principal

## Chapter 10

attractor for animals that mostly court and select mates visually: us.[7] They can be stimulating playthings for both partners but they function as milk factories only after mating has produced offspring. In post-pubescent humans, hemispheric breasts demonstrate fitness for mating. The obvious successor of sexual activity and pregnancy, lactation's milk-yielding breasts discomforted urbanized Victorians and their cultural progeny right through the middle of the breast-fixated twentieth century. (Tit-crazy would more accurately describe mid-twentieth-century American culture as exported worldwide. And, like most things American, bigger was better.) Eight maids a-milking reminds us that mammary glands are more than a secondary sexual characteristic. Male or female, infants require and appreciate breasts (and, unlike adults who would choke, nursing infants can simultaneously breathe, suck, and swallow while on the breast), men admire or crave them, women may be proud of them: all have thought about and come to some aesthetic conclusion about women's breasts. They are precursor to milk.

In any society, at any time, including our own, visual attraction partly explains why the village dance featured as important as the modern version of the mixer or club that shows off the body. One verse's Dancing Ladies nicely coordinates this verse's more subtle allusion to bodily fitness.

In a subordinate, and now thoroughly obscure sense, "maid" indicates a man who has entirely abstained from sexual intercourse. That seems a contradiction to the song's prevailing sense and to this verse's insinuations. Though citations can be found from the fourteenth century, Shakespeare used the word this way in the *Twelfth Night*, 1601, "You are betroth'd both to a maid and man." (V:1) And in 1606 Ben Jonson spoke more directly in *Hymenæi* "View two noble Maids of either sexe, to Union sacrificed." Today we would be startled to encounter "Maids of either sexe," meaning virgins.

The word maid, short for maiden, derives from "common-Teutonic stock; probably with an Aryan original, meaning 'unmarried.'"[8] Sometimes an unmarried woman, a spinster, was called a maid, a usage that survives in expressions like "maiden name," a woman's birth-identity and family name before marriage's sex and children; and "old maid," a spinster. The old maid was not confused with an elderly professional servant (chamber maid). Like the usage meaning virgin, old maid refers

# The 12 Days of Christmas

to someone of diminished or arrested psycho-sexual status. Such a person's social maturation and elevation in community rank (but not necessarily actual psycho-sexual experience) halted by remaining single and, at the verge of womanhood, bypassing motherhood. The word maid, which now seems so old-fashioned, was intimately tied to sexual status, a condition surviving in the almost-quaint "maidenhead."[9] This virginal usage endures in the title "maid" Marianne of the Robin Hood story, also in the "Maid of Orleans," referring to Joan of Arc, or a "maiden aunt."[10] Despite ages of blue-nosed religious moaning about the evils of sex and concomitant exaltation of the virgin state, for heightened standing in the community and assured self-respect, post-nubile maidenhood (spinsterhood) threatened a situation to be avoided.

Despite second-wave feminism, calling someone an "old maid" remains either a pejorative or an invitation to explain a woman's situation and history. Nobody deems that, for a woman seeking a spouse, lack of attractiveness on the marriage market was, somehow, a virtue. The last two centuries of feminist struggle have considerably multiplied a women's options. Yet, there's still an active campaign to browbeat a vulnerable population into thinking of bodily "impurity" following sex. Despite the obviously implicit self-loathing of the pitch (rooted in Christianity's demotion of humanity's mortal form), it's unclear exactly what this foul contamination might be regarding normal body functions. Former times were more honest or, at least in some skeptical quarters, less tolerable of religious nutters.

In 1603 it was lamented, "To die maides! O horrible!" was to die while yet a virgin.[11] That most lamentable fate (in a plague year at the beginning of the seventeenth century) provided a timeless argument whether heard in London stews with lethal disease raging about or the backseat of a Chevy during the Cold War's threat of nuclear annihilation before having gone "all the way."

But knowing what this word means, and meant in the past, is not the same as knowing how it was used in this song and, with notable exceptions, whatever the Church preached about the sins of the flesh, life-long celibacy seemed touchingly pathetic for those living directly from the soil's fertility and animal's fecundity. Or, for those living nearby an emporium of sex, or under threat of execution by plague. Everywhere, milking maids.

## Chapter 10

Slyly sacrilegious, by stressing ambiguous virginity and echoing undertones of the verse of the Twelve Ladies the song purposefully confuses two diametrically-opposed insinuations: a milking maid refers to both a virgin and a lactating mother—one who knows sex and one who knows it not. Eight carnally inexperienced but fully aware virgins combine with sexually accomplished farm girls handling teats, perhaps their own as, with a double-entendre, the song hails an octet of maidens milking an animal or person. After all, a maid could be any female attendant—more formerly called a maid-servant. It all depends on what this verse intended amidst an earthy song celebrating mundane salacious appetites.

If we try to envision the maids as they perform, what exactly are they doing? Because "maids a-milking" ambiguates who is milking what. The carol might insinuate manual stimulation for non-procreative female arousal, as foreplay like the recreational sex of clitoral drumming. Or (depending on the gender of the singer's persona) a male gaze might playfully consume the sight of breast arousal, for the mutual pleasures of voyeurism and proud exhibitionism. Because the exact nature of the stated action remains wholly, and apparently purposefully, indefinite, the implied activity could be handling a person beguilingly to extract something by wiles. We call a "gold digger" a courtesan, kept woman, or a greedily enterprising mistress who might milk money, or jewels and other valuables, from a rich man, her patron. To gain by flattery whatever is desired. That is: to drain out or to finagle.

Actors will milk a part or milk the audience for extra applause. This insinuation extends the sense of forcing somebody to wait in attendance, "cooling their heels" (redoubling one sense of dancing). Because they are not named by a noun-phrase like "milk maids," which is a profession, but are instead called maids-a-milking with the verbal hint that suggests the shrewdest assessment of wheedling promises of sexual fulfillment. These may not be farmgirls but young ladies milking a situation or, more tellingly, a man. This understanding of the word was recorded as early as 1610 when Jonson wrote "For she must milk his epididimis [sic]," which was subsequently referred to when milk was defined as a noun, meaning female "spendings,"[12] and as a verb, "to cause ejaculation"—sexual consummation.[13] The maids, pure farmgirls, guileless without a revealing adjective, may be virginal although the verse's setting suggests a double-entendre directing

# The 12 Days of Christmas

us toward the opposite meaning. Everything depends on who was singing.

When an archaeologist looks down at the outlines of a ruined building, its remains suggest the shape and function of a structure that once stood in the sun; from that imagining of a building and its once-thriving life derives the activity of the street and the surrounding cityscape where the demolished structure's walls once mounted up. Sparse evidence, the mere gumline of former buildings, can evoke a teeming metropolis. Likewise, the more we learn about their peculiar song the more can be reconstructed about the carolers' lives and their intended meaning … gleaned from scant remnants. In that search the long-gone carol singers vitality grows attractive despite their grubby impudence as they thumbed noses at the establishment's propriety and piety.

Aristocrats fashioned the world wherein peasants lived, wherein they were forced to live with few alternatives for self-discovery and expression. Their song attacked the great institutions that taxed them, dragooned them into wars, or preached at them an incomprehensible mumbo-jumbo that simple folk mouthed as insurance from the possibility of Hell. Through all this the singers craved a forthright and half-remembered religion whose gospel required no perplexing doctrine but arose from the truth of the groin, the belly, and the breast—and was confirmed by the whirling heavens' annual cycle.

Through the related meanings of the maids who are milking, an overall sense derives from the song's emerging context of seasonal time, socially determined place, and the performers' identities.

# Chapter 11

## The Night of Birds

> "Religion does not just promote different truths, it advocates different *grounds for truth*."[1]

The milkmaids invoke a world of tamed nature, pastoralism. Humans and animals dwell together. Cultivated land surrounds the farmgirls as they walk country lanes with their buckets of milk. Hedgehogs, badgers, and foxes dart through that landscape's fringes where farm animals graze in barnyards or in fields beyond the village. To a very large extent that landscape still exists throughout the British Isles and it's possible to walk it, with pleasure, stopping in unprepossessing towns blessed with astonishingly fine and welcoming pubs, warm rooms replete with libations to match the hiker's thirst. Over centuries, those institutions—the cultivated farmsteads, the towns and pubs—arose to satisfy a worldview, values lived. With enough tending and care, nature became an artifact yielding hedgerow berries, wool, milk, and cash crops, and orchards. Townsfolk dwelled amid gardened nature, farms near forests that the song represents with birds, some domesticated and others perching wild in the trees.

Excepting the song's five golden rings, only after a week passed did the gifts' character change because at first the carol mentions almost nothing but birds. What do birds have to do with the Christmas season that they should furnish half the song? The carol is but a list of birds and of people known by their occupations. (But, I suppose, the name of a bird designates an "occupation" with behavioral and visual traits and environmental specialization, its niche.) As did Aesop, often the carol's subtle lessons procured animals to stand in for suggestive human foibles, desires, and relationships. Small and great birds staffed this song.

## The 12 Days of Christmas

What milkmaids proposed about nature, birds confirmed. Six of the first seven days introduce birds, each with a different modifier or action.

Each type of bird evoked some particular quality. Their associated actions (verbs) or descriptors (adjectives) altered the named bird—no less than leaping modulates the meaning of lord.

On a thousand street corners, including Oxford Circus, around uncounted snug family rooms after Christmas dinner, in all sorts of unimaginable places where English is spoken, people in the twenty-first century merrily recite obsolete slang about birds. They would feel awkward upon discovering what they are singing and teaching to their children.

If this carol incorporated any religious meaning some pattern should bind the birds to the narrative of Jesus' birth. And various birds (goldfinch, robin) feature in the myths ornamenting the Gospel narratives but the carol's birds mean something else: "Birds were high flyers on the Great Chain of Being and by complexion, hot. Medieval medical practitioners therefore considered them suitable nourishment for … the sick or convalescent, who ate fowl in order to replenish cold spirits."[2] Endorsed by physicians, chicken soup remains the best remedy for a cold and birds, being "by complexion, hot," warded off chills and fostered passion.

The early carolers knew how birds nurtured a fiery nature. "Fowl was … a warming winter food and already traditional at Christmas" by the mid–1330s, the period of caroling's greatest vigor.[3] Maybe birds festoon *The Twelve Days* because they furnished mid-winter delicacies, but why are the birds predominantly female? Their passionate nature's warmth derived from one gender. The colloquial goose refers specifically to a female creature, the opposite of a gander, just as a hen is female. Then as now (despite gender-fluidity) this distinction was hardly a casual reference loosely employed by random pronouns. Every English-speaker's slang still reflects the song's preconception.

Birds play a starring role in sexual jargon and innuendo. In American slang, a pretty young women is a "chick." (And in gentle self-mockery, the genre aimed at this audience calls itself "Chick-Lit.") In England a fetching, charming, or attractive girl is called a "bird." Yet,

## Chapter 11

although male birds customarily relate to salacious idioms, the carol names no specifically male birds. Although a penis is a "cock," neither cocks nor ganders appear in the song.

The carol's geese are female but so are the other birds, even the less obvious ones. For example, although Zeus took the form of a swan to seduce Leda, swans were birds of Venus as were doves and sparrows (hence an innocent disguise for Zeus). While the term swan refers to all such birds, specifically, a male is called a cob (named for the bump on their beak which English, in its earlier and more Germanic version, pronounced the K in knob). A yearling is a cygnet, a word derived from old French for swan (with the diminutive ending, like "ette" in Rockettes). Unequivocal reference to a female names a pen. But in general, though of majestic wingspan, elegance on the water, and fiercely protective aggressiveness, while males are cobs swans may conjure females and the graceful, long-necked, swan remains a primary female surrogate—Swan Lake. A large and belligerent swan might suggest male pride and power if such an association were intensified by its verb. But it isn't. Swimming, "should be considered symbolic for the act of love, with such it has obvious postural and other parallels."[4] Nevertheless, despite sexual correspondences to swimming's wet horizontality, swimming-as-sex does not specify which gender the verse invokes. But the lack can be remedied by a closer look at the language.

Swimming, a very old word, dates from the origins of the English language. Remaining more-or-less unchanged for centuries, it means the actions that propel us through water as we move our limbs. From the Renaissance onward, swimming also meant to glide with a smooth or waving motion.[5] Interestingly, this usage is almost always reserved for women (or used for effeminate men), as in an 1830 citation from Trevelyan's *Life and Letters of Lord Macaulay*, "Showy women swimming smoothly over the uneasy stones." Visualizing a large party, the celebrants circulate about and the men move in an angular fashion while the women seem to swim in space. That expression feels right. Robert Louis Stevenson (1850–1894) reinforced the meaning in an adventure deliberately written in anachronistic language, *The Black Arrow: A Tale of the Two Roses*, 1888, from whose pages comes: "She … swam across the floor as though she scorned the drudgery of walking," a usage by which the author clearly activates the verb's latent gender association. By attempting to cast his prose in the style of an earlier time, Stevenson resurrects the word's flavor as used in the carol. In that sense, the

# The 12 Days of Christmas

verb and the noun—swans and swimming—mutually reenforce a gender valence.

To this cluster of female affinities another meaning of swim can be added, as when a plough advances steadily, to make unimpeded progress (to swim fair). This association invoked and re-doubled undertones of fecundity and nature's sometimes-generous womanly temperament.

Common folk might enter and leave church with their native beliefs intact, despite robust preaching; few entirely abandoned their ancient, tried-and-true, practices. Best to hedge your bets. There was much to lose. The Church claimed the old ways risked a soul otherwise cleansed of sin's burden. But that affliction—a condition unapprehended by taste, aroma, physical pain, or weight—could not be felt or clearly demonstrated: Original Sin. The old ways protected everything else, all that could be seen and that mattered in this life, in a world evidenced by senses that the Church deemed the happenstance accidentals of a transitory bodily existence. The choices diverged starkly. Why risk the next crop or Spring lambing on an abstruse theology based on virginity? The ridiculously evident here-and-now alternative offered present gratification against the appealing if dubious promise of a chaste eternal life.

English churches, especially the Protestant's established Church of England, fought an endless war with caroling. Finally co-opted or assimilated, the vanquished enemy's carol-songs seemed to reform. Caroling seemed to have learned proper behavior, when not driven to, or preserved in, the countryside's remotest corners. But for the peasants, when the earth rested lifeless in mid-winter's cold, milking maids (even those not impregnated the previous Spring and lactating in December) nurtured hope for fecundity. At first milkmaids seem a vision of innocence on the verge of knowledge. But having tacitly gained sexual understanding through their experiences of impregnation (having been leaped) and birth (their own delivery), or handling teats of post-partum animals in their care, the verse's implication of motherhood and milk appear as gendered as the next verses' birds.

Between the Winter Solstice and New Year's, thoughts of ploughing frozen soil were ridiculous.[6] Before irresistibly lumbering diesel tractors worked farmland, you couldn't turn rock-hard soil with a plough pulled by yoked animals, except for small ceremonial tillage. Yet, time did not stop for farmers. To agricultural workers the core of

## Chapter 11

the Winter-long season passed while assured, but somnolent, fecundity rested under the soil, a sense of sleeping potential beneath winter's stillness. That stockpiled life invoked memories of the dormant Celtic fertility goddess Matres who was summoned on Christmas eve.[7]

In the pre–Christian societies that named and worshipped nature's forces and gave thanks to their harvest with libations, "Where crops are gods, tillage is worship."[8] To plow was to commune with mother earth, to make love to nature and hope for increase that came mysteriously and wonderfully from the Spring soil as newborns from the womb. No wispy insight, but nature observed and codified, this poetically religious understanding was institutionalized as The Twelfth Night that "at the end of Christmas ... led into the midwinter fertilization festivals of pagan origin, such as Plough Monday which was the following week."[9] And, what was Plough Monday that it should be observed and celebrated contrary to every Church teaching? "The main purpose of [the] enacted rites on Plough Monday just after Christmas when the ground had to be newly broken, and at harvest, the August period of modern summer holidays, was to ensure continued fertility."[10] That belief, made evident every year when nature burst into greenery and birds into their dawn-welcoming song, contested Christianity. The old mid-winter holiday claimed, not just a truth to supplant other ways but, a "grounds for truth."

Unlike the unverifiable Aristotelian ideas that directed the Church, the tottering foal and sucking calf confirmed for the carol-singers a truth as resplendent and all-pervasive for them as the embrace of a great cathedral. Their magnificently renewing nature as thoroughly drenched their lives in meaning as we're informed by Darwin, Einstein, or Freud. In their universe the swimming plough echoed the swimming swan as the barren season's sterility cycled toward fruitfulness. The verb swimming applied to sex between people and between humans and nature. Such unions yielded long-term increase but also, and more famously, immediate delight. When done correctly, sex is fun, and swimming meant high pleasure and total release as promised by sex. Formal usage also acknowledged the mingling concepts that permeate the song's language, that swimming meant being immersed or sunk in pleasure. Signifying a heightened emotional state, including occasionally grief, "to swim" means to abound in a passion.

Citations of this meaning date from the fifteenth century, and by the early sixteenth (1526) William Tyndale (c. 1490/94–1536) had

# The 12 Days of Christmas

translated *2 Thessalonians* (I:3) in a way that mirrors the carol: "Every one of you swymmeth in love towarde another betwene youre selves."[11] Tyndale's use of language responds to actual speech. Though dependent on his work, the considerably stuffier King James Version of this verse reads: "We are bound to thank God always for you, brethren, as it is meet, because that your faith groweth exceedingly, and the charity of every one of you all toward each other aboundeth." That's a mouthful compared with Tyndale's direct style. His bible spoke the language of the carolers, the very people he hoped to influence. But the carolers required no faith's unevidenced mysteries because they were, to a certain extent, faithless as scientists, seeing how the world confirmed all they believed without having to hold and espouse unconfirmable and invisible mysteries.

Despite its sometimes thundering prose, progenitor to so much modern English, the King James Version represents a step backward from what Tyndale had achieved. Yet, modern English remains overwhelmingly obligated to two books: Shakespeare's collected writings and the King James Bible. It's impossible to write modern English without a debt of cadence and vocabulary to these two books but Tyndale had no qualms about using the verb "swim" as typical English-speakers employed it. By the seventeenth-century Milton's *Paradise Lost*, 1667, used the word exactly as the carol must, to mean giddy delight: "As with new Wine intoxicated both [Adam and Eve] They swim in mirth" (IX:1009). So, once again, this verse's meaning coincides with other verses' implications and tone.

The carol's emerging concurrence of mutually-confirming images and verbs reveals a pattern that's uniform throughout the song. More securely than might first appear, that correspondence signals the recovery of lost intentions. Ultimately, we're talking about truth and who decides, and by what imposed or accepted authority, to shape a confederacy of opinion. Prevailing agreements (on any subject) form and re-form in each era and in every generation—as the worldview shifts. What was obvious to illiterates when they sang the carol of the *Twelve Days* must now be slowly and laboriously reconstructed when it was originally blithely available, if blushingly intelligible to some early listeners who would rather not have known its meaning. Or were extremely displeased to be woken from sleep by its rousing rendition.

## Chapter 11

For most of history, generations passed to their children their society's views about people's place in the world: tradition. As construed by each culture, the world's foundations could be confirmed by looking about and feeling one's own body, which is not so easily substantiated for an airy concept like "original sin." If the compact to believe what your neighbors believe sounds like a description of culture, it's also a way to characterize truth. What people believe to be true will be ratified by their observations of the world. The carol singers certainly thought so, as nothing seemed to contradict their lusts and other desires that teemed visible in nature's yearly cadences. They swam in delight as the plow swam through fecund earth, as Adam swam in mirth with Eve. The carol-singers shared a hearty worldview affirmed by their own bodies that fell into rhythm with the seasons.

If the name for prevailing truth names each era, the carol-singers' world mirrored nature. As a special part of nature, people were an ensouled version of animals and crops, and nature was not something "out there." The idea of such a separation would have been strange because daily observation confirmed nature's continuity, an unbroken relationship that was sung about.

As I sit stirring a latté and watching the street scene, it's pretty clear that I and the people passing, in their chosen clothing's colors, with hurried or languid strides, live in a moment that will soon be history. This moment will be known by the assumptions that bond us. We will have become an era with a title, and that name will identify a cluster of values, truths or convenient fictions about us. In a way that gainsays the idea of a Dark Age beginning to lighten only with the observations of early scientists, unlike splendidly robed clerics and Medieval academics, this carol's first singers knew nature's observable truths that awaited quantification—by Galileo, Newton, and their heirs. The verities they sang about remain true, and emotional continuity across ages connects their lusty singing with moments of exceptional, if brutal, vitality. Such rambunctiousness as prompted and sustain the carol of *The Twelve Days of Christmas* defies authority, and the song remains dangerously anti-authoritarian.

The carol's opponents understood the threat posed by such songs, whether sung by dancing "witches" or in townsfolk's mid-winter carnival of release. Not to sentimentalize the situation: if we reach out sympathetically to these long-gone singers we recognize that their likely xenophobic politics, bigotry, and social values would frighten or repel

## The 12 Days of Christmas

us. Their rough-hewn peasant's worldview was narrow, fallaciously un-scientific and founded on superstitions' unexamined assumptions: alien to us. Yet, in sum, that gone world rests fundamental as groundwork to the Occidental present.

While archaically-phrased, the carol of *The Twelve Days'* swimming swans intimates, with rich alliteration, women dizzy and faint with pleasure. Perhaps post-orgasmic. Not a bad Christmastide item to add to a wish-list.

This present, so congenial to celebrating the Yule and mid-winter's Celtic fertility rites, was definitely not what the Church had in mind to consecrate the season. It also didn't aid modern consumerism: try advertising, selling, and putting a bow on the Swimming Swans' happy, and priceless, consummation. The next verses did gift-wrap and price the Christmas present.

# Chapter 12

## A Goddess: Pure, Pure, Idolatry

Unexpected patterns emerge when we notice that only some of the carol's verses contain verbs. Where they occur the carol's actions compare to, or amplify, some aspect of the verse's noun. Neither arbitrarily nor nonsensically coupled, the united nouns and verbs consistently correlate, and often with subtly sly wit.

Each part of a phrase like "leaping lords" heightens the verse's meaning as both active and passive halves intensify the other's connotation as jargon: ladies dance, swans swim, maids milk, etc. The elegant structure sidesteps mechanical repetition and, like the best art, mixes regularity with variation. Despite the cumulative number carol's repeated tune the song advances no grinding treadmill because expectations about structure, and references established by one group of verses, never become wholly predictable for the next. As if crafted by a single intelligent author the carol masterfully interrupted anticipated patterns with surprises. Yet, all the song's insinuations operate with the same inflection.

Unlike folk art (in any medium) that typically weakly-structures its accumulations, the carol more closely resembles consciously crafted high art's organizational confidence. The song's patterns cease recurring once it established a relationship's formal (that is, poetic) purpose. Even stranger in its strict formalism: despite combining a thing and an action, no verse becomes a sentence. Two words can produce a sentence: I walk; she shops; we talked. None of the carol's two-word phrases form a grammatical unit of declaration, interrogation, or exclamation—although they do communicate. Yet, neither do the verses hint at an uncoiling story with a beginning or middle, let alone a coherent conclusion that wraps up a tale with a memorable adage. It never

## The 12 Days of Christmas

sanctimoniously claims that we are to learn something from singing it; the carol of the *Twelve Days* does not teach a new lesson but reminds of past and promising pleasures.

Ignoring narrative's appealing and self-organizing flow, the carol generates no complete envelope of space or time. In that it differs from a story whose duration connects each image by rooting them in some place, akin to shots in a movie that link, often quite creatively, to the following or preceding impression; instead, a non-narrative asserts only that all transpires within twelve days at Christmas. In their totality, the superficially disconnected verses exclude the very possibility of story-telling. They neither state nor suggest a tale that refers to something outside itself and as a result the carol creates no anecdotes that depend upon a before and after, a story fragment.

Instead of narration, the accumulating nouns and verbs emphasize each other's risqué meanings; those insinuations permeate the carol with a uniformity that suggests a state of riotous drunkenness enhanced this coarse song's enjoyment. As a memory feat of seeming gibberish, a disconnected list later used in the game of forfeits, the carol enumerates enjoyable recollections and seasonal anticipations. With the holiday's complete license, including widespread inebriation, even normally hard-working types could afford to collapse in mid-winter's hiatus and pound the tavern table with each rhythmic line. But, as a song without a narrative structure, latter-day hearers believed it sheer nonsense rather than communicating as an impressionistic whole.

Every verse floats alone, seemingly disconnected although each rises an island in a naughty archipelago invisibly joined by a deeply submarine intelligence. Six geese a-laying is one of those phrases that seems nonsense, that refers neither to what precedes nor follows, yet that verse also mutually intensifies the whole. If the verse's noun-part indicates nothing apparently suspicious, that deception helped the carol outlast repeated campaigns to annihilate old-style Christmas.

As a demonstration of the singers' guile, the song's superficial imagery mentions nothing that's obviously objectionable. This disguise helped because in some eras carolers dodged roving inspectors of the Church and state's unsmiling and oppressive forces. The singers had to evade detection because caroling made them prey to despotic religious cadres and they could even be betrayed by neighbors who overheard

## Chapter 12

ribald indications of the Old Christmas. Celebrants contrived to endure in their venerable practices although their survival strategy of camouflage eventually denatured the boisterous culture they tried to preserve. Outsiders to the old ways, and do-gooders convinced that they were winning the struggle for moral betterment, accepted the disguise and embraced it as a genuinely reformed holiday.

Like many who survive wars of extermination, the song maintained a foolish, mild-mannered, and unsuspicious exterior. Like other survivors of attempted cultural annihilation, the carol hid a potent secret identity, and deferred revenge. That's why the song seems idiotic: it's become a false façade, the cloaked persona taken on by a secret agent. And, at least in popular imagination, what could seem dumber than a goose?

A goose is the general name for large web-footed birds both wild and domestic. Every child knows that geese, though smaller than a swan, are usually bigger than a duck or the carol's also-mentioned partridge, dove, and hen. Goose-flesh and its copious grease are delicacies and were avidly consumed before saturated fats became a concern; brought to the table, trimmed or stuffed, the Christmas goose presented a dramatic holiday treat that taxed neither calorie-consciousness nor cholesterol fears, both future inventions. The Christmas goose's sensational dining-room appearance marked one of the most decorous parts of a venerable tradition when, brought dramatically from the kitchen, the goose centered the Christmas table.

Unconcerned about robust over-eating (a rare experience for many carol singers), as one of his contributions to modern Christmas, Charles Dickens promoted the turkey as the prized holiday luxury food. Yet, by 1825 in Paris, Brillat-Savarin had already extolled the American turkey, a creature unknown in Europe when this carol was born.

Besides providing splendid nourishment, the goose's down supplies the best insulation. Getting six of them would make a fine present. In addition to insulation and celebratory food, geese possess other traits.

When its domain is invaded the common farmyard goose reacts with aggressive territorial hissing and loud snapping—traits that were, and remain, useful for guarding property. In the fourth century, to scorn the classical gods St. Ambrose (*Epistle* XVIII) cited their proverbial (obnoxious or useful) honking. Ambrose recalled an ancient invasion

# The 12 Days of Christmas

by, "the Senones [Gauls who lived near the Seine], whose entrance into the inmost Capitol [Rome] the remnant of the Romans could not have prevented, had not a goose by its frightened cackling betrayed them? See what sort of protectors the Roman temples have. Where was Jupiter at that time? Was he speaking in the goose?"[1] Clearly the reputation of the goose-as-sentinel was well-established in the Middle Ages (and continued as the preferred watchman of Scotch distilleries, most notably Ballentine's aging warehouse).

The barnyard goose perseveres as a sentinel that will "lay in wait" for intruders, loitering and pecking for food until a stranger breaches its territory. Among the peculiarities of geese, this trait proved important in the song, but there's something else interesting about the carol's geese.

The geese of the *Twelve Days* are not assigned to a distinctive type (like "French" Hens) distinguished by their modifier.[2] Yet, even without such discriminations, they acquire many particulars. The song's geese are female—the male is the gander and the young are goslings.

In an ancient and well-observed distinction, without other qualification geese are females and, in addition to signifying gender, a goose is supposedly a stupid animal. This cluster of traits appeared consistent with the carol's foregoing verses: female gender, aggressive territorialism and, paramount, geese exemplify foolishness.

When Samuel Johnson's *A Dictionary of the English Language* appeared in bookseller's shops on 15 April 1755, readers discovered amid its distinctively tall two-column pages Johnson's confession that the goose is "proverbially noted, *I know not why*, for foolishness." [emphasis added] (In modern American usage a different creature usurped its folk-allegorical role as the animal kingdom's moron: the turkey. Yet, a wild turkey is a clever critter who, somehow for a pretty large ground-dwelling bird, manages to sleep securely on a tree branch.) The six geese in the carol may connote six foolhardy or rash females. When reprising the role of a dimwit in 1818 Walter Scott (*Rob Roy* xxvi) describes "A twa-leggit creature, wi' a goose's head and a hen's heart"— that is, both stupid and cowardly. The term figuratively extended to mean a foolish or imprudent person, a simpleton.

Not all dimwits fall for the same schemes; this verse intended a particular flaw, an imperfection of character that summoned all the goose's folkloric qualities.

*Chapter 12*

MERCUTIO: Was I with you there for the goose?
ROMEO: Thou wast never with me for any thing when thou wast not there for the goose.

On a warm and cloudless Spring evening the sky glowed florescent as it does in northern latitudes' endlessly protracted dusk. About a year after beginning to track down the origins and meaning of the carol of *The Twelve Days of Christmas* I found myself back in London and strolling the Thames' South Bank. With some academic colleagues we ambled toward a trendy restaurant, a knot of chatting pedagogues, highly visible by contrast amid a meandering crowd fashionably dressed in the international uniform: black. We were enjoying a picturesque area that had, until quite recently, been an immemorially shoddy zone of abandoned Victorian factories and dockyard decay; a hulking electric powerplant had become an art museum, the Tate Modern. Eastward from the Tate, toward Greenwich, and westward toward the London Eye's slowly rotating cobweb of steel cables, in bygone days the riverbank neighborhood of Southwark had for centuries been notorious as the home of gambling dens, brothels, nests of thieves, traffickers in every illicit good, and the hangout of men and women already wanted on the river's north shore for crimes punishable by hanging, the lash, or branding.[3] My little group of British professors with one Yank drifted eastward casually examining the maze of rehabilitated buildings. With ample time before our dinner reservation we turned on a crooked street and faced the ruins of the once-imposing Palace of the Bishop of Winchester.[4] Its remains oversee renewed Southwark's innocent delights where once whores and their clients caterwauled out songs like *The Twelve Days*. I little esteem the Bishop's memory, a pious hypocrite, his income derived from taverns and sex-worker girls.[5] The sex-workers' tumbled girls toiled for one of Bishop Winchester's many lease-holders, and it was they, the brothel-keepers who paid the taxes. The Bishop's tenants also bequeathed us a verse in one of the world's most popular songs.

Though both terms are now obsolete, Winchester Goose and simply "goose" were commonly understood to refer to prostitutes, which the bygone singers of the *Twelve Days* fully appreciated. If you don't believe me trust Shakespeare whose Globe theater was a stone's throw from the Bishop's digs; he used the word this way.

A(nother) drinking song connects this verse with the Pipers Piping: the shrewd prostitute we encountered in "The Rolling Blossom" who left

113

# The 12 Days of Christmas

**London Bridge and part of Borough High Street in 1616** (*Survey of London: Volume 22, Bankside* (The Parishes of St. Saviour and Christchurch Southwark).

a cheated customer "to stretch his pipe." Shakespeare used this meaning in combination with the goose-as-whore in *Romeo & Juliet* (II:4)

> MERCUTIO: Nay, if thy wits run the wild-goose chase, I have
> done, for thou hast more of the wild-goose in one of
> thy wits than, I am sure, I have in my whole five:
> was I with you there for the goose?
> ROMEO: Thou wast never with me for any thing when thou wast
> not there for the goose.[6]
> MERCUTIO: I will bite thee by the ear for that jest.
> ROMEO: Nay, good goose, bite not.
> MERCUTIO: Thy wit is a very bitter sweeting; it is a most
> sharp sauce.
> ROMEO: And is it not well served in to a sweet goose?
> MERCUTIO: O here's a wit of cheveril,[7] that stretches from an
> inch narrow to an ell broad!

## Chapter 12

ROMEO: I stretch it out for that word "broad"; which added
to the goose, proves thee far and wide a broad goose.
MERCUTIO: Why, is not this better now than groaning for love?

In 1591 Shakespeare's *1 Henry VI* contains such a reference.[8] A few years later, in 1606 *Troilus & Cressida* (V:9) features the line: "My feare is this: Some galled Goose of Winchester would hisse," a line that portrays the scornful sound of an angry goose/whore. The playwright's line cleverly winked to an audience that, while seated in his theater, could likely hear and smell the nearby brothels; Shakespeare neatly combined three traits associated in one animal symbol: femaleness (gender), hissing territorial aggressiveness (a whore on her stroll protected by her pimp), and foolishness. With Shakespeare providing an anchor to usage, for the carol's singers propriety never arrested the song's meander through life's coarser districts. This song was neither born amid, nor intended to be sung by, a decorous company.

Whether in London itself or in the countryside, the singer's had

The so-called Agas Map of London. Attributed to Ralph Agas, this is recognized as the earliest real map (compared to a panorama) of London. Agas probably performed his surveys between 1570 and 1605. The original map (6 feet and ½ inch long by 2 feet 4½ inches wide) was much damaged, and today few good copies exist. On this map can be found the old lanes and streets of London, many of which no longer exist, having been built over after the Great Fire of 1666 and subsequent re-routing of streets obliterated much of the old city's network. But among those old street recorded on this map, many are named for the professions clustered there (indeed, the Great Fire began on Pudding Lane). These street names include Cock(e) street, several thoroughfares called Love Lane/Street, and the candid Grope Cunt Street, where the associated professionals services were rendered.

## The 12 Days of Christmas

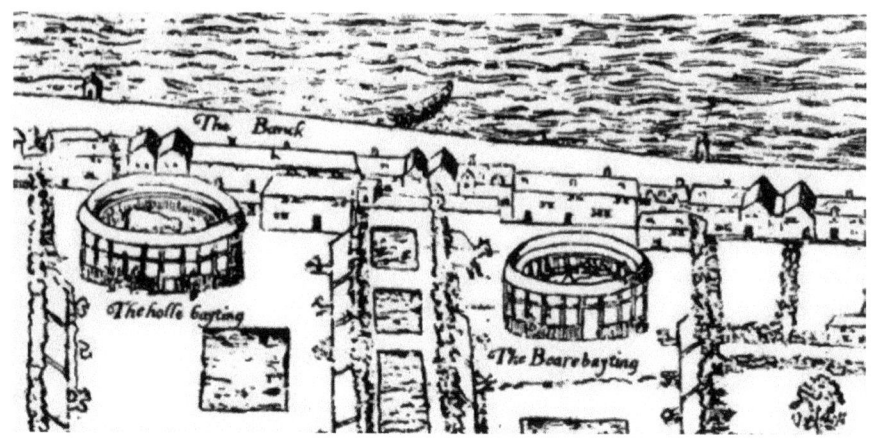

**Detail of the Agas Map showing bearing-baiting and bull-baiting arenas lining the Southwark district of Thameside London.**

long ago left the outskirts of merely rash imprudence and ordinary misbehavior and (figuratively) decamped for Southwark's full-blown debauchery. Those clients for Winchester Geese whored, gambled, drank, fought and Southwark's customers bellowed out a song.

The etiquette of speaking, like every other behavior, should fit the social situation. Something said in respectable company may be approvingly expressed more coarsely elsewhere. In *Hamlet* there's a tutorial in the layering of speech to fit each social strata. Dressed up as a botany lesson, Shakespeare—no botanist but a country boy avid for courtly semantics, whatever his writing's ostensible subject—always has an ear cocked for tuned speech:

> Of crowflowers, nettle, daisies, and long purples,
> That liberal shepherds give a grosser name
> But our cold maids do "dead men's fingers" call them. (V:7)

To translate: "crowflowers [buttercups], nettle, daisies" are agreeable and un-controversial names for plants and their flowers. But "long purples" mean purple orchids, a special case. Their vernacular synonym that "liberal shepherds" use, came about because such rustics live beyond the company of urbane social refinement. These pastoral folk can speak *liberally*, freely, unconcerned about conversational refinements or mannered niceties. In their crude but vivid speech, they "give

*Chapter 12*

a grosser [lewd] name" to those purple orchids. The shepherds called them dog's balls or priest's penis, either term having been common slang. In contrast, "our cold [chaste] maids do 'dead men's fingers' call them," being fastidious of their speech and, as Shakespeare hints, by calling them "cold maids" sexual duds. Or, at least, unwilling to say naughty words.

Purple orchids, a botanically neutral and precise descriptive, offers the writer no poetic value—so he avoided such nomenclature. Instead, invoking a different tone, a courtly woman describes these flowers as "long purples," an acceptably informal name that she passes casually to the listeners. Both the theater's audience and the characters on stage understand her reference, which preserved her dignity. Yet, that same woman obviously knows how peasants and the play's audience speak when she, with false modesty, alludes to a vulgar name that she does not, and will not bring herself to, say. She clearly knows the vulgar "grosser" name that intimated prurience. Skirting indecency, she

"Shepherds Dancing a Carol" from the *Book of Hours* (of the Virgin), Use of Rome. Attributed to the Master of Gijsbrecht van Brederode, mid–15th century, Netherlands, possibly Utrecht, overall dimensions (leaf): 210 ×150 mm; dimensions of the writing laid out in 21 lines: 112 × 85 mm (Bodleian Library, University of Oxford, Douce ms. 93, folio 022r). A century before Brueghel and van der Borcht depicted their riotous peasant dances, these might as well be Shakespeare's "liberal shepherds" who enthusiastically engage in a circle dance to the tune of a piper who stands on the left. The eight rustics dance a carol while, outside the circle to the right, a ninth man sings out or chants the rounds. The fingers of his right hand raised, he perhaps counts numerical verses, maybe even of a song like the *Twelve Days*.

### The 12 Days of Christmas

somewhat prissily says that proper girls call them "dead men's fingers," avoiding other anatomical similes. The carol features just such vocabulary swaps as amused the Globe's patrons.

The carol's lusty singers regaled themselves with witty substitutions, playing the lewd against the acceptable, with astutely layered meanings. That same wit entertained an afternoon's theater audience and after the play's last applause, play-goers filed from the Globe, bound for other destinations. That Southwark mob dispersed to nearby entertainments and, whatever the season, some sought out the neighboring brothels. Some ambled to taverns where, after rounds of drinks and discussion of the just-seen play, knots of homeward-bound friends could amuse themselves with an earthy carol.

## Getting Laid

To some, six geese a-laying, "is obviously erotic, partly from the verb which is still a common canty for it" which seems to amplify the goose as an Elizabethan prostitute.[9] Except for a little problem.

To the modern ear, *lay* and *laid* register as familiar nouns and verbs for sexual intercourse. Thus, everyone but prudes uses these words and the verb serves preferably, or more socially acceptable, than other terms for the same act. So, assuming that "laying" has something to do with the paid services of the geese/whores introduces an easy, but hardly obvious, fallacy. That misconception baits an appealing mis-direction that coincides with the song's essence.

Overall, the image of six prostitutes laying/fucking presents a dazzling array for the mid-winter reveler's jaded appetite—something to mirror the Lords' Leaping. As a gift from the "true love" a half-dozen eager whores would be memorable, a thoughtful hooker-of-alternating-months club subscription—if rationed throughout the year. However winsome this opinion, which superficially bolsters the present case, it's wrong. The verb is not "still" a common synonym for sexual intercourse as lay/laid appears only of recent vintage.

Unfortunately for this otherwise useful reading of the verse, the word lay/laid as "common canty" for (usually heterosexual) intercourse arrives with a modern pedigree, a slang usage originating in the USA in the 1930s;[10] the meaning may be decades older, but not ancient.[11]

## Chapter 12

The carol's "lay" does not anticipate its modern vernacular usage for sexual congress. If only the situation were so simple, that this verse is "obviously" erotic. The carolers enjoyed erotic word games but were not "getting laid." By the Geese of Winchester.

The adjectival form of "lay" means persons contradistinguished from the clergy. To modern ears this innocent-sounding term has shed its loaded implications. Yet, occasionally, the old antagonism flares up at the ballot-box or from a revolutionary's rifle.

When I hear the word "priest" I know it represents a person with expertise. You may be an atheist—and doubt the ultimately transcendent and divine focus of the priest's attentions—while still recognizing the body of learning that the priest has mastered. That recognition makes each of us, willy-nilly, comparative anthropologists because we each come from some faith-community (even atheists) while regarding other belief systems as more-or-less ethical while alien, if not downright wrong and misguided. To the carol singers priests were experts who advised behaviors contrary to what the carol of the Twelve Days professed. That made priests antagonists of the song and its singers, a condition the Church freely assumed.

The carolers' traditions developed from nature's annual solar cycle, especially mid-winter's confinement that awarded cultural expression to a temporary pause, a moment of agricultural leisure. The age-old festival challenged the priest's claims to expertise, his esoteric textual and ritual proficiency toppled by knowledge that every carol singer knew first-hand, as we know our own bodily appetites. Each of us, then and now, must decide if yearnings were cached in flesh by a god who (perversely?) tests our resolve with the promise of a final payday at death or enlivens us to find scarce pleasure where and when available. The revelers trusted tradition-framed, but experientially confirmed, knowledge conveyed in linguistic wit that recognized how reason makes claims to affinities and truth(s) otherwise empirically unavailable.

Reason—though culture-bound and thus everywhere differently weighted and shaped by all manner of local considerations—does not mean higher and precisely formal logic, but the human faculty for thought and pattern-formation. Viewed from a folkloric perspective, the priest's scholastic ways explored a mirror-world without exit, once

# The 12 Days of Christmas

entered, and a world that rested tangential to wider truths. Relying on a form of self-confirming Christian logic (locked into place by stipulated metaphysical presumptions) cannot unravel the carol's way of presenting the universal reality of human behavior. The two worldviews not only diverge but flee from each other because the carol emerges from deductions eschewed by developing middle-class Occidental society, as endorsed and promulgated by the Church.

The Church believed it alone purveyed resurrection and not, as farmers knew, the green corn sprung bravely delicate shoots against late winter; faced by such antagonism the Church was not wrong to assassinate Old Christmas, along with this song and its associated practices[12] The priest and the song contested issues theological and existential in a still-raging battle about the body, as near and as heightened as debating the purchase of perfumed lacy undergarments or as distant as a drowsy yesteryear's classroom discussion of high Christology.

Under severe social and legal constraint, carolers mostly pretended to the aristocrats' moral code throughout the rest of the year. These standards of behavior reenforced a profitable social order. Etiquette erected a bond of Church and state. Formalities respect social tiers, while the song evidences a wild holiday spirit, the moral chaos that contextualizes the words. If you forget the setting for the song it's easy to overlook the intended wit.

In older usage, anything lay was the opposite of the holy; what was "lay" was unsanctified and worldly, secular, even earthy. Lay people have entered no Church orders while non-clerics carry prefixed titles that are often hyphenated (such as lay-priest, or lay-leader, etc.). The joke here is that the prostitute "geese" do carry a hyphenated title, as they are "a-laying" (as other maids were a-milking). But, while a lay-person is an amateur, a professional prostitute gets paid for expert ministrations, being tradespersons today called "sex workers."

A lay member of any calling is characteristically a dilettante, which this verse may invoke. Less than full-time professional prostitutes, geese-a-laying may be girls of loose morals or simply (drunken or horny) women temporarily carried away by seasonal gaiety: borderline sluts or blue-collar trollops. They belong to the category of the sexual laity, lay-persons. They represent the caroler's fellow celebrants.

Just as today, at conventions, carnivals, and festivals—either small local affairs or grand debauches like New Orleans' or Rio de Janeiro's Mardi Gras, a World Cup match or the Super Bowl—celebrants get

## Chapter 12

carried away. In an atmosphere of universal release people do things they might not otherwise, some with subsequent regret, others with delighted astonishment at their own liberated boldness. If what happens in Vegas stays in Vegas, what happened at Christmas used to stay in Christmas. Except for the holiday's lasting reminders: healing wounds from fights, epic hangovers, and swelling bellies.

In a clever game of surprisingly rapid substitutions, some of the carol's nouns masquerade as verbs, and vice-versa. For example, "lay," normally an action, also names a short lyric or narrative poem intended to be sung. That's how Hamlet's mom, Queen Gertrude, describes the death of Ophelia to her brother Laertes: the deranged girl drifted down a stream murmuring snatches of a song:

> ...her garments, heavy with their drink,
> Pulled the poor wretch from her melodious lay
> To muddy death.(IV:7)

A lay (related to the high-art German *lied*) may sound fancy, but when lower classes sang, or at all hours bawled out a drunken song that disturbed the peace, well that's another matter that invited reprimands or incarceration. Strumpets, drunken and disorderly "geese" a-laying, found themselves subject to the law's constabulary and the disfavor of peaceful law-abiding citizens.

Singing lays was mostly a professional's vocation not to be abused by neighborhood rowdies. In contrast, carols were not sung by minstrels: between the fourteenth and sixteenth centuries "there is no record at all of the vocal performance of any of the English carols by any professional entertainer" of the sort who was called a minstrel.[13] At that time, it would have been pretty pretentious, or funny, for carol singers to be "a-laying," singing a lay, and that was part of the humor. The carolers were amateurs, dilettante singers or part-time, seasonally opportunistic whores. That understanding re-unites the singers with the song's many birds. A carol is a song but a lay is also a song, especially bird-song. The sixth verse of *The Twelve Days of Christmas* pictures whoring "geese" singing a lay halfway through the carol.

The carolers might, in their profession's sisterhood, self-mockingly call themselves "geese a-laying": singing geese/strumpets. As a burlesque that caricatured the "geese," perhaps the singers employed a

# The 12 Days of Christmas

verbal effigy that carried pungent connotations, an undertone that echoed actual precedents.

Geese suggest certain attributes (cowardice, clumsiness in their ungainly waddle, resolute territorialism, or stupidity) but when knowledgeable carolers roared this verse—in the days when it was still sung with its authentic meanings intact—mentioning a common prostitute would banish it from pious families' holiday recreation. Recall how *Loves Labors Lost* praises "A green goose a goddess: pure, pure, idolatry." For Shakespeare's audience green suggested immaturity or inexperience (a "greenhorn"), as it still refers to unripe fruit, also youthful ignorance, a not-yet jaded whore/goose. Today, if used at all, this phrase might refer to a teenage prostitute who, shrewdly hardened by her trade, nightly sells her virginity.

Those who sang *The Twelve Days* divided into several types. First were the knowingly bawdy who relished the song's wit, likely as a drinking song.[14] At first, some who knew the meaning undoubtedly refused to mouth such filth. But, increasingly ignorant of its original context and witticisms, newer traditionalists sang it without understanding because in succeeding centuries the straight-laced grasped ever-less of its slangy connotations as its vernacular aged out of currency. Just as Shakespeare's vocabulary is now the realm of experts. Today the carol is universally sung in ignorance of its meaning. Today's grandparents would not instruct the youngest generation in songs containing a standard synonym for fucking or for a hooker, streetwalker, hustler, whore, etc.

Whether in town or village, you might run into the goose a-laying in wait. This was no metaphor. In that long-gone world, as today, a loitering streetwalker "lay in wait" for passers-by. That meaning contributes another, and complementary, significance to geese a-laying. With that extra understanding we savor this verse almost as fully as its early singers, but even this bit of innuendo's rich quotient of associations omits one conspicuous element.

A domestic goose's dawdling seems passive until aroused by an invasion of its barnyard territory, and such inactivity recalls the pretended idleness practiced by a streetwalker. Her doing nothing in particular was active trolling for customers. In either case—goose or prostitute a-laying—ostensibly torpid and witless inaction springs into

## Chapter 12

activity when a stranger/customer approaches. Here the goose's territorialism parallels the commercial (and invisibly bordered) zone of a hooker's stroll, her beat and the precinct within which she trades. Even that highly graphic and enduring reality cannot resolve what the verb actually meant when it referred to geese, unless a-laying just meant dropping eggs.

The ancestor of the verb's modern sexual sense meant: to lay to sleep, to put to sleep, to put to rest, even to put in the last resting-place, to bury in the grave. Figuratively to lay meant to rest, abed, to bed, as in Shakespeare's 1606 *Anthony & Cleopatra* (II) and its lament, "Royall Wench: She made great Cæsar lay his Sword to bed." The verb centrally relates to a bird that produces and deposits an egg but, in a associated sense for human beings, it also signified to "bring to bed" to birth a child. It named the process by which a mother delivered a baby, with the period before and after birth being the lying-in. When this sense joins the undertone of geese as professional prostitutes or (amateur) trollops, the verse's two halves unite with an insinuation neither pretty nor modern. That coarse meaning must be understood in terms of a shady society that lurked a rough underworld beneath lawful society's already nasty but authorized brutality. Or concerns peasants on a once-a-year tear through the bounds of civility.

As an afternoon's amusement moderns do not frequent bear-and bull baitings, or cock pits. Public executions were performed for a constituency expecting gruesome theatricality prolonged to its greatest sadistic extent. When the grand theater of a victim being burned alive proved too rare there was flogging, disemboweling, the stocks as public humiliation with audience participation, inventive physical abuse as community-sanctioned revenge-assault, branding, and public torture. Public humiliation for misdemeanors, the pillory or other cruel punishments intended to dissuade malefactors and, besides the offender's correction, such events offered an entertainment for casually gazing strollers: all are now thought revoltingly savage. (Some of this cruelty persists in non-western societies, a sad fact. A sharp division cleaves societies that allow, and those that shun, sanctioned torture as educative theater.) The thought of such spectacles nauseates a post-industrial moral sense but until recently another aesthetic prevailed.

While modernity was forming, harsh and painful diversions, now considered barbarous, were acted out on the bodies of living people and other creatures; these torments were deemed reliable prompts to merriment.[15] If such spectacles seem alien, so was the coarse atmosphere in which this carol was sung, a once-prevailing mood of the whole community but now relegated to moments of small groups' drunken camaraderie. But, long after the generally approved fondness for brutality waned the carol endured and, an immigrant stowaway into modernity, the song still reflects its native ethos.

## Old Time Indecency

Although some socially acceptable preferences disappear without a trace, as recently as the turn of the twentieth century the *New York Times* warmly reminisced about the quaint old days of gone Christmases and how older folks pined for the amusing practical jokes that lightened the mood of yesteryear with entertainments that a twenty-first century sensibility would regard as scandalous. Among these frolics: for the merry game of "hot cockles, a stick moving on a pivot, with an apple at one end and a candle [was placed] at the other, so that he who missed his bite burned his nose; blind-man's buff, forfeits."[16] Readers of the *New York Times* were supposed to grow nostalgic for burning the old man's nose at Christmas. This was good fun, along with that lingering Victorian favorite, forfeits. Thank goodness, modern imaginations stagger at conjuring the past's coarseness.[17] Christmas in the old days included much that is now rebarbative.

Livelihoods were hard-won and society's unfortunates, who mostly endured without organized community support, counted on unreliable charity. Excluding compassionate gifts for food maintenance, precarious fate and unpredictable justice inconsistently dispensed opportunity meted by class. Few lived long and well. Popular humor erupted cruelly physical when lives offered brief and too-often only bleak episodes in the sun; consequently, understanding this song stipulates the past's harsh buffoonery. In the Renaissance, boisterous women, "geese," were arrested for singing carols on Yuletide—their rowdy pleasure others' insult. That meaning preserves one reference of a-laying: amateurism. But also, to the era's rougher sensibilities it was downright funny to think of whores taken to bed to birth bastards.

# *Chapter 13*

## Intermission

This Christmas carol's texture changes abruptly at verse five, and for no apparent reason, but with satisfying musical effect. The modified tempo, however old, was not recorded until 1909 when the English singer and composer Frederic Austin (1872–1952) added what may have been his own two-bar motif for the verse of the "Five gold rings." The amended verse neatly fit one syllable per musical note of gold-en, rather than singing go-old.[1]

After four nights of singing about birds (a partridge in a pear tree, 2 turtle doves, 3 French hens, 4 calling birds) the true love earned golden rings. Then two more birds arrived (6 geese a-laying, 7 swans a-swimming). Why were rings sandwiched into a list of birds? While there's nothing wrong with rings, which make a fine gift (that to moderns bespeak devotion, engagement, marriage, super-bowl victory, graduation, membership in a fraternal organization, etc.) nevertheless they intrude disturbingly out-of-place in this song.

The parade of birds and their appealing liveliness enchants with varied twittering calls and diverse, if sometimes gaudy, plumage. Female birds flaunt attractions that tinge the song with suggestions of active, perhaps rowdy, sexual lives. Their vitality contradicts metallic rings—inorganic, hard shiny crafted artifacts—lifeless adornments thrust amid achingly mortal life. The song's catalogue would appear just as abnormal if a list of man-made objects suddenly mentioned a single animal: attention would fasten on the deviation because that jarring anomaly seems devoid of obvious connections or interactions with the surrounding verses' emotions and animation.

Unlike the ladies, lords, maids, and the many birds, the rings gleam dead tokens that the song treats as insensate, without verb or

## The 12 Days of Christmas

context—except being given by the True Love. Also, the inert rings emerge on the Fifth Day bracketed by ebullient human activity (leaping, piping, dancing, milking) and vivacious creatures who perform life's endearingly raucous actions (calling birds, hissing and laying geese, swimming swans). The carol-singers constructed a stark contrast that weighs the lively against immobility.

The carolers lived closer to nature than modern city-dwellers and (although they lacked the word for it) they likely understood what a biologist would call "irritability," the capacity to respond to stimuli. That capability separates creatures—capable of pain, pleasure, and fear—compared to unfeeling things helpless to respond with motion to perceived sensations. As mere jewelry, vanity's ornament, the human worth of golden rings evaporates in ill health or at death. "You can't take it with you." (Yet, many cultures believe that you can. Accordingly, they fill graves with golden goodies, food, weapons, and servants in the flesh or as models—all to accommodate a post-death existence. The ego, that simply cannot believe in its own finality, invented the immortal soul to convey personality past death.) Besides lacking a verb and being inanimate there's another major difference at this verse.

Rings represent the carol's only items that might conceivably—even remotely, under normal circumstances—be considered gifts exchanged by real people. That's no small consideration. The rings appear exceptional compared to the carol's other gifts that cannot, or seem unlikely to really, be bestowed.

Precisely because nobody literally "gives" milking maids or leaping lords, while rings are routinely given, a hint emerges that the song guardedly organized its references, coherently if enigmatically. Since the carol's other gifts suggest encrypted souvenirs of the holiday, the rings may not be what they seem either.

If golden rings signified marriage to the song's True Love, that image hardly seems controversial today. But that was not always the case. Rings did not invariably indicate such devotion. In bygone days this symbol implicated wanton sexuality and not, as we think it, primarily the wedlock-sanctioned conjoining of families.

The Church began to uniformly oversee marriages only in the twelfth century, which raised the total number of sacraments to seven. Before that, and for quite a time thereafter, marriages were concluded

## Chapter 13

as secular binding contracts to unite families (with superficial and optional deference to the Church). The rings represented the pagan "wed" that bound the couple; that exchange took place before the marriage ceremony. The wed had nothing to do with authorization by the Church, whose blessing was mainly considered unnecessary—sometimes an extravagance. Anyway, if they stand for marriage five rings is polygamy, which certainly devalues Christian marriage.

A musical jest about the recently arrived sacrament incautiously, perhaps foolishly, tested the limits and reach of heresy. A good rule in a theocracy, or in a kingdom ruled by divine right—whereby the king contrived to derive sovereignty from God, an indirect theocracy—don't make fun of a sacrament. Not only would such a musical prank anger the Church but approval of adultery showed sympathy for what eventually became criminal behavior. For the slight gain of momentary amusement, such mockery provoked the Church's ire already inflamed by caroling, Yuletide misrule, and merrily celebrating lustful behavior. But the carolers risked little because the song baited the authorities in a way that's inconspicuous to modern listeners.

The nuptial ceremony, the sacrament of wedlock commonly evoked by rings, was ridiculed by recalling how the Yule sanctioned temporary marriages and permitted, even encouraged, licentiousness to overrule the bonds of wedlock. But to perform these

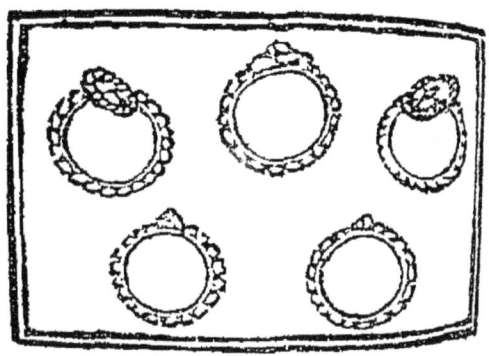

**Five Golden Rings.** Anonymous illustration of "five gold rings," from the first recognized publication of *The Twelve Days of Christmas*, 1780. This illustration accompanied the earliest known version of the lyrics. The simple artwork appeared in a children's book, *Mirth Without Mischief* (printed in London by J. Davenport, George's Court, for C. Sheppard, no. 8, Aylesbury Street, Clerkenwell). The book's lyrics appeared without music. Somehow believed to be of French origin, the publication titled it, "The Twelve Days of Christmas Sung at King Pepin's Ball." Presumably that ascription referred to Charlemagne's son Pepin the Short (714–768) the first Carolingian king of the Franks.

## The 12 Days of Christmas

renegade weddings, that the Church tried to stamp out, required an agent and there was, then, a class of reprobates willing to perform the rites:

> Hedge-priests, monks out of the cloister, men who for one reason or another had left the schools and taken to a nomadic life, had been a trouble to the church since the fifth century.... By the beginning of the thirteenth-century vagabond scholars had become a pest which had to be sternly dealt with [and] commonly linked with jugglers, buffoons, and other low strollers [w]hen they could be caught, they were deprived of their tonsure, thus making them in effect outlaws with no place in the social order.[2]

Unbound by their independence from proper society, wandering non-priests needed a meal. Hunger prompted renegades educated by the Church who looked, and could act, like clergy.[3] As ecclesiastical renunciates, even outlaws, they were as predisposed to celebrate the old pagan holiday (with which many were familiar and had grown up) as to observe Christianity's melancholy veneer. So they officiated at Yuletide's temporary unions.

Such impertinent Christmas alliances violated the spirit and letter of Church-sanctioned weddings while maintaining only the slightest trappings of matrimony. Aristocrats could largely function above the law and privately flaunt the Church's observance as the highborn had their kept mistresses and bastards while Yule gave the peasantry temporary exit from the lawfulness of marital fidelity's sacrament. The antithesis of married constancy, Yuletide encouraged temporary marriages as either an oxymoron to circumvent the Church, or utmost cynical perversity that served the couple's mutual carnal satisfaction.

In response to this affront and other laxities, as the Middle Ages waned the Church took an increasing interest in overseeing the institution of marriage but, far from intending primarily to cultivate elevated morals, by superintending marriages the Church protected its new franchise.[4] Naturally, not everyone was pleased. Some readily perceived that what had formerly been gratis and regulated by (heads of) families and clans was now to be licensed by a sole provider, a third party outside the family. Not surprisingly, trying to monopolize the market for a what many recalled as a previously free service (in both senses, of lacking outside authorization and of soliciting parishioners' contributions) incited taunting, some in the form of songs.

In keeping with the song's tone, drenched in derisive humor that

## Chapter 13

jeered at sober authority, the golden rings did not betoken actions of high moral fame. Today that may be difficult to imagine but in centuries past their understood symbolism brought out attempts to suppress the use of such rings. The infidelity that golden rings could symbolize prompted Puritans to stifle all gaiety surrounding marriage ceremonies.[5] In Tudor times, marriages were forbidden to be performed during the six weeks of the Christmas season. (That ban, perversely, left the field clear for unsanctioned libidinous unions.) Yuletide singing about marriage and golden rings was like singing about the pleasures of cigars in a no-smoking zone. If that seems rather mild protest there was more at stake.

Dour Protestant restraint endlessly tried to reduce the levity attendant upon the old-style mid-winter festival, but prohibitions only encouraged more outrageous and extra-religious bawdiness: ersatz and ephemeral marriages. That was the verse's real subject. Reaction to the dull prospect of the stern Church-sanctioned version of Christmas (or the even drearier outright suppression of the holiday) resuscitated mid-winter's ancient carnival because that festival permitted, even encouraged, "temporary marriage" as part of the fun.

Today the gold rings signal domestic virtue, legalized sexual congress, roving bachelors calmed, household stability, and conditions to legitimate children otherwise born bastards. But wedding rings were once an inflammatory token to devoutly religious folk. When the carol was already known to have been sung, marriage's golden ring provocatively blazed an emblem that the ruling religious elite tried to suppress. If the carol's image referred to marriage, many heard this verse as repugnant. If it didn't refer to legal marriages the verse blared even more disgusting. By the time of Cromwell's ascent to Protector in 1654, the Puritans had not only taken aim at the regular marriage ceremony but at the wearing of golden rings.

Only in 1656 the English Parliament repealed Cromwell's strictures that required quiet marriages performed before a justice of the peace. The new matrimonial legislation allowed most marriages to return to churches; the Anglican *Book of Common Prayer* was banned and a solemn new *Directory of Public Worship* instituted a hushed simplified ceremony. Even then, wedding rings were discouraged and their use rebuked as, "A relique of Popery and a Diabollicall Circle for the

## The 12 Days of Christmas

Devil to daunce in," which could not sound odder to modern ears—except recalling the carol as an enchantress' circle dance.[6] This verse summoned visions of ring-dancers performing an obscene song, and the rings' suggestion of extra-marital sex or even marriage-authorized sex. According to the ruling prudes, the carol—the carole, the devil's dance—and the wedding ring accompanied sanctioned debauchery. Not surprisingly, there was a breadth of opinion on this matter.

Despite the law, many families continued to insist on the wearing of such quasi-religious ornaments, signifying the bond of marriage, if not love.

Compared to the Roman Catholic Church's marriage sacrament, Puritan marriage enacted a legally sealed contractual rite that reflected a sober, utterly unmystical view of the world. Common folk celebrated a marriage with a wedding ceremony that meant community-wide gaiety, good wishes all around, gifts, a feast, and a cheerful party with drinking—followed by sex performed without regard to consequences. A Commonwealth Preacher, William Secker, in 1658 issued an immensely popular sermon which, with considerable courage in the face of lingering official rebuke, defended an age-old practice gone underground. Without becoming theologically lenient or tolerating social laxness, Secker flaunted the edicts, and his sermon was titled *A Wedding Ring Fit for the Finger; or the Salve of Divinity Upon the Sore of Humanity; Laid Open in a Sermon at a Wedding in Edmonton.*[7] The work widely circulated in America and England, indicating that American Puritans were no more monolithic or unopposed in the new than the old world. This verse, that implicitly taunted Puritan sobriety, suggests how the carol of the *Twelve Days* grew as popular in America as in England.

Today, gold rings may promise future fidelity but this verse rewarded proven sexual compatibility confirmed over five unquenched days. That period of erotic liberation soon extended to twelve consecutive daily couplings. The carol's sheer gusto and ingenuity of sexual unions recalls that a gold ring unambiguously "suggests wedding to us, but, beginning in medieval times and through the Renaissance, gold rings were often given by the aristocratic or well-to-do to followers for services beyond the call of duty."[8] Perhaps to those enthusiastic "geese."

Golden rings never manifestly indicated marriage; casual or commercial sex could be rewarded with golden rings, which further widens

## Chapter 13

the distance between modern assumptions about propriety and the past's audacious naughtiness.[9] As George Burns quipped, "It isn't pre-marital sex if you have no intention of getting married." It's hard to improve on such sagacity.

Not all inventive and playful coupling led to marriage, then or now, but in former days singers crooned about extra services supplied by a subordinate (today called sexual harassment or, if desired, unethical workplace liaisons). Popular ballads recognized how money influenced women's sexual conduct, and men's. The conventional wit of the time was that a woman's virtue could be had for a penny or two, and was assured with a keepsake like gold rings,[10] as in the lyric:

> Sir John gives me glittering rings,
> With pretty pleasure to assay—
> Furs of the finest, with other things:
> I have no power to say him nay[11]

Those five rings dangled a mighty fine present for a person who, dazzled by gold, has "no power to say him nay." But the goodies may have been distributed, shared among other compliant partners.[12] Expanding from the dual partners (male-female or master-servant) a total of five rings might suggest a party, carousing and group sex—an orgy.[13] Also, a ring or circle was simply another way of referring to the vulva.[14] So, for example, an alternate reading titles the play as *Much Ado About [A]n O Thing*, the so-called pudendum.[15] Peasants and the literate set recognized the arithmetic, that between them a heterosexual couple's anatomy features five rings, openings admitting intromission of a digit or other member. But the clever double-meaning of ring-openings was not lost when needed for a good laugh.

In a play whose original cruel comedy has mostly faded for us, indeed becoming almost morally irretrievable, the final scene of reconciled lovers in Shakespeare's *Merchant of Venice* ends with Gratiano's last uncouth, though witty, line addressed to his bride:

> Well, while I live, I'll fear no other thing
> So sore, as keeping safe Nerrissa's ring.

Of course, sore also means irritated, bruised and inflamed, perhaps from hard use with Nerrissa. Leave 'em laughing.

After resolving a cliff-hanger Shakespeare knew what his audiences wanted: the relief of a guffaw at a bit of sex, hence the double-entendre ring. Keeping Nerrissa's ring safe (guarded, concealed, and secured

## The 12 Days of Christmas

against others by a husband's frequent use) will chafe. The audience suffered no illusions about this joke. Curtain down.

Master authors wrote witty and off-color jests while common people toyed with rudimentary verbal pranks, but their word-play used the same material, the semantics common to an era. While mostly the works of canonical literature come down to us, studied and lovingly preserved and revered, folk wisdom's songs and fairytales addressed similar situations. Rings, metal and anatomical, matrimonial or salacious, offered the joksters fair game in high art and low. Peasants consummated both genuine and mock, or temporary, Yuletide marriages and understood "ring" in its many allusions.

Marriage rites' seasonal association continued for a long time because weddings were often mid-winter affairs. Yuletide and Christmas as linked with weddings endured at least until the eighteenth century when, "George Washington married Martha on Twelfth night or 'Old Christmas' eve in 1759."[16] Because they were observing an ancient tradition, that date served a wealthy couple rarely thought of convention-breaking when it came to social situations. Political revolution was another matter.

Yule was the customary season for weddings and rings, which was one of the reasons that various Churches discouraged or forbade weddings at this season—citing the sanctity of the season of Christ's nativity as their prohibition's alibi. Yet, counterfeit weddings remained staunchly part of the festival and, if one such consummation was pleasurable, why not five? The phrase that comes to mind, "the more the merrier" uses a word now routinely exercised, more or less exclusively brought out of retirement, for wishing a Merry Christmas.

Yuletide's ferocious excesses surpassed the merely gleeful; amateur hedonists prospected for memorable goodies amid frenzied immoderation. But times change. For moderns, golden rings recall affectionate bonds, especially of marital fidelity (whose breach prompts concealing the ring under the motel bed, so powerful is its message of inviolability). The sympathetic association hailed from pre–Puritan days and survived hypocritical piety because common folk retained the rings' sentimental associations. At the song's hinge-point, they brandished a flagrantly drawn-out challenge against the ring-custom's pietistic curtailment.

In a clash of two kinds of conservatism, these rings illustrate a

*Chapter 13*

folk-rebellion that rebutted Puritanism's excessive cleansing of cherished tradition. Revolts against the Puritans' sullen worldview issued not just from the lower classes but included an insurrection from the agricultural peasantry (who could actually become quite prosperous and remain peasants) and New World yeomanry. In 1659 the General Court of Massachusetts Bay Colony imposed a hefty five-shilling fine on those apprehended for "observing any such a day as Christmas ... by forebearing of labor, feasting, or any other way." Reproving such Puritan excesses the British government in London forced a 1681 repeal of the law banning Christmas festivities. From 1687–1689 the holiday was again openly celebrated when the Massachusetts Bay Colony had its charter revoked. With the charter restored in 1689, once again local authorities suppressed Christmas. This tug-of-war against what each side found repugnant included views of marriage, its wedding rings, and old-time Christmas festivities.

## The Kill-Joys

Not only did Puritans attempt to stifle merriment accompanying marriage ceremonies but especially to expunge the great mid-winter Yule holiday (that occasioned many weddings, legitimate and binding, or temporary) and, concomitantly, to suppress seasonal caroling that highlighted the festival. Such songs flourished in a lewd community-wide celebration that utterly validated the Puritan's fears. The cause for their moral anxiety survives in graphic descriptions of pre-restoration Yuletide.[17] In those days people frequently "blackened their faces or disguised themselves as animals or cross-dressed, thus operating under a protective cloak of anonymity" according to Yule's old ways as recorded by John Ashton, a late-nineteenth-century historian who reported an episode from Lincolnshire in 1637 when:

> the man selected by a crowd of revelers as "Master of Misrule" was publicly given a "wife," in a ceremony led by a man dressed as a minister (he read the entire marriage service from the Book of Common Prayer). Thereupon, as Ashton noted in Victorian language, "the affair was carried to its utmost extent."[18]

Christmas, marriage, and unconcealed fornication (not just adventiously performed in unobserved public spaces, but in front of a

# The 12 Days of Christmas

crowd)—all united in the symbol of the five rings sung as the carol's pivotal stanza.

The song perfectly companioned that season's events when, before an audience of their neighbors, a crowd-pleasing "Master of Misrule" and his "wife" openly mocked both Church-sanctioned marriage and the clergy, carrying the partying "to its utmost extent"—fucking for an audience as a live sex show which, to put the best face on it, perhaps derived from some ancient fertility rite inherited from the Saturnalia or Yule. There's an interesting correlation to be derived from this outdoor performance.

Unexpectedly we learn that the carol of the *Twelve **Days** of Christmas* does not recount clandestine nighttime deeds carried out with guilty stealth under cover of darkness. No shame. No guilt. Nothing to hide veiled by darkness. All done under the sun. In front of your cheering neighbors. No doubt well on their way to inebriation.[19] And the congenial crowd inspired to their own present erotic deeds after relishing the performance of the mistress and her misrule-master, who must have been proficient at *something* to have been so chosen.

For twelve successive days beneath winter's feeble silver sun, activities now associated with the evening were practiced unashamed in public. The celebrants of old-time Christmas felt they had nothing to hide and, in the festival's original mood, indifferent to the nights, the carol's inventory proceeds listing indecencies performed in broad daylight. Only Christian mores superimposed on the celebration required the furtive observance of mid-winter activities, perpetuated illicitly in the dark. If Puritans do it with the lights out the Yule's misrule shines a celebratory spotlight on the usually hidden.

People un-ashamed of pleasure-seeking, sometimes gave golden rings for especially outstanding and memorable sexual exploits. Accordingly, the seemingly gratuitous word "Day" served as more than a numerator, a way of counting.

Once launched, the song's pattern continues relentlessly to the end, with one surprising anomaly. An unanticipated oddity broke the salacious carol's reciprocating noun-verb form with a pattern-shattering irregularity whose slight modification (unlike a flaw in a diamond) added appealing contrast.

Variety supported the song's poetic matrix. In managing this

## Chapter 13

formal trick the carol seems surprisingly sophisticated. A first-rate artwork establishes regularity that, lightly touched with variation, whets expectations. Ingenious breaks in the established pattern test the anticipated structure with tasty inventions. Too many expectations met and the work bores its audience who can anticipate what will come next, but too many unexpected variations produce incoherence. And, balancing theme and variation, the carol of the twelve days exhibits this classic trait of well-balanced art.

The five rings formerly implied something completely different from (if not the exact opposite of) their wholesome meaning today, and at verse five the carol takes a decided turn in structure.

Sung with a pause in the song's break-neck speed, the ring-verse locates the song's balance point but not its center. It perches asymmetrically because more verses follow the golden rings than precede them. A real mid-point would mirror-image the number of verses, equally weighted and flanking the rings, but at this verse something does change to give the song a before-and-after feeling.

Following the rings, the verses serve as the song's second half, and the latter verses feature a simple formula: a named object and its modifier. The verbs vanish.

## Chapter 14

## Fourth Night

Bits of choice jargon trace the carol's early history through a turbulent adolescence. The song somehow survived political and religious wars fought from pulpit, parliament, and with sword. Even cultural warfare's otherwise sworn enemies (Catholics, Protestants, Puritans, Royalists, Parliamentarians, and pious new world colonists) agreed on one thing: they all tried to smother the verses of mid-winter caroling. The song's opponents were not wrong in their antipathy.

No innocent bystander, but an active partisan in that cultural battleground, every recitation of the beloved carol reinstated something old and authentic. A lusty rightful heir could dethrone an ersatz holiday of good manners. Then, an improbably de-natured Christmas, up-dated and quasi-religious, dragooned the bawdy mid-winter drinking song into its toned-down festivities. But instead of issuing its death warrant with this conscription, modern Christmas saved the carol of the *Twelve Days*.

For centuries popular religion's rousing pre–Christian "Christmas" wrangled with theological Christmas. The Church's version had meant to oust the older and lively Saturnalia which, seeing no reason to die, relentlessly fought back. To the dismay and disgust of clergy the old ways persisted in winning hearts and loyalties over the cheerfully re-branded innocuous Christian observance.

More than a specifically and exclusively Christian holiday, the Christmas season is celebrated around the world, even in places like Japan that are not Christian. Christmas triumphed where Christianity had not. But this modern materialist holiday confutes what the Church intended for joyful reverence and fellowship; it also palely resembles the old-time festival—being rather a diluted version of the ancient

## Chapter 14

masquerading, drinking, gift-giving, pranking, and fornicating (under the excuse of mid-winter snuggling or an office party gotten out-of-hand). Today, Christmas promotes good cheer as a moral value that celebrants are supposed to spread throughout the year. Modern Christmas proposes an ideal, though not really a religious paragon: generosity growing from wildly extravagant gift-giving and a shallow convivial forgiveness. And that, above all, promotes consumerism. In contrast, the Twelve-Days carol

**Old Time Caroling.**

relates how human beings behave when unconstrained by an establishment vested in regulating civic behavior.[1] So, the next verse offered no surprise when, like the other gifts, four calling birds seem innocent—on the surface.

In Old English "birds" meant the juveniles of any feathered animal. (This distinction still obtains in some dialects, as in Scotland where large birds, e.g., hawks or herons are "fowls" while small birds and chickens are "birds.") In 1593 Shakespeare alludes to "That Princely Eagles Bird" (*Henry VI Part 3*, II:1). Regardless of the parental species, offspring are called a bird, and the *Twelve Days* was probably well-formed by Shakespeare's day when—much as Americans universally refer to youngsters as kids, and do not mean baby goats—the word conjured chirping fledglings as vulnerable infants, never great soaring

# The 12 Days of Christmas

wings. With linguistic wit the song's birds simultaneously evoke helpless nestlings and something else. Finding the alternative stands us face-to-face with the original carolers.

In former times "bird" meant the young of any creature. The young animals might be maidens or girls, because bird used to be confused with bryd(e), bride. Once again gender reigns consistently throughout the carol: the bird is female. Modern British slang revives the earlier sense.

In the UK, bird refers to a girl or a woman, always as sexually available—or at least imagined to be sexually active—but the word never implies a prepubescent female except affectionately. This usage goes back quite aways. Eric Partridge noted that "bird's nest" was used by Shakespeare to mean the "Pudend and pubic hair,"[2] as in *Romeo and Juliet* (II:4) when the Nurse, half-protector/half-procurer, counsels that: "I must ... fetch a ladder, By the which your love Must climb a bird's nest soon when it is dark." The fluffy pubic thatch may be called many things, but to endearingly name it a bird's nest makes its owner a bird.

The women-as-bird proffers sex for the penis as a cock. Referring to his farmyard realm's coop, prissy Americans substituted "rooster" as a less offensive avian word (although the term is much older). This timid linguistic forgery glances at the cock's job on a farm, to rule the roost. Referred to as a cock, the penis is also a pecker—in the wit of folkish synecdoche. In one version of the Southern blues, the singer of *Corinna* laments: "I got a bird that whistles/ I got a bird that sings/ but without Corinna, life don't mean a thing." The singer is not talking about a pet canary but a friendless, and he claims talented, penis.

In familiar or disparaging British street jargon, a "bird" is not a lofty word suitable for upper classes, except to sarcastically abase a gentlewomen, as was already practiced upon dancing ladies. In American slang, girls are chicks. Not a term used across class lines this usage exactly parallels the tone and application of the British "bird."

As a linguistic fact-of-life regarding sexual organs, the song's avian associations proliferate. We might hope the situation less vulgar, less sexually charged, or more nominally religious, but such stuffy evasions fracture the carol and cannot reconcile the song's true subjects.

While the carol mentions various birds (geese, swans, hens, partridges, doves) this verse's young birds are qualified as calling, perhaps

## Chapter 14

crying out for food. With a concealed double-meaning the verb's usage proves consistent with the carol's unrelenting emphasis. We might wish for some tonal variety or a wider scope of observation as the verses juggernaut along, but the song's monomaniacal fixedness recalls pornography's monotony, an ordeal of boredom for the uninterested. And revulsion for others. Without diversity this song regards seasonal sexual pleasures and doesn't wander off into other considerations except as political sidelights about class and temporarily-relieved subjugation. It recalls a vanished Christmas few can now imagine, and none expect to see revived.

Joining bird and call in the same verse performs some clever word-play. The innocent names of birds identity both a thing and an action. As a verb it means to pursue bird catching or fowling, to bird, go birding (which in this context might be transposed as *cherchez la femme*). That is, "to bird" implicitly entails "calling." The carol startlingly self-confirms its intentions and presents as careful a bit of craftsmanship as ever represented an authentic culture. Recognizing that a call is not only a loud vocal utterance, when the carol was new-minted a call also referred to a decoy-bird or a lure, a secondary meaning that echoes piping. In 1595 Shakespeare's metaphor was understood in *King John* as a summons:

> CARDINAL PANDULPH: if but a dozen French
> Were there in arms, they would be as a call
> To train ten thousand English to their side (III:4)

More to the point, a play by Shakespeare's disciple, Philip Massinger, *The Parliament of Love*, 1624, contains the line: "This fellow has a pimp's face, And looks as if he were her call, her fetch." So, the song's "calling birds" could be decoys to solicit girlish favors, outright pimps. Without fear of misunderstanding, "a call" would have meant a procurer or panderer. A loitering pimp, lounging against a building and eyeing the passing trade, presents a piece of urban furniture as old as cities but realizing that such a fellow was a whore's "call," that pimping was a calling, recasts this verse.

The act of calling means stopping at a door or place on the way to somewhere else. These are not extended stops but brief, even momentary, interruptions on the way to arriving home or ending a journey. A bird that is calling never rests for long, and might be homeless, which introduces a subtly shaded undertone. Those who come calling go away:

## The 12 Days of Christmas

a call girl. A call can be a brief and usually formal visit when we make or pay or receive a call. Therefore, four birds calling could be a quartet of young women making a brief planned visit. (This meaning survives in the nautical "ports of call.") The arranged appointment could be a rendez-vous the women thought up or they could have been summoned; to be called or to receive a calling also figuratively means an invitation, bidding. Again, Shakespeare supplies a citation in his 1592 *Venus and Adonis:* "Tapsters answering every call." This sense brings us right into the present day.

When authorities broke up whoremaster Heidi Fleiss's Hollywood call-girl ring of the 1990s, general wonderment arose that celebrities, male movie stars of tremendous fame, purchased the services of her stable when these same renown'd gentlemen could have walked into any bar in North American and picked up and bedded any woman around, to mutual satisfaction. What eluded envious plebes reading press accounts of her business was that Ms. Fleiss did not offer just sex (however varied and expert) but the promise that her discrete sex-workers, unlike star-struck pick-ups, would *leave* in the morning and not gossip. That is, they made "calls" then moved on without entangling emotional claims.

Though all call-girls arrive, perform, and then depart, Ms. Fleiss's case proved paradigmatic. Her clients' celebrity demonstrated (better than ten thousand ignominious "Johns" could have) that the true nature of the provided service, essentially a sex-worker's "calling"—a specialized laborer's vocation not dependent only on talent, beauty, and acquired skills (although that helps)—makes calls and then, noiselessly and without fuss, vacates the premises. Anything else is unprofessional. The song's "calling" and "birds" counterbalance. Striking one word from the verse topples the other side of the equation. The verb needs the noun and the object suggestively colors the (allusively obscene) action, thereby each half reciprocally amplifying piquant evocation.

Unfortunately for moralists or those desperately hoping to retrieve this song and save its innocence for an idealized Christmas, it cannot be dragged back to the shores of rectitude from the raging surf of sin; it's impossible to diminish this verse's naughtiness, or the carol's accumulating sense, no longer an undertone but clearly the main event.

Insights into the carol's older usage explains why people would enthusiastically gather to sing apparent nonsense.[3] Their reasons hardly differ from present needs, and we are not brighter than our ancestors;

## Chapter 14

we seek coherence as they did. In some far-off time people sang about what mattered to them and, having espied the carol's subject, we should defend the original carolers' interests. Not only are the long-deceased noiselessly seething against ridiculous misrepresentations of their gone world, but for centuries powerful interests worked to eradicate true caroling's record.

Unearthing this carol's place in Christmas champions the rights of bygone singers of bawdy songs. A legion of supporters already advocate on behalf of wholesome carols, but the disproportionate attention lavished on those immaculate songs misrepresents the situation of early carolers' concerns. Whether you are attracted or repulsed by the world beckoning from this song, the strong cider- and beer-sodden festival and its carol deserve a fair hearing. We cherish, and do not shy from witnessing, Brueghel's equivalent representations.

Though now obsolete, a calling summoned to answer to a charge, an accusation, or impeachment. This usage survives only in the legal sense of being "called to the bar" as admission to the status of a barrister, an attorney. But we still use "calling" to denote an occupation or vocation. In that sense—when calling refers to a career choice or a tradesman's job—the verse becomes tinged with a meaning something like: these "birds" were professionals. They were expert, and they were ready. To arrive. To perform. To leave. Not that such professionalism mattered overly at Christmastide as sex-workers were less segregated than in modern times.[4] Medieval "prostitutes, especially those who practiced prostitution on a casual basis, were not a separate subculture, nor were they limited to one particular geographic area; they inevitably formed part of the life of the entire community."[5] So our song considered both screwing's professionals and amateurs.

As an interestingly precise contrast, the women of this verse were not "lay" or amateur practitioners as the geese may have been. The dilettante, the beginner or maid(en), the professional crafts(wo)man of sex workers—all happily jostle in this song, as cozy and merry together as modern carolers singing enthusiastically on some street corner sprinkled in sifting snow.

However monomaniacal the verses, echoing and fortifying their meaning throughout the carol, the images are not redundant and each refers to a distinctly particular situation.

### The 12 Days of Christmas

Anticipation, even eagerness when expertly feigned, intensifies the sense of being at someone's call. Without sounding official, juridical or stodgy yet including a sense of being governed, the word meant to be subject to command and ready to answer a directive or relevant summons. A brief call subtly differentiates from continuing service, as implied by the, already cited, phrase "To dance attendance on their Lordships pleasures" (*Henry VIII* V:2) Ultimately, this difference implies immediate availability, which survives in the phrase "at [someone's] beck and call," figuratively to be subject to another's authority, direction and will. Hired work. These multi-valent inferences aggregate around a collective meaning. They form a more nuanced description than seems initially possible from such a flippant verse.

The true love's gift: two pair of young women who functioned like call girls. Short planned visits were, perhaps playfully, governed by the singer's (erotic?) desires, stamina, and imagination. Essentially: Let's Party! messaged old Christmas, without any of the new-fangled encumbering moral baggage.

# Chapter 15

## Hens Improved: French

Outlandish images ornament the song. But, if initially discouraged by the verses' opaque gibberish, the situation gradually clears. Certain attention-grabbing phrases prove more accessible than others and centuries later their connotations remain recognizable. Some terms endure in our spoken language; others clearly hail from an expired world. Although human needs haven't changed much over the centuries (while today's expectations for necessaries would seem mind-bogglingly princely to Medieval peasants) apparent similarities between outmoded phrases and their modern counterparts conceal traps. The preceding verses proved amusing and vulgar, but the third day's seems wholly innocent. What was funny or ribald about the French? Three French Hens seems an approachable image that suggests only pleasant, even cordial charm, perchance a gracious present. Nothing bizarre portrayed here; no violently active verb like leaping, energetic motion like dancing, or sexually suggestive acts like milking or even swimming. The carol's antique connotations of *being* French or of *giving* somebody (your true love) something French defies modern usage.

In modern parlance, French hens would be 'three French chicks.' Scholars recognize that, "a hen is a bed-partner, and a French one would for the English have connotations of considerable activity"—invidiously compared to a good stolid English girl.[1] Even without an animating verb, a noun saturated with energetic hints contributes to the carol's uniformity of tone.

This verse's raunchy image of a trio of adept bed-partners carries a wonderful suavity into the song—a working-man's idea of sophisticated luxury as a late-Medieval Hugh Hefner might promote. If not quite the (now-obsolete) Playboy ideal of the silk smoking jacket and snifter of

# The 12 Days of Christmas

brandy, the song also conjures aspirational images of skillful practitioners beyond what local homespun rustics could expect of quick, seasonally expedient, sex ignited by rough drink. Nuances appear, which evidence distant yearnings for refinement and a growing awareness of internationalism that fed an incipient worldliness. Long-distance trade began to touch every village. English wool returned as French wine.

Beyond the shire's narrow Medieval country ways the carol yearns for gifts farther afield than England's homegrown social struggles. Instead of merely ridiculing your neighbor or the next town, this folksong burlesques a foreign trait. The verse values erotic accomplishments that, even if merely legendary in Globalism's sunrise, were privately esteemed and desired though publicly discouraged by sexual hypocrisy.

The song assiduously dodges the language of Anglo-Norman aristocracy—slighting any such words. Between about 1350 and 1550 England found itself in a peculiar linguistic situation: the few relatively literate Englishmen were routinely bi- or trilingual, while the rest of the population spoke a vulgar tongue, (Middle) English. That version of English was not even fully recognized at the royal Anglo-Norman court. Though ruling the English nation, courtiers only gradually weaned themselves from speaking a dialect of French. At first the overlords' proclamations assured that the governed understood they were commanded by foreigners until, over time, the rulers themselves became "English" and deigned to speak the native language. The carol singers emphasized their English-ness with a linguistic provincialism that thwarted any remnants of hifalutin Norman-French.

The song enrolls simple (often four-letter) Anglo words: bird, call, drum, first, five, four, gave, lady, leap, lord, love, maid, milk, nine, pipe, pear, ring, swan, swim(ming), tree, true. This core vocabulary avoids Latinates so diligently as to suggest both a purposeful evasion of Norman French and an avoidance of Church Latin's grave sounds, with all the deliberate pomposity so conjured.

Concurrent with the carol singers' witty efforts, others worked at refining everyday language's bluntness into something subtle enough for sharp literary witticism—no job for amateurs. Professional authors, largely non-aristocrats, accomplished that distillation of colloquial speech. We know their names as they propelled the literature of modern languages away from Latin's Medieval norms and limits. Just when

*Chapter 15*

the names of visual artists, sculptors, architects, and painters emerge from the shadows of anonymity, so do the celebrity poets. Concurrent with caroling's most fecund period, the troubadour's high noon coincided with the work of Dante Alighieri (1265–1321) who championed his native Italian.

Like English, Italian had been scorned as a serious literary medium. Like Dante's vernacular, English strove at considerable social disadvantage with Latin and Anglo-Norman French; in England either Latin or Anglo-Norman French could muster international audiences of the educated while what became standard English warred with itself in local variants.[2]

One dialect eventually represented a national voice after the English identity formed following centuries of bloody incursions into Celtic-speaking Scotland, Whales, and Ireland by the "leaping lords." But only gradually was English deemed a tool of this unification. As the use of spoken French declined at court and in official documents, a London/East-Midland dialect gained acceptance throughout the country. When British dialects merged into a recognizable "English" the foreigner could be mocked as the overseas stranger. Oddly dissimilar in manners and dress, foreigners could be invidiously portrayed as the "other." Especially, the French.

Parodies in the vernacular language staked out emerging national literatures that could, and did, ridicule other countries for their differences—readers and writers no longer united by Latin across political borders. Moderns surfeited with entertainment find nothing special about a lampoon in vulgar English but formerly such jokes were completely fresh and their onset dawned abruptly. Basil Bunting confessed, "I can't think of any good parodies in English before Shakespeare." You need a despised "other" to identity the exact boundary between the culture that every native carries in their head and that distinguishes them from people elsewhere and populations doomed to either inferiority or impossibly perfect legend. Those far-away peoples are rumored to do things oddly. The new era's dawn glimmered as surely from its satire and pornography as high art.

The Middle Ages ended when provincial imaginations conceived newly accessible places open for business, lands that were no longer merely hazy legendary settings for stories. Reports of these lands came

## The 12 Days of Christmas

back from missions of diplomacy, trade (with its handmaiden, exploration), and following Crusades. A small diagnostic of this change, as colloquial languages climbed upward toward national literatures, appears in the importation of "french" hens who contributed a special editorial tang. They marked a cosmopolitan awareness that legitimated everyday local speech. And ridiculing the lascivious French sets a clear marker in time.

The emerging national language wielded by paid specialists, writers of vernacular who flattered their audience's former dialectical isolation, appears in the *Merchant of Venice* when the Italian-speaking Nerrissa asks, "What say you then to Fauconbridge, the young Baron of England?" who seems a mono-lingual dolt.

> PORTIA: You know I say nothing to him, for he understands not me, nor I him: he hath neither Latin, French, nor Italian, and you will come into the Court and swear that I have a poor penny-worth in the English: he is a proper mans picture, but alas who can converse with a dumb show?

Her contempt portrayed the Renaissance view of properly refined accomplishment, both at the level of tradesmen and aristocracy. Common countryfolk remained skeptical.[3]

Just as the carol form was gaining vigor, in 1362 English was adopted as the language of pleading in courts of law. Now unschooled commoners (complainants or criminal defendants) could understand courtroom exchanges, even if they didn't like the proceedings' fairness or the results. By the late fifteenth century the language battle ended and English appeared in more documents than Latin or French. With their speech clearly segregated from the continent's predominant modes of expression, the English developed a sense of the others as "them," people with different, questionable, customs, values, and who talked funny. Specifically, the English defeat in the Hundred Years War (1337–1453) prompted vilification of anything French. French Hens was no compliment.

Perhaps a French-hen indicates something proverbial about Gallic temperament, especially in contrast with the robust English celebration of Yule. In particular, things "Frenchified" were deemed "infected with the venereal disease," as in the eighteenth-century slang expression "the

## Chapter 15

mort is Frenchified," meaning "the wench is infected"—a sober warning about three French-hens.[4] The French gout (or the Ladies Fever, also called the Frenchman or French Pox) was the name for the disease which the French themselves called Naples canker, *mal de Naples:* syphilis. A French pig was another name for the venereal bubo that Shakespeare cited as the Winchester Goose.[5] Actually, Shakespeare employed both vulgarities, as in *Henry V:* "New have I that my Nell is dead i' the spital Of malady of France." (V:i) Even in wholly anachronistic situations Shakespeare knew he had a sure-fire guffaw when—as in the late, and probably co-authored play *Pericles, Prince of Tyre*—in an ancient Mytilene brothel on the island of Lesbos (IV:2) the doorkeeper inquires of the madame:

> BOULT: ...mistress, do you know the
> French knight that cowers i' the hams?
> ....
> BAWD: Well, well; as for him, he brought his disease hither[6]

If bad stuff happened, the French brought it. This was a guaranteed laugh line. In the *Merchant of Venice,* the French suitor becomes a joke merely for being...:

> NERRISSA: How say you by the French Lord, Mounsier Le Boune?
> PORTIA: God made him, and therefore let him pass for a man, in truth I
> know it is a sin to be a mocker....

But sin can be a frolic. And mockery provides sinful fun. Sometimes Shakespeare had only to mention the French to get an automatic chuckle, and the carol's singers would not pass up such inherent mirth, or at least knew a punch-line when they heard it.[7] This disparaging usage apparently suffused every mention of the French as unwholesome, which makes three hens considerably less appealing than on first introduction. So, the song contains sarcasm, sex, and humor.

The hen-bird of any species is the female, which reenforces the song's choice of gendered slang and the vernacular's intimations. With an admirable (or maniacal) mental focus, the song remains fixated on celebrating the festival's multi-day riot of misrule and sex. The carol unwaveringly concentrated on what the singers knew of their own experience, perceptions and lessons neither reported nor preached.

The singers' truth was not our truth that derives from accepted

# The 12 Days of Christmas

disciplines: science, art, jurisprudence—trustworthy sources of the modern world. But, neither was the carol singers' truth strictly religious or scientific, but experiential.[8] Their world claimed its community-sanctioned effectiveness and verity from the recurring evidence of crops' fertility, the heavens' predictable annual rotation, and human urges corresponding to seasonal cycles (after all, centuries before Louis Pasteur, nobody knew how mash to turned to beer, apple juice to hard cider, whey and curds to cheese, or sticky dough to risen bread). Largely because the carol-singer's body had not (yet) separated from nature, each caroler was her own expert on what felt right, what accommodated best the seasons, and the body's hungers.[9] Cut off from the seasons by central heat and air conditioning, watching the changing leaves through multi-pane windows when not looking down at a book or a computer screen—these breaches from the outside world impose sensual remove that contrasts with the immediacy of the singers' awareness of their bodily faculties which were, all too often, uncomfortable and itchy.

Nowadays such bodily knowledge concerns sybarites. But also womanizers and ascetics like cloistered monks and nuns whose every awareness monitors the flood of bodily sensations in a kind of reverse hedonism. Then there's the bodily knowledge of sluts, drunkards, sexually fluid identities, and other sensual explorers prowling the outskirts of mainstream propriety. If practiced wholesale today, the carol singers' community mores would be judged very differently. Yet, their knowledge of the zoological and botanical world would be admired.

By c.1325 English-speakers readily distinguished between the "Partriche, fesant henne ant fesant cocke"—a standard comparison to differentiate the sexes. The distinction remained useful through 1540, when Richard Hyrde observed, in his *Vives' Instruction of a Christian Woman*, "I my selfe ... haue seene the cocke swan kill his hen, because she followed another cocke." Without the modifying word cock the swan was presumed to be female (as verse seven supposed, with the other verses supplying contextual emphasis). From the early to the mid–1600s hen solely distinguished the female from the male; in 1660 it made sense to say: "Soon after we got a hen sparrow." Old-time carol singers who heard that phrase would have understood it because for centuries "hen" appeared as a suffix to indicate female birds: Guinea Hen, Grey-Hen,

## Chapter 15

Heath-Hen, Moor-Hen, Pea-Hen, Water-Hen. The male was designated the cock: Heath-cock, Peacock, etc. A male victim was hen-pecked.

The sorts of double-meanings in which this song glories remain common, if hard to detect in simple terms of otherwise bland appearance. An everyday word of three letters opens an unsuspected door and a vista to the past, because the hen indicated a bird's femaleness and a French-hen stated gender tinted with a foreign nationality.

As figurative usage about persons—especially a humorous or low colloquial allusion to a wife—a woman or a female was a "A hen-hearted" person. A hen-hearted person could be of either sex, although the hen's reticent and dithering qualities were especially disparagingly when attributed to the male. (Today, calling a man a "pussy" impugns his virility, especially his courage, by comparing him to the softness of female genitalia and feminized reticence.[10]) An 1890 dictionary simply defines a Hen as "a woman, specifically a wife or mistress," with such scornful derivatives "Hen's-Arsehole" as the mouth.[11] This insult invokes the hen for the least admirable female qualities, like proverbial gossiping or being a timid bed-partner who would have to be shown what to do (not French). That miserable prospect could be modified for the better, because French-hens would be acquiescent, blithely animated, and uninhibited, although poisonous sexual partners.

The song might be considered a string of co-references, features that only make sense because they refer to each other on the same semantic level. Most of our speech operates that way, except when we use air-quotes to show an inserted statement out-of-context or, for really good conversationalists, to signal sarcasm by speaking *in Italics*, a good trick. But the song's uniformity of expressive tone adds credence to the intentionality of the entirety. So, once again, behind that carol's mask as an artless ditty of innocent nonsense, *The Twelve Days* lampooned the pretenses of the Church's Christmas. A gift that flaunted three saucy French-hens mocked the self-righteous (or merely righteous) under whose noses or windows this lewd song was roared, perhaps defiantly with alcohol-laden breath. Yet, an interesting gift.

# Chapter 16

## Sincerity and Tenderness

A comforting pause softens the carol's runaway smut.

The second verse conjures a charming image. It doesn't function as respite from exclusively offensive material because the carol's spectrum of possibilities also sets a place for tender emotions, a time to cuddle when not drinking or screwing.

Formerly, and still today in many dialects of English, "dove" indicates all the pigeon species native to or known in Britain. This gentle creature betokens endearment. The carolers invoked it with sharp-eyed precision. The class of bird includes the Turtle-dove (whose name derives from the song of its call, turr-turr), called the Ring-dove, the Rock-dove, or Rock pigeon which the singers meticulously named and organized as the carol sorts birds. Their unambiguous references distinguished one type of bird from another, because some of this bird's relations enjoy fame and others infamy.

The feral Rock Pigeon is a fancy name for the strutting bird that pollutes and ornaments urban parks; it has adopted window ledges and architectural features as its precarious home instead of nesting in cliff faces, where many believe it belongs, exclusively. It is the rat-with-wings whose feeding was banned from Trafalgar Square after such feedings were prohibited in New York's Bryant Park; yet recalcitrants still scatter bird seed in public spaces. Depending on your view of the matter, hordes of them adorn or befoul Saint Mark's square in Venice. Generally referred to without differentiation (except by ornithologists or hunters) most species of this family are called pigeons with the name dove restricted to birds that resemble turtledoves. That introduces no small difference.

Reenforcing a particularity as old as the Bible, the *Twelve Days*

## Chapter 16

recognized that a turtledove and pigeon are not the same creature.[1] Each had its own associations, some ancient and others still invoked.

When used as a simile, a dove indicates a gentle or guileless person, especially a loving woman or child. (The Bible preceded modern usage with the same metaphor for meekness: "O deliver not the soul of your turtledove to the multitude of the wicked: forget not the congregation of your poor forever." *Psalm* 74:19) A dove also describes an innocent or simpleton, as in Shakespeare's 1596 *Taming of the Shrew* (III:2) "Tut, she's a Lambe, a Dove, a foole to him."[2] Yet, not all meek people are esteemed, let alone cherished and, however defenseless, the person referred to as a dove may be scorned for being feckless, lacking self-assertion, vulnerable, cowardly or overly timid.

When everyone pursued their own satisfaction, unrestrained during the Christmastide riot, elevating the meek assumes a distinctly religious notion alien to some singers. At mid-winter, at least temporarily, a different ethos held sway. For cynics throughout the year, the defenseless can be reviled for being unworldly and ineffectual, and therefore undefended for cause (according to a worldview and political "philosophy" that still snubs the un-deserving poor and the ill-fated). Innocence does not reign a virtue in all times and places, and even the God who helps those who help themselves evidently thinks twice about helping those who do not avail themselves.[3] The dove indicates both a cherished gentle soul of the singer's fondness and also a guileless patsy. As usual, the singers were seemingly hip to both connotations and chose the word precisely because it lived both a charming and charmless Jekyll-and-Hyde existence.

As an appellation of tender affection, the dove is a nickname that dates at least to Chaucer's time, when c.1386, in the *Merchant's Tale* he could write "Rys vp my wyf, my loue, my lady free ... my dowue sweete."(897) Two hundred years later, Shakespeare maintained this tone in *Hamlet*, 1602, "Fare you well my Dove."(IV:5) The carol of *The Twelve Days* conveyed to modernity the dove as a darling naive, among those rare unchanged medieval usages still current: a cherished lover.

While tempting to equate turtledoves with chaste love or purely spiritual reverence, evidence for that construction crumbles. Doves, according to scholars of these matters, are the carol's only symbols "that have retained their medieval and Renaissance erotic significance. They were birds of Venus."[4] Turtledoves do not signify virginal "Platonic" esteem. They indicate everyday unchaste love—fervid desire.

# The 12 Days of Christmas

In Shakespeare's 1590 *Midsummer Night's Dream,* Hermia's vow to Lysander avouches how the bird's naivete, as servant and companion of the goddess of love, certifies her consuming passion:

> I swear to thee, by Cupid's strongest bow,
> By his best arrow with the golden head,
> By the simplicity of Venus' doves
> By that which knitteth souls and prosper loves (I:1)

She wants to be united with her lover, with whom she is infatuated to distraction. She wants coupling. And the carol's second verse features such a hoped-for twosome.

From Christianity's earliest days the dove represented gentleness and, recounting the baptism of Jesus, the dove stands for the Holy Spirit.[5] If the carol were actually a song of religious veneration as some hope it was—and not about erotic release and the attendant celebration—the doves might have appeared in the third verse: all things trinitarian serving as Christian images.

Associated with the holy spirit in Renaissance religious iconography (and more recently with peace) doves could have represented the Holy Trinity if placed in the third verse, but there are two, not three doves in the song. Moreover, the three French Hens are most certainly not trinitarian in any religious sense.[6] Instead, the doves introduced a retrospective, a nostalgic bit of old-time Christmas when families gathered over food and drink in a bond of blood and milk kinship. Ferreting out this representation of the past and a fuller appreciation of this verse, follows a close look at the birds themselves. Details of the doves that would have been conspicuous to the original singers are less obvious to modern city-dwellers.

Turtledoves are also called ring doves, or ringed-neck doves because, similar to the Collared Dove of England, a fine dark line encircles their throats[7] Once sacred to Demeter—the goddess of harvests and the earth's fertility—doves have long symbolized fidelity and tender love. Though gentle prey animals subject to the depredations of raptors, doves stand for fierce devotion and affection, not chaste Christian love that elevates prissy virginity, but pagan fecundity. The dove bespeaks love and fealty to energetic nature's miraculous fruitfulness. Their symbolic associations rose from an awareness of the teeming

## Chapter 16

undomesticated world that surrounded farmsteads; properly respected and propitiated, those forces worked with farmers. With mid-winter drinking, feasting, bodily rest and carnality (all practically summoned by nature to convene at the same time) those who toiled at animal husbandry and in agricultural communities observed the essence of a formerly sacred, but now heathen, festival. Still, there's the question of why two doves and not three.

Two doves portray sympathetic and responsive lovers. Devoted, mild, and vulnerable they persevere as defenseless quarry for fiercer animals. Like the song's other birds, they also stand for human conditions within ancient society's ideas about community care and company. Associated with fecundity and loyalty, their number is significant in the carol.

Four calling birds summon to a party; three French hens parody licentiousness and creative lust; but a loving couple bond in affectionate fidelity, mutually attentive as a unit within the larger security of their age-old faith community. As a paradigm of tenderness, the doves form an annual pair, caring for each other's needs; they mate with gentleness that bespeaks family-rearing, a model to be emulated. Advised by their race's ancestral customs, extended tribal beliefs bound small farmsteads to a social network across the landscape, and in that field of premises peasants coupled supported by kinfolk and town. From birth they attended to each other with, this verse hopes, the ideal represented by doves. A delicate verse about lifelong emotional attachment appears amid fierce mayhem, a pause while mid-winter's alcoholic frenzy abated.

The song's most tender and guileless figures, the turtledoves' devotion leads directly to the climate in which the last verse makes any sense as sung on the first day.

## *Chapter 17*

### First Night's Naughty Bird

Descending from the twelfth verse, the beginning of the carol's inventory suggests that the first day's most-often repeated gifts should take pride-of-place:

> On the first day of Christmas
> My true love gave to me,
> A partridge in a pear tree.

Supporting the meaning of every other verse, this keystone image warranted twelve repetitions. If this chorus-like verse seems meaningless to us it riveted the attention of the *carolle* dancers who sang it unrelentingly on every "day" of Christmas. It must have been something those long-gone singers cared about, and cared for.

Nobody would actually want twelve ornamental trees. Peasants could not buy the ensemble, a parade of a dozen fancy topiary with birds perched in the branches. So many partridges roosting in boughs would cram a palace's conservatory. Perhaps it's humorous to limn a fantasy about the fripperies of wealth.

Much depends on the verse's meaning; but if the bird and the tree stand for something else there is no obvious place to begin to understand what the two things mean together. The conundrum of deciphering a partridge in a pear tree "must have given rise to hours of deliberation," mused one folklorist.[1] Pondering about this verse will continue as long as searchers only poke around the warm jollity of a Victorian Christmas and the game of forfeits. The song proffers one conspicuous clue.

Every other verse's gifts are counted in sums equal to the day of the festival. The twelfth day featured 12 Ladies; then 11 Lords; on the fifth

*Chapter 17*

day, 5 Rings, etc. The first day's gift should be only one present, a single thing. Instead, the first day's remembrance seems double. But the festival's initial day may only apparently confer multiple gifts. It's our job to winkle out how two became one.

Two objects, a pear tree and a partridge, somehow combine as a single thing. No mere academic concern about grammatical agreement-of-number, consolidating the first day's gifts introduces the song's consistent message. Just as the carol begins, this verse establishes an imperturbable theme with a reference that baffles moderns who perceive two items where one was meant. Best begin by examining each of the two images.

## When Is a Tree Not a Tree?

The Christmas tree was not introduced into England until centuries after this song was already deeply invested in the seasonal celebrations.[2] As recently as the early nineteenth century the tree-bedecking custom was so new that many Europeans had never seen this Teutonic re-packaging of the Yule log.[3] When thirty-eight years old, Charles Dickens published "A Christmas Tree." In December 1850, he began by remarking on a novelty unknown in his youth: "I have been looking on, this evening, at a merry company of children assembled round that pretty German toy, a Christmas tree." Dickens referred to the royal family's quizzical adoption of a previously unknown custom: Prince Albert's importation to Windsor Castle in 1841. Even on the threshold of the twenty-first century, modern-day "Romans cannot decorate a Christmas tree to save their lives—the tradition is a 'barbarian' import."[4]

Having nothing to do with the English celebration of Christmas, the "Christmas tree" arrived too late on the scene to be mentioned, or even ridiculed, in the carol. The pleasure that moderns take from decking the tree was unknown to the carolers and eliminating this seasonal association removes an obstacle that bars further understanding of the verse. By erasing this false, but beloved, detour we can backtrack to the main path.

If the tree in which the partridge sits is not the Christmas tree, it could be any kind of tree, even a surrogate for, or allusive reference to, a person, as in Shakespeare's *Richard III* (1594): "The Royall Tree hath left us Royall Fruit" (III:7).[5] Perhaps, in this sense, the carol's pear tree is a person.

A tree is not always tall woody herbage. The first verse might ignore a tree's cool shade in Summer. The carol likely disregards leaf-shedding gold in Autumn, beautiful silhouettes festooned by puffy snow, and even glowing new buds; because other things are called trees. Any stout piece of wood from a stem or branch (either unworked in its natural state or shaped by a carpenter for some purpose) may be called a tree—depending on its use. It's not the material, wood, but how you wield it that counts.

Old-fashioned "tree" phrases often meant something other than a large plant that grows lumber. Many tools are called "trees." These kinds of implement "trees" appear in word-combinations with pole, post, stake, beam, or wooden bar. So, we have: axle-tree, chess-tree, cross-tree, door-tree, draught-tree, roof-tree, swingle-tree, shoe- or boot-tree, etc. Also some wooden shafts are called trees: a spear, lance, or the handle of a tool. Such usage opens a panorama of varied references to people, things, and animals. Citing a tree never necessarily referred to a symbol for a living botanical, with or without perching birds.

Tree-like labels for tools pre-date the industrial revolution by centuries but few such articles remain in common use. As spoken language's senior citizens, some rare old-time tool names weathered metal machinery's geared and steam-driven invasion of the workshop and these, among the carol's linguistic fossils, help relate an antique situation.

Particularly suggestive, a block upon which a boot is shaped or stretched is a boot-tree. Whether made of metal, wood, or plastic, when forced into them shoe-trees maintain shoes' shape. A shoe-tree bears no fruit; its name derives from its placement—inserted into a shoe. The punning analogy suggests the verse has nothing to do with juicy edible harvests plucked from an orchard's branches. The pear tree not only stands for a person (as Shakespeare and others created such metaphors) but the pear awards the tree a female gender, as women are said to be pear-shaped. Accordingly, the "tree" blocks or molds the pear from the inside. Could this be any clearer? Like a shoe- or boot-tree a slang

## Chapter 17

pear-tree shapes or spreads the pear by being inserted into it. A pear tree refers to no sort of vegetation reaching for the sun. There's only one thing that it could be, and sunshine has nothing to do with it.

The pear tree represents the entire ensemble of fruit-impaled-on-trunk (as clothing surrounds a clothes-tree or headgear encircles and bedecks a hat-tree). A penis inserted into a pear-shaped woman quips the song's pear tree.

Often given a life or a pet name with its own identity, it hardly takes a master of Freudian symbolism to recognize the shaft of the penis as a tree trunk: hence a tree, or "tool" when so inserted. Here the drinking-song's essence consolidates its witticisms. A slyly obscene joke.

Proportions definitely matter to give scale to the imagery; this verse ignores feral woodlands and domestic orchard to pun on anatomy. Not cultivated fields or forests but flesh. The carol visualized a particular form of intromission that each startled generation re-discovers to delight at its own inventive cleverness (but known from ancient times, like all sex). When modern, post-eighteenth-century, pornography came into existence, the genre often portrayed that position featured in the carol's first verse.

In pre-modern times, aristocratic amusements bandied the otherwise often-sequestered erotic genre; nobility could afford high-class versions. Others—rural peasants, urban manual workers or tradesmen, and the outlaw classes—had their own, usually coarser and cheaper, erotic entertainments. Each class addressed obscenity with it's own cant and imagery, some ribald some quite refined. Then, as now, there were many ways to sing about sex in forms as varied as the harsh words of Rap "music" (a form of chant), a suave Mel Tormé ballad (actually a form of art), or the closing lines of *Tristan and Isolde.* Some vocalized about sex in a carol whose words yield their meaning if we are willing to follow its unseemly hints.

Traveling back into less-decorous times we may wince at what we find but honesty should jettison anachronistic, post–Victorian, propriety and pretentious manners that blind observers. Accordingly, a partridge—whatever that meant in this song—in a pear tree was not a gift that came from the florists or the pet shop, and was not two things. The verse imagined an action needing two people to perform, and one of them, the carol's "true love," provided it to the singer. Every day. For twelve days. The carol singer could be male or female.

### The 12 Days of Christmas

# A Bird by Any Other Name

I began by recounting how one bleak day while hurriedly trying to cross a cold street this carol suddenly appeared fresh and absurd. At first the carol seemed indecipherable, perhaps deliberately unintelligible except to those sharing some forgotten joke that excluded present-day singers, however cheerfully goodwilled. A mist of light snow swirled around the shoppers, a shoal of colors that parted for the red bus as a great fish parts a school of small fish.[6] A very old song's first verse exploded with the weirdness of its eccentricity and, after the first day, serves as the chorus.

Unearthing the carol's meaning(s) did not proceed in order from day 12 down to 1, but that is how the story must be told. Over the next couple of years after that moment in Oxford Circus, the carol's story began to knit together. The verses' meanings arrived as they ripened, disarranged from the song's sequence, but slotted back into order.

Transmitted to us by unknowing messengers from a bygone era, the first day's verse completes the cycle, which it also begins. As the first, and in a way a final, stanza/chorus it unfolds an audacious panorama of plebeian desires. That same yearning was recorded elsewhere, too.

ROMEO: I would I were thy bird.
JULIET: Sweet, so would I:
   Yet I should kill thee with much cherishing.
—*Romeo and Juliet* (II:2 in Capulet's orchard)

Invoking the partridge prompted nods of recognition around the singers' circle as, "the partridge in medieval and Renaissance belief was a very naughty bird."[7] Unsurprisingly, the song begins with a wayward reference.

On the very first day the carolers announced that their singing disregarded: the Three Wise Men, the cozy manger tucked into a livestock shed, a "Mild Young Virgin" (as later ages would have her), the aged Joseph marveling at somebody else's child, blazing supernatural light glowing around the Babe, awe-struck shepherds joined by a trio of visiting kings, and maybe angels whispering hosannas in the

## Chapter 17

background—none of that concerned the carolers. From their carol's first words the singers let listeners know that their off-color concerns reeked of bad taste and matters inappropriate to modern Christmas. Moreover, this verse's bawdy meaning indulged other references, because wit evidences itself in the cleverness by which a known idea, word or image, transforms into something else; like the nominal tree, the partridge begins the song with a clever double entendre.

In the days when most people lived close to nature and saw the world with eyes whose attentiveness to zoological detail spelled the difference between plenty and starvation, nature's small traits were the lore of foragers and hunters—and all were sometimes hunters, for recreation or survival. (Some were gatherers also. In addition to agriculture, wild mushrooms, field and forest greens, and other undomesticated scavenging played a large role in diet; to mistake one mushroom for another meant life or death. Universal knowledge of flora and fauna typified pre-industrial society and such erudition still matters in low-technology groups, sometimes called "primitive." Hunter-gathering only survives into the industrial age as the fishing industry.) So, we learn that "partridges and their fellow ground birds routinely abandon *terra firma* in favor of trees and other elevated spots for safety."[8] Partridges can roost in trees. A partridge in a pear tree is not an impossibility.

An attentive stroller in the countryside could have noticed a young partridge clambering into a pear tree. But such sightings, however frequent or uncommon, do not prevent the verse carrying other meanings because it would be witless to sing of the obvious: what many had seen and all could know.[9] And who would want twelve trees and birds.

The religious holiday of Christmas might have supplied a citation from Gospels, but—unfortunately for those wishing to rescue the carol from the tavern and brothel—Christian scriptures provide the song no alibi.[10] Without a pertinent biblical proof-text, the partridge we are hunting has flown the coop of Scripture and Christianity.[11] Escaping the Bible, this bird nevertheless represented a desirable Christmas present.

A partridge (especially of the genera *Perdix* and *Alectoris* or similar related creatures like the Ruffled Grouse or Bobwhite) tendered an attractive gift, being a plump old-world game bird. Yet, however welcome as mid-winter victuals, cooking the bird itself likely proved secondary to its insinuations. All of the European partridge (*Perdix*) family

## The 12 Days of Christmas

were commonly invoked with a smile as the slang term for a prostitute, a promiscuous woman or girl. Among those references: since a partridge and a quail are similar birds, if the song were old enough, the song's originally intended hearers would have realized that the quail, was "a common Elizabethan term for a prostitute."[12] We find this usage in *Troilus & Cressida* "An honest fellow enough, and one that loves quails." (V:1) Are we surprised to learn this procession of indecent verses again implicates a hooker?

A parade of whores marches through the song, not necessarily in disrepute but as fellow-singers of the carol. Consistently, throughout the song, birds allude to females and the women are either various kinds of whores, objects of sexual desire, or eager bed partners.

A century later partridge still meant a whore as quoted in a song from c.1700: "Go home, ye Fop ... and for half Crown a Doxey get, But seek no more a partridge here."[13] This naughty connotation stuck durably to the word. In the late 1950s, the sublime Everly Brothers recorded a song in which a girl (significantly in the carol's context, called his "lovey-dove") is compared to a partridge-like quail; like *The Twelve Days*, their song slyly abounds with birds—itself significant as the Kentucky bluegrass region, and America's greater southern Appalachian highlands, are celebrated for preserving Elizabethan usage.[14] Though surviving in an American regional patois, just because the term was used allusively in Elizabethan English does not mean that the same usage is not earlier.[15] Not only was the carol of the Twelve Days carried across the Atlantic in the settlement of the New World, the carol may pre-date the formation of Renaissance English. Every day for twelve days the carolers invoked this bird and celebrated its very name that hinted at naughty implications.

The English name partridge, originally *partrich*, derives from the Old French *perdriz*, from the Latin *perdix* that the Romans borrowed from Greek. The Greeks called the bird *perdix* because it made a sharp whirring sound when flushed from cover; that singular noise gave the bird its name. The sound stems from the Indo-European word-root:perd, "to fart." Odor plays no part in the word's evolution, only a mimicked sound[16] Describing the bird, early hunter-naturalists borrowed a word-root that refers not to its being fetid but to an explosive noise, the burp of suddenly released air. In German we find *fertan*

## Chapter 17

and in Old English *fartan, feortan,* to fart.[17] Though we seem to have traveled far from the song's sprightly bird, sound not scent leads us forward from associations odiforous.[18]

Until modern times such onomatopoeic references would have been clear to people who stalked their game and knew the identifying sounds of birds and their calls. For a hunter the mnemonic value of remembering the partridge's farting sound meant the difference between having dinner and going hungry. Catching one would make a dandy present and the offer of a corpulent game bird, even daily throughout the holiday,

**Petard.** A precursor to artillery (and more akin to a mine) a small bomb of gunpowder packed into a cubical wooden box or bell-shaped metal container was attached to a wall or gate, or placed in a tunnel beneath the target. This early explosive device derived its name from Middle French *péter,* to fart or break wind that erupted in a sulfurous fart-like explosion. Though dangerous to the intended victim whose walls were to be breached, with only a primitive knowledge of metallurgy and explosives, the weapon could be equally lethal to the sappers and military engineers who set them.

would be welcome. But beneath the text's camouflage-by-nonsense (equivalent to wartime's visual dazzle-camouflage) plain meaning yields a coherence when secondary usages are considered; slang saves the day. While farts always intrude socially, ungracious and unwelcome, the word's associations prove positively pleasant.

In this song's context the sudden release of gas/air intimated a gratifying situation. The carol associated a partridge-fart with the anatomical pear-tree ensemble, connecting neither with the Church's idea of Christmas.

## A Fruit by Any Other Name

> I roused you under the apple tree;
> Your mother conceived you there.
> —*Song of Songs* (8:5)

The song's choice of tree is hardly neutral, as a pear tree in northern Europe, "had the same signification as a fig tree in southern Europe. Both were erotic, commonly feminine symbols."[19] The pear tree is gendered; it is female. Like the birds that seemed sexless until their specific identifiers were examined, we find gender in a place apparently innocent of sex. And not just sex that neutrally indicates one reproductive half of a species, but here associations surface that refer to procreation itself. And its preceding ancillary delights.

In general, "Pears traditionally represent fertility. According to ancient Welsh lore, a young girl who walks backwards to a pear tree on Christmas Eve, and then walks around it three times, will see the image of her future love."[20] In particular, the equation pear = woman, refers to the obvious, that women are normatively flaring-hipped and pear-shaped.[21] This distinction maintains even today in medical literature when "apple-shaped" women exhibit a higher rate of heart disease than "pear-shaped" women. Other, similarly-shaped, fruits carried female connotations that begin to suggest exactly what the song conveyed by invoking the pear.

For example, the French call by the name *cul de chien*, literally "dog's ass," the fruit, which in English is "called the medlar, which is distinguished by the way it puckers suggestively at one end. (In fact, this same fruit sometimes goes by the English name *open arse*, because of

## Chapter 17

its likeness to the vulva.)"²² Shakespeare exploits the fruit's suggestive shape to produce an extended erotic metaphor in *Romeo and Juliet* as Mercutio comments on his lovesick buddy:

> Now he will sit under a medlar tree,
> And wish his mistress were that kind of fruit
> As maids call medlars when they laugh alone.
> O, Romeo, that she were, O that she were
> An open-arse, thou a pop'rin pear

Shakespeare's jokes are multiple in this jibe but, like our carol, coordinated to a unified lascivious effect. Little is really new; the three Andrews Sisters sang *Don't Sit Under the Apple Tree with Anyone Else but Me*—an apparent warning against the most blatant infidelity—which followed their singing of *I'll Be with You in Apple Blossom Time* (to which a Freudian might add, You bet!)²³ Mercutio taunts, "that she were, O," the open shape of the O referring to the vulva, which "maids call medlars" (imagining, with the usual male delusions, how women talk). Then, "O that she were," equates a woman to a vulva/vagina; this predicate-nominative where she is (just an) O arrives either as a coarsely funny bit of wordplay or a degrading bit of pre-modernism: *she* is simply an O, a hole. Remember that variant title: "Much Ado About an O Thing." Shakespeare used this simile elsewhere in his plays, and we have already seen in *Romeo and Juliet* (II:1) the ring/circle summarizes the vulva in the phrase "his mistress' circle," iterated in *The Merchant of Venice*'s "ring." Evidently, pre-modern audiences never tired of this joke so we shouldn't be surprised to find it repeated in our carol. The more sly ways to pack in words for vulva, apparently the better. Also, to be fair, the more frequently playwrights drifted double-entendred terms for penis into their texts, the more likely to be well-paid.

To moderns such ribaldry offers pre-ironic humor. It's crude, full of winking and nudging, but executed with supreme linguistic zest. If not an utterly discomforting realization when regarding great art's lofty stature, first acquaintance with such lewdness can be mortifying. We may not like it but we live with the enduring results of popular taste and mob preference. The alternative—rephrasing, ignoring, or cleansing slang words for vagina, penis, or vulva—may please prissy readers or play-goers. (They are moral descendants of the carol's first unwilling auditors of "dansin and singin off fylthe carrolles on Yeull Day.") Bowdlerizing may even satisfy present-day readers merely seeking a respite in flight to storied realms of good taste.

## The 12 Days of Christmas

In these lines, Mercutio/Shakespeare might not even refer to the vulva but to the anus. He who wishes "his mistress were that kind of fruit" would make it accessible to a "pop'rin pear"—a phallic-shaped fruit from Belgium. Vulva and ass available for love-making advises Mercutio is best as Romeo yearns "under a medlar tree," which gives him an upward view of the fruits' bottoms.[24] Conclusively, with French finality on matters of cuisine, *Larouse Gastronomique* suggests that the sweet-sour medlar only becomes edible when over-ripe. The impatiently dripping fruit, custardy and lubricious, represents the perfect emblem of lust's target: yielding, firmness gone as the fruit acquiesces, yielding all spent resistance.

Besides the medlar other fruit trees suggested sexualized anatomy. The spurious practice of Medieval typology assigned essential similarities based on outward appearances.[25]

Woman = pear invokes the pear/medlar as lusciously overripe and happily consenting, if not eager. The metaphor presumes

"Medlar, poppy anemone, and common pear or popprin pear" illustrated in *Mira calligraphiae monumenta*, fols. 1–129 written 1561/1562 Created in Vienna, Austria, 1591–1596. Joris Hoefnagel, Flemish-Hungarian, (1542–1600), Georg Bocskay, Hungarian (d. 1575). Tempera colors, watercolors, gold and silver paint, and ink, Leaf: 16.6 × 12.4 cm (6⁹⁄₁₆ × 4⅞ in.) (J. Paul Getty Museum Collection, Ms. 20 [86.MV.527], fol. 13). Between 1561 to 1562 in the imperial capital of Vienna, Georg Bocskay, a Croatian-born court secretary to the Holy Roman Emperor Ferdinand I (1503–1564), created a model book of calligraphy, the *Mira calligraphiae monumenta*. In an extraordinary collaboration, some thirty years after Bocskay completed his calligraphy Ferdinand's grandson in the Habsburg line, Emperor Rudolph II (1578–1637) commissioned the painter Joris Hoefnagel to illuminate the manuscript. With a sensitive eye for each page's design, as laid out by Bocskay the book's scribe, Hoefnagel inserted images of fruit, flowers, and insects, and he arranged the layout to augment, and not detract from, the calligrapher's work.

## Chapter 17

her enthusiasm. As an extended sexual metaphor the pear+tree represents more than a woman's swelling hips. The complex shape this song describes results from a special viewpoint of intercourse (usually available to men, unless playful mirrors are handy). The "pear tree" couple performs a specific sexual position, a form of coupling that illustrates the carol's primary verse.

When a women sits astride a supine man in coitus the man views the characteristic female pear-shape penetrated—and "he will sit under a medlar tree."²⁶ The male partner beholds the woman's torso and buttocks impaled upon the trunk of his penis: a pear tree. (I know. This is an indelicate matter but, according to their contemporaries' disgusted testimony after being inflicted by such rowdy performances, the carol singers were not exactly following Emily Post.) The song's pear-tree merrily aggrandizes the penis by calling it a tree, a stout perennial—size counts, and flattery helps because the opposite, insulting or mocking penis size deflates the holiday spirit. The penis is neither a shrub nor a bush, common synonyms for the vulva, especially its luxuriant pubic hair (that Shakespeare called the bird's nest).²⁷ The drollery of the carol's cardinal phrase celebrated energetic and liberated sexuality, and reveals a buried depth of honesty beyond modern prejudice.

The impertinent carol once entertained people who, with relatively few options to amuse themselves, created an endlessly witty song. Adding yet another layer to the orgiastic wit, the verse provokes, a visual pun.

Medlars, illustrated in: *A Book of Fruits & Flowers. Shewing the Nature and Use of Them, Either for Meat or Medicine* **(published in England, 1653).**

## The 12 Days of Christmas

If asked to visualize a pear, most of us would spontaneously imagine a brown, green, or a yellowish fruit. Those are the pear varieties we mainly see today. But in older usage, "Pear-Coloured" meant red.[28] The song depicted the engorged vulva with a portraitist's loving precision. Nobody's private parts are green. The unmentionable can be sung by peasants when it cannot be spoken in public. But then again, considering heightened emotions, opera sings poetic verse conveyed with passionate musical intensities that cannot be realistically spoken, even in a stage play.

Only a special viewpoint yields a vantage of the song's implied ensemble: man under and woman riding in reverse. Pre-modern examples of that image are mighty scarce (although Romans had no qualms about such depictions, beautifully painted). Until the advent of explicit movie loops (short pornographic films often shown in peepshow arcades) and specifically the sub-genre of point-of-view (POV) style videos, modern art rarely showed this conjoining. Perforce, the male saw this ensemble because the view is unavailable to his female partner without using a mirror. Hence mirrored rooms, a plaything of aristocrats.

When mirrors were extremely expensive handmade luxuries, the Palace of Versailles flaunted a grandly Baroque gallery, Louis XIV's 73-meter-long "Hall of Mirrors" (1678–1684). Seventeen tall windows flooded the room with daylight while at night the mirrors amplified the room's glittering candlelight and showed off to best advantage the costumes of mingling courtiers who crowded near the king. That was one political use of mirrors, but among Versailles' garden pavilions a less famous private upstairs chamber offered an adult playroom with mirrors to maximize a tryst's visual delights.[29] Past ages knew every way of connecting bodies and the ways to optimize those unions. Some carnal celebrations took extravagant aristocratic forms, which required considerable preparation and were very costly. Peasants bawled out songs for free.

The verse's wholly obscene point-of-view infrequently inspired mainstream visual representations. Shunned by tasteful graphics, this anatomical monument was arrogated to pornography and the pornographic genre has always been subject to both limited production and regular waves of censorious destruction, known as "cleansing" to its

## Chapter 17

adversaries. Few representations of this way of conjoining bodies survive in occidental art because the life of pornographic artwork usually lasts no more than one generation.

Embarrassed heirs of pornography collectors destroy the unwanted and disgraceful accumulation of erotic imagery while appreciative heirs preserve the works, but the former vastly out-number the latter. In each generation some illustrations fall victim of zealous scouring and the number of works diminish until a single inheritor in the line of custodianship decides to relegate the offending creations to the fire. Each generation is a sieve through which pass fewer and fewer works of pornographic art of quality workmanship, regardless of sensitivity or comprehensive treatment of the subject, or the creator's artistic fame; nothing avails against the fervent censor's stern decree.

The superb Renaissance collaboration of the poet Pietro Aretino (1462–1556) and the engraver Marcantonio Raimondi (1480–1534) produced a beautiful and, in its time, renowned book of sexually celebratory sonnets and illustrative prints, of which not a single intact copy survives.[30] We know this volume of poems and pictures only from replicas, or even copies of copies. (Reproductions suffered the same fate as the original because, regardless of artistic quality, they bore the same flaw of depicting moral effrontery.) In Raimondi's and Aretino's book, Sonnets X and XIV provide the male perspective that the carol extols in its first verse.[31] This beautiful upper class and intellectual version surveyed the same materials as the blunt peasants' song of the 12 Days.

The carol inventories several feasible sexual couplings, possibilities that, however disconcerting to find in a Christmastide entertainment, should not be prejudicially eliminated from the notorious Yule holiday because "Christmas was the time when such [obscene] songs were most often heard." It's easy to imagine the singers trying to out-do one another in effrontery and audacious impudence. A kind of contest of obscenity governed proceedings as roving groups of singers, or tavern-bound drinkers, sang the pleasures of "chambering." The song salutes instinctive appetites as each verse—and all the verses together, without gender discrimination—recognize the full range of human physical expression and desire.[32] That sexual frankness poses a dilemma for modern Christians struggling with carols to be sung in church.

If the carol celebrates the pear-tree as a form of heterosexual

## The 12 Days of Christmas

coitus, what about the "partridge," the farting bird? The bird and tree can be united into one symbol and thereby resolve the meaning of this verse and, eventually, the whole carol.

The partridge evokes the sound of air expelled from a distended vagina and the verse's complete allusion refers to a fart (in a pear tree). Here the verse's seemingly separate items merge into one. The combination of the two images recalls how picture-writing works by over-laying and juxtaposing drawings. An ideographic representation (such as found in written Chinese) combines concrete things to portray a concept, an action, or a general noun. This verse's bird + tree limns a mid- or post-coital vaginal burp or fart. Coarse? yes. Indelicate? yes. Humanly accurate, and therefore in the mainstream of poetic creativity? yes, again. The Shakespeare family's "old friend and neighbor Elizabeth Wheeler memorably told the Puritans on the benches of the church court in 1592: 'Godes woondes a plague of God on you all, a fart of onse ars for you!'" which translates as: "God's wounds[33] ... a fart of one's arse for you!"[34] The insult distinctly qualifies the kind of fart and implies more than one type of Elizabethan fart, isolating an arse (ass in American) from a vaginal fart or burp.

Again, the song unblinkingly observes life—not as lived by some enchanted incorporeal lover or that idealized goal of courtly love, a dreamily beckoning mistress of refined manners.[35] The carol's "true love" has a body that makes noises that the singer fondly accepts without qualification.[36] The carolers conceded their bodies as temporal and real, not transient and irrelevant shells gambled for a theological promise. We find earthy folks at the song's core, celebrants who recall with affection their lover's corporeality.

The partridge's call, the feminine shape of the pear, the conjoined pear tree—all blend their associations into one thing.[37] A partridge in a pear tree is, simply, the result of a good athletic fuck that opens the vulva and vagina. The contented recipient could be either male or female since "My true love gave to me," and it's hard to know who is happier.

Unlike the florists' trimmed shrubbery with a bird included, however poor, the donor could, without monetary cost, readily procure this

## Chapter 17

welcome gift. The partridge-in-the-pear-tree offered a special treat as the woman-above position gave theologians fits by overturning the Church's idea of nature's order. It therefore represented an exceptional, and private, rebellion that Medieval women could make against restrictive social organization.[38] Singing the verse over-and-over hurled an exceptional affront at the establishment. Professional prostitutes of the time rarely engaged in such behavior "for 'technical' reasons (this position is more tiring for the woman and its contraceptive efficacy is dubious to say the least)" while, should the prostitute or client be questioned by the authorities about couples practicing woman-on-top positions, suspects claimed deniability "for 'moral' reasons, [as] clients observed the necessary hierarchy between the sexes."[39] A logical uniformity drove the wild carnival.

Just as Christmas instituted temporary social chaos governed by the Lord of Misrule who overturned the social order, body positions overturned the sexually normative. The Church-sanctioned man-on-top tableau, the "Missionary Position" was touted by missionaries to the more inventive populations they encountered.

During the Yuletide season servants could impersonate lords while the Church fumed while Adam's heirs happily fornicated beneath Eve's daughters. The "true love" offered playfully varied sexual positions. The true love also provides this dear present less expensively than a professional sex-worker. The true love could afford the gift every night of twelve.[40]

# Chapter 18

## Who's Counting?

The inexpensive gifts—affordable during the holiday season, universally appreciated, never returned, always the right size, never redundant, and given under cover of the general melee—could be happily bestowed throughout the year. The number of gifts match the year's daily calendar count only because the first gift tenders a single item, not a bird + tree, but one thing. Again, however distasteful the possibility that looms before doubters of the song's lewdness, this unity challenges skeptics to find another explanation for this verse. After all, a "Hole in One" names a single sporting event indicated by more than a simple noun.[1]

There are 364 gifts in the song, the same number as days in the year, minus one: Christmas Day or New Year's day.[2] The carol treats the gifts (and perhaps the year) as a unity.

| Gift | Days Given | Number of Gifts |
| --- | --- | --- |
| 1 partridge in a pear tree | 12 | 12 |
| 2 turtle doves | 11 | 22 |
| 3 French hens | 10 | 30 |
| 4 calling birds | 9 | 36 |
| 5 golden rings | 8 | 40 |
| 6 geese a-laying | 7 | 42 |
| 7 swans a-swimming | 6 | 42 |
| 8 maids a-milking | 5 | 40 |
| 9 pipers piping | 4 | 36 |
| 10 drummers drumming | 3 | 30 |
| 11 lords a-leaping | 2 | 22 |
| 12 ladies dancing | 1 | 12 |
| | total | 364 |

## *Chapter 18*

The "true love" could receive a favor every day of the year, keeping the spirit of Christmas throughout the seasons—but not in the twee Victorian sense.

A proof of the gifts' sequential presentation derives from the verse of the 9 pipers. Before modern times (and the piping Renaissance, likely begun on the Isle of Skye) pipers were soloists. The nineteenth century introduced a novel innovation by massing pipers in military pipebands. Until recently nine pipers would not have played together which means that in the days when the carol was sung with its meaning intact, pipers arrived throughout a 36-day sequence playing (pibroch) one-at-a-time. On the other hand, dairy maids not only milked the livestock on a daily basis but on larger farms also made butter and cheese; eight of them would be appropriate to manage a herd of over 150 animals. So sizeable a cattle operation required considerable pasturage and additional servants supervised by the farmer's wife—an ideal farmstead and a Christmas fantasy where numbers counted.

Received together during the holiday as a single bout of sensual gormandizing, the gifts would soon have been expended in a dizzying orgy. Instead, during Christmas the carol awarded (or pledged, as gift certificates) favors judiciously unwrapped during the entire year. To fulfill the complete annual cycle the song considered the apparent expense of the true love's Christmas gifts.

In various allusions over several centuries, the pear was formerly anything of very small or contemptible value, as today we might say that a trivial amount is "Not worth a fig." This phrase derives from the Italian *fica*—a slang term for vulva, descended from unattested Vulgar Latin. (Language imprints vivid phrases whose long memory travels down through time.) An obscene gesture illustrates the equivalent French phrase *faire la figue*, when the fist is brandished with the thumb held between the first and second fingers to form a vulva. The gesture boasts an ancient and exalted heritage. Dante Alighieri (1265–1321) used the figa gesture in the *Divine Comedy:*

> When he finished speaking, the thief
> Raised both his hands aloft each making the fig,
> Crying: "Take that, God, for at thee I aim them."
> ("Inferno," Canto XXV line 2)

## The 12 Days of Christmas

A couple of centuries later, when a Pope compelled Michelangelo (1475–1564) to paint frescos on the ceiling of the Sistine Chapel (the project lasting 1508–12) he featured the muscular Cumaean sibyl, who sits consulting an open book while behind her stand two little angels (putto), a blond and redhead; the redhead mischievously "gives her the

**Michelangelo di Lodovico Buonarroti (1475–1564), Cumaean Sybil, fresco, 1510. Sistine Chapel, Vatican.**

*Chapter 18*

**Michelangelo, Detail of the Cumean Sybil showing an attendant putto giving the "figa."**

finger," makes the fig.³ This sign of anger or contempt flashes the equivalent of the (mainly American) extension of the middle finger from the fist, associated with the phrase "giving [or flipping] the bird," a surrogate penis meaning "Fuck you!." Once again, a bird and sex.

Down to the present time, the triad of bird, vulva, fruit, united in a constellation of coarse but widespread usage. As the fig on the continent (in former times and still today) indicated the cunt as quintessentially detestable and worthless, in England the pear stood for trivial value, repulsive in insignificance if not merely dismissible, and often female. The carol's singer implies that this gift, of little value or cost, though cherished, will hardly tax the giver but it will satisfy the recipient—who places it at the head of the Christmas wish-list. And who would give such a token as, "My true love gave to me"? Only one person. Received from anybody else such a gift could be a calamity if discovered. Only one's "true love" gave such a gift without involving infidelity or adultery. Not that the past more rigorously observed standards of sexual devotion than presently practiced or preached, but the song unrolls a Christmas wish list ... such as few send to Santa.

The English Parliament only outlawed adultery in 1650 when it became a felony punishable by death. Fornication became a crime punishable by three months' imprisonment. Before then, illicit sexual consolation with someone other than a spouse was, at least theoretically, a risky legal adventure, but people always found ways to accommodate such yearnings. The song's moral universe ignores cuckoldry, which

# The 12 Days of Christmas

was not even considered a hinderance. Instead, the carol condones temporary fidelity and sequential liaisons for pleasure. It celebrates exactly the sort of behavior sermons decried as brawling, disorderly drinking, and gambling, accompanied by exhibitionist and orgiastic sex.

Amid Yule revels, that permitted (almost) everything, otherwise lewd thoughts were uttered aloud without reproach and singers bellowed the gift of "a partridge in a peartree" as the song's rollicking finale. The dozen "fruit trees" arrayed an orchard, itself pre-modern slang for "The female pelvic region, with especially reference to the pudend and the womb."[4] (Nothing antique here. These same succulent associations feature in the title of Rita Mae Brown's 1973 novel, *Rubyfruit Jungle,* a delight to lesbians, and many straight males.) Centuries earlier, this unashamed carol posits neither sexual victim nor sin; no one took advantage or was sexually exploited, and all seems merrily consensual. The woman might be pleased or embarrassed by her vagina's sounds when capaciously opened in vigorous love-making. In this last frank observation, full of rowdy gusto, the carol's egalitarianism celebrates lust and fecundity, which means that these final words proved equally suitable when sung by a man or women. The "me" (in the words "gave to me") could be the one who emits the vaginal burp or the one forming the pear tree. The singer's sex remains unspecified. That startling final realization helps to imagine how the song was once sung or, at least, what it described.

The true love presented each gift throughout the holiday, in person, when families traveled sometimes a considerable distance to be with their relatives to exchange keepsakes. Young lovers freed from drudgery could give and receive such a gift over two weeks, blissfully expending pent-up lust in the old equivalent of Spring-break—minus Fort Lauderdale's lingering aroma of sunscreen, lousy beer, and iridescent drinks with cute names.

After a hearty dinner and much drinking with kin and friends gathered near the hearth, came lively singing, then bedtime, and for some of the young unmarried couples, bundling in bed, followed by the exchange of this gift. The most desired gift, it is rarely rejected. Awarded on multiple nights it's cherished by the receiver and giver; unlike a returnable holiday sweater (jumper) in the wrong size, pattern,

## Chapter 18

or color, the antique idea of pear-color accurately described a gift where one size fits most everybody.

Had only a single verse been obscene, the carol could not have been sung in polite company. But beginning with "leaping"—as a common and unambiguous term once used both in high and low society for an act whose modern name is absent from current Christmas carols—to the song's rollicking finale, the subject-matter's references blare a consistent expression. The song's naughty working-class puns must be accepted as all-or-nothing because polite speech cannot be peppered with occasional obscenity and still be generally acceptable. Neither can a song.

However tempting to cherry-pick the carol's least objectionable, or the most successfully poetic, erotic images, such references could not exist in a proper song about the Christmas season or to accompany a family's game of forfeits. Transported whole from the time before the suppression of Christmas, this unlikely aesthetic survivor's decipherment stands or falls as an entirety.

# Chapter 19

## Conclusion

Recovering the carol's spirit and its original appeal required the reader to wade through a sewer of historical usage, which some may find deeply objectionable. And not just the language. Robbing a favorite holiday event of its innocence seems an unfounded mortification. But the song's unpacked citations of antique slang really were spoken, before the Renaissance and into fairly recent times. And we have many records of such usage, if not a really old copy of the carol that would clinch the argument. Painting a picture of the carol's wayward singers would not be nearly as convincing were it not for the many citations of exactly this language, and those quotes persuade us of the slang's authenticity and widespread use (as by Shakespeare, among others). In aggregate the emerging meanings and insinuations conjure uncouth wassailing celebrants behaving contrary to the modern holiday's endlessly and ruthlessly imposed chaste merriment. That contradiction between past and present naturally persuades righteous protest to so jarring a deformation of the beloved season's memory and supposed traditions. Instead of supplying the current holiday with a direct ancestor of impeccable breeding, a decently courteous forerunner deserving our pride, the carol, drenched in unvarying lewdness, steadily sprays those obscenities into the unresisting and blameless air.

From verse to verse if the carol belies the fantasy of Merry Olde Christmas of fellowship and worship, it restores actuality, however different. The disjuncture—between the historical reality and a dreamy ideal of the past that goads present striving to match that paragon—is understandable, because large forces worked to install the usurper on the festival's throne. Our imaginings of the past were furnished with plush novels, soppy illustrations, and modern media's virtuous

## Chapter 19

enactments of snowy sleigh rides delivering heaps of presents. Indoors we were taught to imagine a polite game of forfeits in a Victorian family's warm sitting room where, over a punch bowl crowning a food-laden table, these chorused, though misunderstood, verses were welcomed in the cheery atmosphere.

When every verse of this old carol reveals lewd vernacular meanings (even if only secondary meanings) the burden of proof shifts to those who would maintain the carol's pristine innocence as an innocuous tongue-twister. Here the ghostly "Spirit of Christmas *Really* Past" intervenes to remind that, like the glittering bedecked tree, today's chaste Christmas arrived only recently, a new invention.

Most of us grow up assuming that the Christmases we recall repeated ancient rituals, if only watered-down versions of the "real" Christmases of Dickensian and later Victorian times;[1] surely those holidays celebrated age-old, authentic, customs. But the account of that past grew murky and unrecognizable. We know little of lewd Christmas carols as, "Naturally enough, such songs were infrequently written down."[2] Those who could write would be loathe to dignify and preserve recollections of a festival that literate society struggled to suppress, repeatedly, and through several generations. Victors write history, so goes the commonplace; in this struggle the victors were literate and they forced folklore's oral tradition to capitulate before the formidable printed page—Homer never had to compete with other media.

The pen may be mightier than the sword, a highly dubious proposition (try finding a library of Cathar writings), but even scribbling trounces thin air, that manger where folksongs were born. Unprejudiced records of folk-pornography and citations for the *Twelve Days'* bawdy meaning survived only by luck. In life as in art, the successful abound in happy breaks, undeserved windfalls they think they earned from a benevolent fate that compensates for their every screw-up. The world's losers can't buy luck, and anyway they're broke. The rich, victorious and powerful, not only write history, they publish it.

An equally beloved song, the popularity of *Greensleeves* may date from the 1570s yet, "not one broadside copy of its survives from the sixteenth century"; sheer usage destroyed the sheets as they were passed from hand-to-hand[3] Just as bowdlerization befell the eventually-published *Greensleeves*,[4] busybodies happily eviscerated the *Twelve Days*. The people who could write didn't care about how whitewashing bawdiness misrepresented the situation. In fact, they'd be loathe to transcribe it. Readers and writers—scribes, clerics, lawyers, and academics—were indoors during mid-winter trying to ignore what was going on outside: a riot. So, documents of the Yule carnival remain scarce. The song's birth certificate was lost along with other accounts of popular culture, although some artworks convey the unbridled tumult.

One scholar notes that "There's no telling what the verses [of *The Twelve Days]* were before they were written down since they were passed from generation to generation."[5] On the other hand, a thumping rhythmic tune froze its cadenced lines into a fixed form and, once achieving a mature form, the song may have barely mutated over its long life.

Songs like *The Twelve Days* can travel down through centuries unchanged as the phrases coast into a future where no one remembers what the words meant—the form remains the same but its function changes. Regard how durable are ditties like "Ring Around a Rosie," a relic, probably born amid the horrific Black Death; as part of the culture of childhood its meaning is lost on today's toddlers who are taught this rhyme, or garbled variations. Its words remain unaltered from the first generation who witnessed its grim description of mass death: "all fall down!" Likewise, few recall the city-planning dilemma that prompted the chant "London Bridge is falling down," about a viaduct built between 1176 and 1209.[6] That song, too, persists unchanged; every word remains intact although its references are forgotten.

The carol's era-specific slang tattered with age, each generation discarding bits of the subject-matter's forgotten meaning. The song of *The Twelve Days* transformed into a ghost recognized by fewer and fewer who did not know it when alive. The carol wandered the earth, sung everywhere English is spoken. Its realm far exceeds the expanse of empire: on Christmas the sun never set on this carol.

## The Ghost of an Idea

The transition faded to white. Not quickly as cards or doves disappear from a magician's hand, but gradually. Old madcap Saturnalia, later Yuletide, transformed into religiously observed Christmas. Then, although the Catholic Church, Puritans, and the law suppressed lusty

## Chapter 19

Christmas, the holiday would not be extinguished because it served a need. Popular demand revived it until, after successfully resisting extermination, its last bawdy vestiges smothered beneath plush Victorian gaiety. A tasteful sneer strangled Christmas into compliance, followed by its oh-so refined murder and burial. Once killed, a zombie shuffled onto the stage and that version prevails undead, pretending innocence, outwardly dainty. The artificial replacement dates only from the nineteenth century when a master composed its birth announcement.

The holiday we know was first captured whole in one of our culture's most visible artifacts, Charles Dickens' *A Christmas Carol.* In this supreme literary exposition of modern Christmas Ebenezer Scrooge should not be regarded as merely a stingy old man, a caricature of greed whose nasty habits will almost inevitably lead him to a bad end. Dickens loathed the old man's scrounging and soul-destroying capitalism because Scrooge, who makes nothing tangible, presides over a private bank. While Scrooge lives his old age as an avowed miser, yet self-justifying reasons for money-hoarding make him a more interesting character of his era, and not merely a warped misanthrope.

Scrooge transcends a blunt lampoon of avarice because Dickens aimed higher than securing the simple tale of a gloomy businessman redeemed by jollity. Dickens' historical debate about Christmas mainly passes unmentioned by casual commentators and never appears in the story's many dramatic adaptations.

Dickens engaged a controversy whose protagonists' arguments tumble from its pages because the short book presents an intellectual contest. The author announced his intent in the first phrase of the (sometimes-omitted from re-prints) *Preface:* "I have endeavoured in this Ghostly little book, to raise the Ghost of an Idea." That is, *A Christmas Carol* muses on intellectual alternatives, ideas. It is—more successfully than a ponderous self-conscious doorstop like Mann's *The Magic Mountain*—a book of ideas. In the guise of various characters Dickens weighed the merits of several abstract possibilities. His characters participate in a formal debate as contested as the Oxford Union, because the story considered the obligations embodied by lifestyle choices. But luck delimited the options that allow individuals to express values. Providence predestined some for salvation after death, while in this life It smiled on those It showered with resources; It allowed some to

# The 12 Days of Christmas

enjoy good health and ample nourishment and to bask in social esteem, while unlucky others were fit for the prisons and workhouses. Elsewhere (India) that hierarchy of benefactions expressed itself as tiered castes whose assignments were explained by karma, the sum total of the effects of past actions. (This notion survives in the Conservative capitalist's judgement of the impoverished, that their poor decisions explain their condition, as if the victim had been allowed all agency. Which is what Scrooge presupposes.) Questions about how civilization seemed to cruelly distribute social and material assets raised core issues that are too easily papered-over by the story's implicitly Christian goal of personal redemption.

Dickens, who had seen Olde Christmas disappearing over the horizon, debated the archaic versus the new forms of Christmas celebrations, and how that remodeling might signal a civilization's turning point. Having suffered degradation in his youth he sorely believed his world needed reformation. If overlooked as a book-of-ideas, the small volume will be mistaken for an uplifting amusement written only for money.

In the book's disputation Scrooge practices the rigorous Christianity of methodical living, an outlook that suppressed the old Yule spirit. His Puritanical slighting of Christmas purposefully neglects the re-born holiday's rowdy aspects, its forced materialism and hysterically conspicuous consumption.

> "Nephew! ...keep Christmas in your own way, and let me keep it in mine"
> "Keep it!" repeated Scrooge's nephew. "But you don't keep it."

But he does. Scrooge well remembers a quieter, though still very pleasant feast of his youth—forcefully recalled for him by the Ghost of Christmas Past. Scrooge is not stupid. Dickens fashioned him grimly Malthusian, but witty and less theologically opaque than many who spend their lives in commerce. Scrooge holds religious ideas, and they are old ones:

> "Spirit," said Scrooge, after a moment's thought. "I wonder you, of all beings in the many worlds about us, should desire to cramp these people's opportunities of innocent enjoyment"
> "I!" cried the Spirit.
> "You would deprive them of their means of dining every seventh day, often the only day on which they can be said to dine at all," said Scrooge. "Wouldn't you?"
> "I!" cried the Spirit.

## Chapter 19

"You seek to close those places on the Seventh Day?" said Scrooge, and it comes to the same thing.... "Forgive me if I am wrong. It has been done in your name, or at least that of your family," said Scrooge.

Scrooge practices the virtues of religious toleration, the innate (in America, "inalienable") rights of the individual as promoted at the end of the seventeenth century by John Locke's notion of the *market* that values dignified labor. Locke preached that "every man has a property in his own person: this nobody has any right to but himself. The labour of his body, and the work of his hands, we may say, are properly his. Whatsoever then he removes out of the state that nature hath provided, and left it in, he hath mixed his labour with, and joined to it something that is his own, and thereby makes it his property."[7] That is, a person's efforts—value-adding labor in the extractive industries, in skilled trades, or by applying human intelligence to a dilemma—produce bounty. Therefore, as directed by God, unequal wealth is justified. Disparities in affluence or poverty evidences the just outcome of a cosmic plan.

These ideas supply the basis for patents, copyright, labor laws, and a host of other modern notions that today seem both obvious and as ancient as how we celebrate Christmas. John Locke's lifedates (1632–1704) fall within a generation of Scrooge's and therefore Lockeian ideas represent the formative spiritual material of Ebenezer's youthful influences. In Scrooge's mind, Locke's concept of wealth creation (through manual labor, creative thought, or daring investments) indicate divine benefaction, a blessing. Greed may not be "good" but wealth is. How, Scrooge wonders, can the dispersal of wealth, squandering the outward indications of God's grace, be a blessing? The conflict leaves him, rightly, confused. As it does modern Conservatives.

In a latter day, Thomas Malthus (1766–1834) preached notions similar to what presided over Scrooge's formative years.[8] Resources, Malthus argued, being limited, and expanding more slowly than the population, the only equitable distribution must be guided by the hand of Providence that awards some with material favor and outward success. Scrooge, not smug, thoughtless, or unfeeling, practices what had been a joyous philosophy he has simply forgotten how to enjoy. He is a free-markets man. Dickens' story changes him, but not in the way most people assume, and it helps to recall the tenor of that old-time carol, *The Twelve Days of Christmas* to understand where this character was coming from.[9]

## The 12 Days of Christmas

At the end of the tale, Scrooge throws himself into the rambunctiously happy holiday as proof of his conversion from old-time piety and determinism. Painfully abrupt as St. Paul's conversion, Scrooge renounced of all he believed and participates subject to a thin lacquering of Christianity slapped on the revived—and essentially intact—ancient festival. The holiday's games, like the amusements his nephew plays with his guests, augment or replace forfeits' raunchy version, or drinking games. The wassailing was up-dated to a civilized toast to health. If expurgated modern caroling supplanted the old, the antique indulgence of exchanging presents lived on, along with giving little boxes and dolls and taking surcease from work. If possible, candles glowed everywhere, just as Romans favored at Saturnalia. Visits from friends, whether Magi or not, were welcomed as callers admired decorated trees from Germania that centered a toned-down version of Celtic feasting and drinking, general forbearance, and a naughty touch of misrule. Scrooge was converted to neo-pagan merriment by three ghosts who behave as gently as Maoist re-educators rather than as examples of rhetorical Christian sobriety. They resemble Odin more than Augustine.

Scrooge (who wants to keep his counting house open on 25 December but reluctantly grants Bob a day of paid leave) represents the Puritan's lingering view of Christmas, a fading memory in Dickens' time. Scrooge plays his foredoomed part in a contest between the earlier Puritan and the holiday's newly revived, though tamed and sanitized, gaiety. He represents a man both elderly enough to recall the old congenially low-key holiday and he's also a diligent moralist imbued with the work ethic. Dickens' story drives the final nail in the coffin of the Puritans' suppression of lusty Christmas, replaced by a tolerably and tentatively decorous version. Written in 1843, with Scrooge pictured as a quite elderly man, his up-bringing in the eighteenth century took place in the burgeoning moment of early Methodism.[10] Scrooge was taught, and learned, that Providence rewarded year-round toil and he is confused that divine fate should now advantage and sanction year-end merriment ... and leisure.[11]

He was taught that heaven treated people as they deserved, that the rich earned an earthly stipend by hard work, that the poor were inefficient, negligent, or shirked their calling to exploit God-given resources. This debate about dynamic or static resource-allocation is hardly over.

Scrooge, an apostle of thrift, balks at his nephew's squandering pent-up money on partying, capital whose source seems to be Scrooge's

## Chapter 19

Father Christmas with the Yule Log and Wassail Bowl (*Illustrated London News*, 23 December 1848). The wassail held strong drink and was passed around for toasting. The word derives from Middle English (wassayl). The "wass" (in Old Norse) relates to words about being like was, were, and the tense-cue will. The "ail" refers to hale or healthy. To wassail was to salute a companion with a drink "To your health!" or, "May you be healthy!"

Compared to the respite, warmth, light, and drink he brought, the figure of Father Christmas himself hardly had to seem appealing to be welcome, as evidenced by this almost-gaunt mistletoe-wreathed figure toting a log as he trudges along with his walking stick. He bequeathed his chubby descendent, the appealing elfin figure of Santa Claus, his robe's wide cuffs.

beloved dead sister. (His displeasure reminds us that a "spend-thrift" specifically designates, not merely or generally a wastrel but, someone who dissipates an inheritance, who *spends* someone else's *thrift*.) In Dickens' story, the theological rug has been pulled out from under Scrooge and now, very old, frightened and bewildered, he has been assaulted by a tag-team of scary propagandists who, at the brink of the grave, terrorize him into reversing his belief system. The drama of his conversion plays out in countless theatrical and movie recreations of the book. Nobody much seems to bother with rendering Scrooge as sympathetic, although Dickens paints him as a very complex man, nor do many readers wonder about the source of his initial assumptions. What seem the character flaws of greed and insensitivity may reflect a formerly legitimate religious stance: the piety that tried to kill Christmas and its caroling.

## The 12 Days of Christmas

Dickens puts the story's crucial words in his hero's mouth, for the old man is a hero, casting his old ways aside and setting out on new moral seas to which he is neither accustomed nor furnished with a chart, though he hopes to come at last to a safe harbor. That is the promise.

Scrooge's new-found anti-determinism is evidenced by his realization, albeit coerced, that contrary to his long-held beliefs, "Men's courses will foreshadow certain ends, to which, it persevered in, they must lead.... But if the courses be departed from, the ends will change. Say it is thus with what you show me!" He implores the ghost of the future to give him some sign that this credo, so strange in his mouth, is correct because he is no longer sure of what he is supposed to think at this terrible moment and wants some reassurance from an all-knowing spirit that an excess of last-minute consumerism and lavish charity will constitute the good works needed for his salvation. Good-bye Calvinism. It is inconceivable to Scrooge that buying and spending will save your soul.

At first a spectator, before the ghosts make him a hero, Scrooge was caught looking the wrong way at history's tennis match when the ball of Christmas reversed course, from sensuality to austerity and back to a revival of hedonism re-packaged as "Christmas cheer" or the "spirit of Christmas." And, as an incidental casualty, the debate dragged the carol of the *Twelve Days* hither-and-yon, finally lugged into re-alignment with intellectual and religious fashion. And out onto Oxford Street.

The wheel of Christmas had come full circle and Dickens was just the man to announce the change. What he recalls as an amiable, joyful holiday in Scrooge's youth was itself a reaction to a sternly joyless and sexless holiday (in reaction to what riotousness preceded it). Ghosts had to rehabilitate Scrooge's rigorous interpretation into condoning a winter carnival of release, over-consumption, over-stimulation, and charity. That evolution continued apace, intensified beyond Scrooge's worst imaginings. Today the bountiful holiday revives mid-winter's bygone candles and pagan generosity, but not much else. For too many that spate of gift-giving departs leaving crippling debt from flamboyant gestures—along with old-time hangovers and, reminiscent of the ancient festival itself, embarrassing office-party indiscretions.

Because Christmas now marinates in sheer materialism (and

## Chapter 19

Father Christmas (*Fun Magazine*, London, issue 763, 24 December 1879). Toning down the raucous Yule season as a time of carousing, Victorians re-used the old accoutrements of Father Christmas. Prissy folk conscripted his wassail bowl to deliver presents ... to "good little boys and girls" who had hardly figured in the ancient festival. The holiday's emphasis on children and consumerism grew rampant by the nineteenth-century's last decades. Dickens' sympathies for England's indigent helped propel this re-configuration with the author's loathing of childhood abuse and poverty—well-founded from bitter personal youthful experience.

charity driven by guilt about materialism's victims), shouldn't the song of the Twelve Days become the holiday's most appropriate anthem, in praise of unrestraint? It shimmers with self-indulgence eradicating abstinence. The impediment to accepting the carol's revived meaning arises from the character of Christmas as pure consumerism, the blossom of an industrial-age society that generates vast sums of money from a holiday that drives whole economies. But the presents listed in *The Twelve Days of Christmas* are (horrors!) actually free.

The song that once antagonized social propriety and the Church proves the nemesis of modern business ... unless you're in the sex trade: one of the Dancing Ladies, French Hens, or (Winchester) Geese a-Laying, who caterwaul a filthy song.

Usually rare songs performed by early-music revivalists, carols at Christmas reign common as autumn's leaves sifting down, and it wouldn't hurt if carolers everywhere and their audiences at home or on street corners understood the words. Not that it's necessary to understand the words. For several centuries the carol's been bawled with fellowship and joyful incomprehension. Like other songs that unite people in a shared moment, the carol can be sung without thinking about the words. But one day, on one street corner it occurred to me to ask what these odd phrases actually meant.

**Detail of Father Christmas. Presents replace wassail. Father Christmas also has changed, becoming fatter, jolly to the point of manic laughter, an acclaimed celebrity who no longer brings strong drink for the adults but dolls and toys.**

# Chapter Notes

## Chapter 1

1. Some may take offense at such language. That's the point. As appropriate, plain modern vulgarities replace those of olden days that were, in their time, equally, indecent. To set this song into its context the words' sheer effrontery must be revivified, which requires contemporary language of the same potency as the song's original vocabulary possessed in its era. Shakespeare used the unadorned word in *Much Ado About Nothing* when Benedick describes how Jupiter took the form of "some strange bull leapt your father's cow/ And got a calf" (V:4).

2. Shakespeare set the tone early in his career. In *Romeo and Juliet* (1591–95)—that first adventure of teenage lust—the horrified Juliet protests she would rather be raped than sully her avowed love for Romeo. The author, yet unsure of his audience, indulges a double-entendre: "O, bid me leap, rather than marry Paris" (pause, for the double meaning to set in, that she would rather be raped than lie with him) "From off the battlements of yonder tower" (IV:1) with a little Freudian phallic imagery tossed in.

Then, in *Othello (the Moor of Venice)* like Othello and Casio who love Desdemona, Iago confesses (II:1) that "I do love her to;/Not out of absolute lust ... but partly led to diet my revenge,/ For that I do suspect the lusty Moor/ Hath leap'd into my seat." Because, as Shakespeare seemed to know, when lust manifests in vaulting ambition and rage, rape is often described as violence about control rather than uncontrolled eroticism.

3. Galambush (2005) 271.

4. Living examples of subculture's racy, if ephemeral, coinages offer a touchstone for the vitality of the song's (now mostly extinct) references. Jargon, like today's rhyming slang of lower-class British society, epitomizes such quaint private speech with allusions invisible to outsiders who do not normally speak in rhyming slang. Codified in 2002 in John Ayto's *Dictionary of Rhyming Slang* (Oxford) the earliest reference to this weirdly inefficient idiom dates from the mid-nineteenth century. Yet, eighteenth century records makes limited reference to this cipher device. The carol ignored such rhymes but familiarity with slang's sly poetic ribaldry enlivens the colorful song whose off-color meanings may, now as then, provoke blushing.

5. Partridge (1947/1968) 116.

6. The 1778 *English Gazetteer* (ed. 2) s.v. The south bank of the Thames: "Southwark, In the times of popery here were no less than 18 houses on the Bankside, licensed by the Bishops of Winchester ... to keep whores, who were, therefore, commonly called Winchester Geese." As early as 1161 Henry II promulgated his "Ordinances touching upon the government of the stews in Southwark." A royal edict of 1310 shut all the brothels and streetwalkers, "common woman," thrust out of their establishments and caught plying their trade within the city walls could be punished with 40 days in prison (the duration that yields the word "quarantine" from the Italian, *quarantina giorna* forty days of isolation, suggesting a hygienic consideration). Even

then the brothels had been thriving in the outer borough for half a century administered by their Catholic landlord the Bishop of Winchester. That cleric earned enormous sums from their supervision and licensing. Such businesses prospered in a legal jurisdictional limbo outside the City proper. In 1504 fear of syphilis provoked Henry VII to close the Southwark bordellos, although business recommenced the next year. In 1546 by Henry VIII issued a proclamation intended to finally eradicate the brothels and the crimes they bred but, according to Shakespeare's testimony and others, they continued to thrive.

## Chapter 2

1. Restad (1995) 109.
2. It's a good thing that countryfolk came pouring into the metropolis bringing their rural ways and archaic beliefs. After the Black Death of the mid-fourteenth century, waves of infection swept congested cities that could not—with local citizens' reproduction rate, high infant mortality, and massive plague deaths—replenish a critical mass for cultural and mercantile vitality. That vacancy attracted a rich cultural mixture flowing toward tragedy-created opportunity. "Until the nineteenth century, towns were so insanitary that their populations never replaced themselves by reproduction, multiplying only thanks to the influx of rural surpluses" (Porter 1997:23).
3. Manzione (1996) 90.
4. Greene (1962) 17.
5. Fallows (1995) 1.
6. For some carolers Christianity was newly arrived in Northern Europe, despite claims for its antiquity in the triumphs of St. Patrick or the so-called conversion of Clovis (d. 511, the first king to unite the Frankish tribes). Only in 1387 Lithuania converted to Christianity. Since they wouldn't advertise the fact, nor would any literate person have recorded it, we have no idea how long pockets of local paganism hung on in England. Pre-Christian British practices may have long persisted as full-scale religious expression, with a surreptitious priestly class or quirky below-the-radar local conventions that were tolerated because misunderstood. The fragmentary bits of ancient traditions were malevolently labeled "witchcraft" or demoted to "folk customs" deemed harmless, in either case misinterpreted by Church authorities.
7. Rossiaud (1988:150) quoting a poem first collected by Montaiglon.
8. Camille (1998) 115–116.
9. Greene (1962) 17.
10. Camille (1998) 115.
11. Greene (1962) 16–17.
12. At the same time, a more scientific view of the world strove to objectively examine behavior and phenomena. Such new and hifalutin scholarly conjectures never touched the grubby lower-classes and their ecstatic circle dance, but in the upper reaches of academia, "In pre-modern European culture and society, dance was regarded as having a bearing on health ... [and considered] its effect on the general well-being of its practitioners ... [accordingly] It was quite common to recommend it when a balanced development of the human body ... was required" (Arcangeli 2000:3). The peasants who danced the carole on Yuletide did not consult expensive specialists to balance their humors.

## Chapter 3

1. Hollander (2007) 107.
2. So, for example, to set the season apart, in many communities, especially in Southern Europe, lavish seafood menus feature on Christmas Eve, so as to avoid the former luxury of meat-eating that highlights the next day.
3. Croft-Coke (1956) 58.
4. A hint of old Rome's temporary inversion of slave-and-master, the heart of Yuletide, survives on Boxing Day when masters defer to, or at least show appreciation for, attendants and underlings' loyal service. Boxing Day's boxes carry a faint recollection of Saturnalia's ancient practice. On the first weekday after

## Notes—Chapter 4

Christmas, usually 26 December, English postmen, garbage collectors, tradesmen, and servants expect to receive gifts, usually of money, called "Christmas Boxes" (although, in addition to cash given as an annual tip for faithful toil, house servants, who worked on Christmas Day, might take home boxes of food leftover from the feast). The custom remained informal until Parliament created Boxing Day an official Bank Holiday in 1871. Since Boxing Day falls on the day after Christmas, it coincides with the feast of St. Stephen, which helps explain the words of the nineteenth-century Christmastide carol based on a 13th-century tune. "Good King" Wenceslaus (907–935) of Bohemia—having feasted, woke refreshed, and wishing to review his realm's condition and distribute alms—stepped out on the feast of Stephen.

5. A figure lingering half-remembered amid the Germanic midwinter festival's newer version, among the names of the great one-eyed Norse god, the long-bearded Odin (in Old English, Woden), was "Yule father" or "the Yule one." The assembly of gods were called "the Yule ones." Odin had suffered for mankind. To give the world knowledge of Runes (the word) he had hung on the world tree in agony.

6. Camille (1998) 250.
7. Camille (1998) 87.
8. Greene (1962) 17.
9. Nissenbaum (1996) 7. Nissenbaum does not unpack Rev. Henry Bourne's grimly witty substitution of a literary conceit of multi-lingual associations.
10. Society-wide rowdy behavior loosed a cascade of disruptions. Constraints thrown off, an underclass encouraged defiance of niceties, with predictable results. William Harrison (1535–1593) described in his Tudor *Description of England:* "gentlemen as lie in wait for fat booties by the highways, and which are most commonly practiced in the winter season about the feast of Christmas, when serving men and unthrifty gentlemen want money to play at dice and cards lewdly spending in such wise whatsoever they have wickedly gotten" (1587:239). Christmas—high season for gambling, drinking, obscene caroling, fighting, and whoring—also notoriously marked an annual period of thievery.

## Chapter 4

1. Nissenbaum (1996) 6.
2. This may be similar to Bavarian Märzen (March Beer), a dark malty brew whose production has been strictly defined by edict since 1553. This beer is typically manufactured during the winter, drunk for Oktoberfest and (apparently, according to this ballad) into early Winter. Stored in a cool resting place, old-time March Beer approximated today's lager beers, compared to more typical English ales (but unlike hoppy IPAs casked for long-distance travel).
3. Smith (1980) 171.
4. That quarrel endured through 1929 when, with the same humorless practicality, Communist Russia banned Christmas, calling 25 December the National Day of Industrialization. The old holiday had the last laugh when the Soviet Union went out of business on 25 December 1991.
5. McCarntey (1999:35). In a scientific sense, by which a justly maligned age operated, "in the 'feast of fools' medieval society came to terms with mental alienation through the carnival notion of the world turned upside down—madness as dionysian release" (Porter 1997:128). Both diagnostic and therapeutic medicine merged with religion, folk culture, and superstition.
6. Graves (1948/66:289) continues, explaining "the otherwise unaccountable connexion of asses and fools." More importantly, the Fool resides at the heart of old topsy-turvy Christmas.
7. Smith (1980) 172.
8. Jonson's comedy, *The Alchemist,* 1610, mounts a satirical view of alchemy's deceptions and its gullible patrons in the 17th century's earliest moments; zealously lampooning his contemporaries, the playwright also documents current morality, both mainstream and extreme. (Samuel Taylor Coleridge

maintained the play contained one of literature's three perfect plots.) As a part of revived cultural vitality after dramatic stage presentations were restricted, Jonson intended his play to anoint the urban theater's complete re-endorsement. Formerly a marginally disreputable amusement, in 1597 the Lord Chamberlain's Men were refused authorization to use the theater in Blackfriars as a winter playhouse because of the neighborhood's objections. At that date a stage within the city walls, even under royal patronage, was infamous. But, now without objections, between 1608 and 1610 the company appointed the King's Men regained control of the playhouse and *The Alchemist* was among the first plays performed there. Though devised for production at Blackfriars—served up for a hip urban audience who would recognize the types being ridiculed—plague in London compelled the company to tour; so *The Alchemist* premiered at Oxford in 1610 playing in London, on its intended stage, later the same year when the depiction of Jacobean London (and the very neighborhood surrounding the theater) could be held up for knowing derision.

9. Rigorously Old Testament Christians of the Radical Reformation, Anabaptists—direct ancestors of the Amish, Hutterites, and Mennonites—rejected standard Christian customs such as participating in civil government, taking oaths and, most significantly, wearing wedding rings. During the 16th and 17th centuries Roman Catholics and Protestants could agree only on oppressing Anabaptists who followed a literal interpretation of the Sermon on the Mount and Believer's baptism. Thus they proved easy targets for Jonson's humor.

10. Nissenbaum (1996) 20–21.
11. Quoted by Nissenbaum (1996) 7.
12. Greene (1962) 18.
13. In response, the Church peddled its own interpretations. Rankly unsupported supernatural claims (theology) vied with naturalist observations as, "magic functioned with religion" and "Roman Catholicism etched onto believers' minds the notion of miracle cures and the healing powers of sacraments, relics, Latin incantations, invocation of saints and holy waters" (Porter 1997:41). Each side of the debate fostered its own worldview. Witches' and Christian magic, though equally well supported, neither compared to the practical zoological and botanical wisdom of agrarian lore's efficacy. Through the Middle Ages the competence of Christian interventions in science, agriculture, or medicine lacked the peasantry's banked-up accounts based on practical observations. Christianity would be a hard sell for people attuned to the land's rhythms, especially its mid-winter release that so wonderfully synchronized the seasonal cycles and calibrated with failing daylight, ready drink, leisure, and meat. Other than threats, the Church could offer little adequate response.

14. Anybody who thinks it's easy paring back every moral stance accumulated over the last two thousand years has no idea what Federico Fellini accomplished in his *Satyricon* (1969).

15. Young (1988) 155.

## Chapter 5

1. After its own prissy fashion, the Victorian period saw the peak of the caroling revival after interest re-kindled in the second half of the 18th century. The renewed attention produced collections of traditional broadsides (which included "The first Nowell" and "A Virgin Most Pure") as well as translations of foreign carols ("Patapan," a French noël). The holiday's general reconfiguration spurred a movement that mined the English folk carol's rich tradition, but exploited only certain, tasteful, resources extracted from the past. Such academic interest long preceded popular reconsideration of caroling, an ignored pastime for almost another century.

2. Restad (1995) 109.

3. A melancholic longing in many hearts seeks the lost nostalgic possibilities of an ideal Christmas. Dickens set an impossible bar to fulfillment. Following that same yearning, Irving Berlin's

## Notes—Chapter 5

1940 reminiscence conjures an imaginary tableau in *I'm Dreaming of a White Christmas*. The retrospective song, a willed revery, paints a slightly hallucinatory scene "just like the ones I used to know," that follows Dickens' summoning an old-time party. Berlin's first (usually omitted) stanza concedes "There's never been such a day/ in Beverly Hills, LA," and they were mighty rare elsewhere. That lack prompts the lament.

4. The song preserves archaic usage for a verb sometimes spelled "troul" that means to heartily sing a round's successive verses. Its word-root descends from a primeval sense of to run, tread, or ramble through. While the song's current English lyrics date only from 1862, the tune itself retains a much earlier Welsh melody of a winter's carol.

5. As Alan Lomax reported in his definitive guide to North American folk songs, "Among the carols sung on [Christmas eve] was *The Song of the Twelve*. Versions of this ancient mystic song have been recorded everywhere in Europe ... its origins may be found in Sanskrit, but all European versions are probably derived from a Hebrew chant for Passover (*Echod mi Yodea*) ... [from which] a number of forms soon developed [including] *The Twelve Days of Christmas*" (Lomax 1960:467).

6. Leach (1950) vol. II:1134.

7. Husk (1868) 181.

8. A late nineteenth-century source (Gomme 1894: vol. I:137) explains that:
Forfeits are incurred in those games in which penalties are exacted from players for non-compliance with the rules of the game; "Buff," "Contrary," "Crosspurposes," "Fire, Air, and Water," "Follow My Gable," "Genteel Lady," "Jack's Alive," "Old Soldier," "Twelve Days of Christmas," "Turn the Trencher," "Wadds," and others.

The book was the product of initiatives begun by the Folk-Lore Society, formed in 1878; Mrs. Alice Gomme's volume is one in the series, *A Dictionary of British Folke-Lore*, edited by her husband, Sir George Laurence E. Gomme, proponent of the historical Blue Plaque markers.

9. Decker notes that "forfeits was played on twelfth night (now celebrated as the Epiphany) of Christmas back in the days when it was an extended winter celebration" (1994:58). The "extended winter celebration" was a holdover from a decidedly non–Christian holiday that lasted until 2 February, aka Groundhog Day. There shortly followed another light-centered holiday, originally celebrated on 14 February, and still observed by some Christian rites on that day. The blessing of the candles on Candlemas-day is also called the Purification of the Blessed Virgin (Greek, Hypapante), Feast of the Presentation of Christ in the Temple.

10. Dickens (1940/1966:99). This edition preserves the irregularities in spelling and punctuation found in the first edition of 1843.

11. Decker (1994) 58.

12. "Several versions of the game have been noted in the mountains of East Tennessee" (Lomax 1960:238).

13. While uncommon, alternate versions have been found, the basic pattern (cited above in the text) presents the song's essential or what has become its "standard" form. Luckily for research, "There are not dozens of versions of The Twelve Days" (Palmer 1991:5). Naturally, there's always an exception.

For some reason, of all places, the *New York Times* cites an alternate, a metrically inferior proxy for the song that switches verses 10 and 12 (Olson 2014:B3). So, we hear of "12 drummers drumming" when the sharp plosive and abrupt sound of ten introduces drumming's clamor. Contrariwise, "ten" before lords-a-leaping lacks the slippery final consonantal V. Excepting such untoward abnormalities, the carol knows few, and minor, deviants.

14. Considering the Post-Colonial period's lack of sustained and organized opposition, "explains why so few of the English carols, and none of the ritual dances and ceremonies survived in American folk tradition" (Lomax 1960:238). No one felt the carols and dances needed defending.

## Chapter 6

1. This brisk dance and its name derived from the French *courante,* based on the verb *courrir* to run (from the Latin *courrere).* From the late 16th century and for the next two hundred years it was a fashionable court dance for aristocratic couples. Its lightly skipping steps, borrowed and refined from lusty Italian folkdancing in triple time, used quick running steps in time signatures of 3/2, 3/4, 6/4 or even 3/8—counted as 3s (not like the modern 6/8, counted as 2 or 6); hence Shakespeare's galloping *"swift* corantos." Though it raised a sweat, the dance was not inherently erotic, but it was usually preceded by a pantomime of wooing which set the tone and fixed the erotic message as the dancers heated up. Like lavolta, it provided a form of dirty dancing: foreplay.

2. Popular in France during the sixteenth-century and later, galliard means gay and rollicking. The dance was executed in a moderately quick triple-time and, like the lavolta, performed with exaggerated leaps that suggested wantonness.

3. Smith (1980) 168–9.

4. Partridge (1968:91) made this observation and cited another example from *Much Ado About Nothing* (III iv).

5. Farmer & Henley, 1890.

6. Also in *Richard III* (3:7)
BUCKINGHAM: Go, go, up to the
 leads; the lord mayor knocks.
[Exit GLOUCESTER; Enter the Lord
 Mayor and Citizens]
Welcome my lord; I dance attendance here;

7. Because Medieval brothels often operated on the premises of the community-owned bathhouses (a place to stew in hot water) the establishments were called "stews" or "stewhouses."

8. Greene (1935/1977) lvii.

9. Hoping for renewal in the year's darkest pit, the cold-season's fertility festival's release tested all manner of restraint. Leaving behind the Middle Ages, both the Church and the emerging nation-states gained coherence and bankability from the suppression, sublimation, and re-direction of animal urges. Those, so-called "base," energies can be productively (and profitably) channeled, or at least non-destructively deflected into sports and entertainments, warfare, religion or, more recently, consumerism. The anti-social upheaval implied by unlimited sex—enacted every Yuletide until suppressed by colluding Church and Christianized State—became the anthem of Peter Weiss's crazed proletariat who, with enraged gusto equal to earlier Yuletide's carolers, caterwaul (1966:92):
 What's the point of a revolution
 without general copulation
 copulation copulation copulation...

## Chapter 7

1. Which the New International Version translates as: "In breeding season I once had a dream in which I looked up and saw that the male goats mating with the flock were streaked, speckled or spotted (*Genesis* 31:10). Here mating = leaping.

2. There's an absurdity to modern urban children learning to read by turning the colorful pages of picture books of farmyard animals that many will never see. Yet, those animals names remain the core vocabulary of young readers. The idea of farmyard animals could only arise once people left farms, because for farmers and their children such familiar creatures are livestock.

3. That this prerogative never really existed hardly matters. The singers believed the *droit du seigneur* or the *droit de cuissage* had been an entitlement exercised by the nobility at some point in their recent past. As part of this communal fable, Shakespeare invoked the threat of the *droit de seignor* in *2 Henry VI* (IV:7), almost as a tax on the maidenhead—a "pole" tax. At the very time that the canon of Christmas carols was most energetically in formation, "beginning in the thirteenth century many other references to the same 'right', under a variety of names, added it to the arsenal of weapons with which to combat lordship"

(Bourreau 1995/1998:4). Despite the myth's persistence, there is no evidence that the *droit du seigneur* was ever practiced, or would be long tolerated.

4. Leap-ore was "also called round ore" (*The Century Dictionary* New York: The Century Co, 1889-) why I do not know. Familiarity with the grades of tin ore would have been common knowledge to many pre-modern Britons as tin has been mined in Cornwall from pre-historic times. Much of the tin in Greco-Roman bronze masterpieces was mined in England. In the great shadowy international web of pre-historic trade routes, tin was a major export item, though probably not leap-ore which was not worth shipping.

5. An Anglican, sympathetic to Presbyterians, John Trapp wrote a massive and, despite its unwieldiness, popular commentary on the Bible. His readers were attracted to his terse writing studded with quotable lines: *Annotations upon the old and new testament*, 1646–47 (from vol. 5: "Commentary on the New Testament Epistles & Revelation," App. 684).

6. E. B. (c.1690–98/1899).

7. The word "merry" (related to mirth and, somehow deriving from old Teutonic for short or brief) itself proves interesting when associated with Christmas, as inveterately happens as part of the traditional greeting. The word relates to joy and the licentious. For a discussion of this etymology transformed to wholesomeness see: Wardroper (1995:178–9).

8. Our own day still recognizes that not all leaping/fucking evokes bliss and not every sexual vulgarity refers to conjugal joy. When it indicates the defective or sub-standard, the "curse-word" status of leap re-doubles when it equals fuck. A famous bit of U.S. Army slang from World War II is S.N.A.F.U. (pronounced "snaffoo" and never said as a string of letters) an acronym standing for "situation normal, all fucked up."

9. Around the year 1670, Sir John Scot (or Scott) authored *The Staggering State of the Scots Statesman (1550–1650)* that contains this line: "He … grieving that he had not that power in court that he thought his birth and place deserved, leapt out, and made sundry out-reds against the king" (153).

Though a term originating in the sixteenth century, British English still refers to a cock-sure fellow—a vulgar over-reaching social climber, obtrusive among his betters—as a "bounder." That pejoration carries all the original meddlesome connotations of audaciously leaping unwelcome into a situation.

## Chapter 8

1. This last phrase does not mean that the musical instrument is a shabby or elderly example; "old" is gentle vernacular, a slang construction typical of the American South, and whatever word follows "old" is addressed affectionately or familiarly.

*I've Been Working on the Railroad* has been traced to an African-American "Louisiana Levee" song; others think that Irish work gangs in the West based the song on an old-fashioned hymn. This folk song's origins are unknown. Texans adapted the tune as their state anthem, *The Eyes of Texas are Upon You*. Because the skin-headed banjo, an instrument invented in North America (though ultimately descended from the South Asian family of rababs) was associated with African-Americans, this song carries a decidedly underclass mood, with implied racial-sexual mythology.

One theory holds that the verses of "Dinah" and "Someone's In the Kitchen" are interpolations, or that Dinah could refer to either a woman or a locomotive, and that the horn signifies the call to lunch; none of these hypotheses holds up if the song is a ditty of veiled lewd meanings referring to exactly what railroad workers craved, sentimental sex.

The first line about "working on the railroad" probably refers to laying track; the drudgery and monotony of "All the livelong day" also represents an extended period of any rhythmic physical exertion, setting the tone for what follows.

A healthy early morning erection, "Rise up so early in the morn," precedes the action. While the captain (of the work crew) asks for the engine to blow its horn, this blowing quickly becomes something else as Dinah is repeatedly asked to blow.

If Dinah were an engine, it would be impossible for someone to be "in the kitchen with Dinah" and that someone is "Strumming on the old banjo." The singer "know[s]" that someone is in the with Dinah, either because Dinah is promiscuous and somebody is always in her kitchen, or because it is the singer himself who is in the kitchen. (The idea of the singer vocalizing in a psychotic persona can be found in other folk-songs, like "Peggy O".) Unlike *The Twelve Days*, this work song is decidedly male in spirit and Dinah is no randomly chosen name; she is the Old Testament figure known only for having been raped ("And Dinah the daughter of Leah and Jacob, went out to visit with some of neighborhood girls. And when Shechem the son of Hamor the Hivite, prince of the country, saw her, he took her, and lay with her, and defiled her" [*Genesis* 34:1–2]). The name Dinah stands for violent sex followed by the cooing of the maniacal rapist, a stance somewhat softened by the worker's gently confessed but unquenched lust.

The song begins with repeated action that fades out with an endlessly repeated, but more pleasant, action.

> I've been working on the railroad
> All the livelong day
> I've been working on the railroad
> Just to pass the time away
>
> Can't you hear the whistle blowing
> Rise up so early in the morn
> Can't you hear the captain shouting
> Dinah, blow your horn
>
> Dinah, won't you blow
> Dinah, won't you blow
> Dinah, won't you blow your horn
>
> Dinah, won't you blow
> Dinah, won't you blow
> Dinah, won't you blow your horn
>
> Someone's in the kitchen with Dinah
> Someone's in the kitchen I know
> Someone's in the kitchen with Dinah
> Strumming on the old banjo, and singing
> Fie, fi, fiddly i o
> Fie, fi, fiddly i o
> Fie, fi, fiddly i o
> Strumming on the old banjo

## Chapter 9

1. Baines (1973) 13.
2. The song was a favorite at London's Beefsteak Club and of the Anacreontic Society as late as the period of transportation of criminals to Australia, 1787–1853 (see: Wardroper 1995:178–9). The Anacreontic Society also sang the rousing drinking song *Anacreon in Heaven* whose tune—with verses replaced by the rhymes of an American lawyer, Francis Scott Key—became *The Star-Spangled Banner*.
3. According to the Sigmund Freud Museum (UK) this unattested line has caused some consternation, and the museum's website plaintively asks:

> Where did Freud say, "Sometimes a cigar is only a cigar."? If you know the answer to this one, please let us know because we have no idea.

Long before Freud's time, Shakespeare larded a play already spangled with windy references. Banter in *Othello* combines blowing, and passing wind/gas through the anus, with other anatomical analogies; in this extract (III:i), the homonym "tail" is the penis and the wind-instrument may be the farting buttocks near which hangs the bagpipe-like penis/scrotum:

> CLOWN: Are these, I pray you, wind instruments?
> MUSICIAN: Ay, marry, are they, sir.
> CLOWN: O, thereby hangs a tale.
> MUSICIAN: Whereby hangs a tale, sir?
> CLOWN: Marry, sir, by many a wind-instrument that I know. But, masters, here's money for you: and the general so likes your music, that he desires you, for love's sake, to make no more noise with it.

## Notes—Chapter 10

For "love's sake" not the more usual protestation "for God's sake!", as the pipes and love were intimates.

4. Cipolla (1977) 2.

5. A female friend, an artist who lived in a small New England town after she had decamped from New York City, told me that lacking most other diversions she'd discovered everybody in that town took turns sleeping with everyone else, covertly to be sure, but every possible coupling was tried. The metropolis offered many diversions while the rural and agrarian heartland rollicked porn heaven. And always has.

6. I've previously explored this problem in: *Rumpelstiltskin's Secret: What Women Didn't Tell The Grimms* (Routledge) 2020.

7. "Animals could not be slaughtered until the weather was cold enough to ensure the meat would not go bad; any meat saved for the rest of the year would have to be preserved (and rendered less palatable) by salting" (Nissenbaum 1996:6). Smoking, by hanging meat in the chimney, or air-drying would work; pickling also preserved meat but pickling might (varying with the technique) require salt which, depending on location, could be expensive. Either salted, air-dried, otherwise pickled or smoked, preserved meat was not fresh like just-slaughtered livestock. Hanging meat to ripen was another matter, also best practiced in deep winter (Rand 2017).

8. Christmas was not the only ecclesiastical season to undergo reversals of public piety. "England ... after a period of strict observance during the middle ages, had become more and more relaxed about dietary prohibitions after the split with Rome during the 16th century, and with the Revolution of 1648–49, the Lentan laws quickly became obsolete" (McGee 1984:132–33). Christians who were willing to ignore the grimmest Lentan restrictions found levity easy at Christmastide with its countervailing spirit of great Yule.

9. Still proud of its Medieval buildings in the Tudor style after Europe had long since moved on to Neo-Classicism, England's first Renaissance structure survives in remnants of the Palace of Whitehall, Inigo Jones' 1622 design for the Royal Banqueting House.

10. And, for the record, however wild the mid-winter festival, certain acts were off-limits, though known and considered. Like cannibalism, as practiced by long-haired savages.

11. No need to wander into Queer Theory to enjoy this song, and no need to exclude it either; prevailing theology and assumptions about anatomy defined and separated the sexes. Antiquity accepted sexual expression in a continuity between homo- and hetero- sexual pleasures, so long as one—usually the male—remained untainted by adopting passive positions in lovemaking that partnered him with a social inferior.

12. In addition to attracting a widespread and general readership for the good stuff, "the book has sold more than 30,000 copies to anti-pornography organizations, [but] it has run into unexpected resistance among religious bookstores. Although their sympathies lie [with the report's conservative impetus] ... many are refusing to stock or display the book for fear that the vulgar language in it and its graphic descriptions of sexual acts will offend their customers" (McDowell 1986:C13).

## Chapter 10

1. Most Christmas celebrations fall short of the modern family-centered ideal. An almost-fantasy—of congenial and benevolent relatives and friends gathered in warm fellowship and feasting—has become so mythologized as to remain among the dying's fond moorings to life. An anatomist attending her mother's deathbed cheered the ebbing patient, without real hope of rousing her from the semi-consciousness of a terminal coma: "We went through our repertoire of hits, from Disney films [and] a range of Christmas songs (despite it being the height of summer)." That performance conceivably included *The Twelve Days,* sung in a coolly sterile hospital room with only an old dying

## Notes—Chapter 11

woman for audience (Black 2018:84). Just so anodyne, but tenderly cherished, has once-fierce caroling become.

2. The Beatles *I Want to Hold Your Hand* (Lennon/Mcartney 1964) never meant just that because "When I touch you I feel happy, inside/ it's just a feeling that my love, I can't hide," which meant that while wearing that era's skin-tight trousers arousal became visible so it might as well be called love.

3. Maines (1999) 6.

4. Russett (1989) 44.

5. Two examples illustrate this varied usage. In 1765: the *Museum Rusticum et commerciale: or select papers on agriculture, etc.* informed its readers that "The eating of the first shoots of rye makes ewes milk extraordinarily" (IV:225). In the next century Charles Scott's 1886 book, *The Practice of Sheep-Farming*, advised that "Some of the breeds of sheep milk very heavily" (178).

6. Sharia imposes incest prohibitions constraining those who have nursed from the same woman's teats.

7. No one, despite the hype, has demonstrated actual human pheromones but breasts were selectively bred from aesthetic preference. They have grown more prominent than needed for the infant's nutritional necessity; great apes, several times a human's weight, nurse with visually insignificant breasts. Human breasts became the most variously shaped and sized organs in the animal kingdom. Their astounding diversity of contours and profiles, range of volume, variety of proportions, and the absolute weight variations—all this would be biologically intolerable were this same deviation to characterize the liver, adrenals, thyroids or any other organ. The wide variation occurs because no other human gland performs the display function (like a peacock's tail) to entice a mate. For purpose of sexual display and courting, such variety charms and attracts different partialities, which encourages genetic diversity. Breasts' importance for mating selection (lust) suggest that this verse's inference required only a glancing allusion to make its point. For a starkly convincing visual demonstration of the mimicry of human hemispheric breasts and buttocks, see Morris (1977:240).

8. Partridge (1947/1968) 142.

9. This term, that derives from the Old English word for the status and circumstance of "maidenhood," referred to a maid's physical condition.

10. Sometimes this understanding was used in jest, as when Shakespeare has Falstaff sarcastically spout:

There's no more faith in thee than in
a stewed
prune; nor no more truth in thee
than in a drawn
fox; and for womanhood, Maid Marian may be the
deputy's wife of the ward to thee
(*1 Henry IV,* III:2).

Eventually, as often happens, slang forgot or mocked its original source and a Maid Marian was simply a loose woman, a wanton (Farmer & Henley 1890:270). The old reference grew irony-steeped to contrast with the story-book character's goodness.

I've described another set of symbolic possibilities involving a maid and milk (see: Rand, "What the Kitchen Maid Made: Vermeer's Kitchen Maid," *Bulletin van Het Rijksmuseum*, Amsterdam, Autumn 1999). This article's original title, before translation and editing into Dutch and then re-translation back into English, was: "What the Milk Maid Made."

11. Thomas Dekker 1603.

12. Farmer & Henley (1890) 311.

13. Certain female porn stars who specialize in it, and other adepts, are said to "squirt" as the legend of female ejaculation lives on, celebrated by ardent women.

## Chapter 11

1. Baggini (2017) 17.
2. Camille (1998) 84.
3. Camille (1998) 87.
4. Smith (1980) 168.
5. Two lubricious examples:
Written before 1553, Nicholas Udall's *Ralph Roister Doister, a comedy*, jokes:

## Notes—Chapter 11

"Ye shall see hir glide and swimme, Not lumperdee clumperdee like our spaniell Rig" (Arber 1869, II:3. 36). And from a composition authored before 1563, *Jack Juggler, a new interlued for chyldren to playe, named Jack Jugeler:* "She minceth, she brideleth, she swimmeth to and fro."

An associated meaning, to move, or appear to move, as if gliding or floating on water seems an extension of the verb's central sense. Hence it can mean to move, waft, or be suspended in the air or ether, occasionally and theatrically by mechanical means.

6. The English martyr, William Carter (1548–1584) began a ten year apprentice to the queen's printer, on Candlemas Day, 1563, that is, after the Christmas revels ended and business returned to usual. Candlemas is today celebrated as Groundhog Day, a holiday that returns the festival to its pre-Christian importance in the agricultural calendar. This, now-secular, holiday derives from German superstition that if a hibernating animal casts a shadow on 2 February winter will last another six weeks but spring will quickly arrive if no shadow is seen. In America. the holiday's allure remains widespread, drawing reveling visitors to Punxsutawney, Pennsylvania. Consistent with the past's mid-winter revels that incited riotous conduct, local authorities have banned alcohol that day in Punxsutawney. So much for centuries of Christianizing.

Like so much of Christian ritual, the roots of the 2 February holiday issue from unconquered Pagan culture which, given half-a-chance to celebrate light amid darkness, will erupt in the joy of fecundity. The *Catholic Encyclopedia* dourly notes the Eastern Rite's celebration of new fire, part of the Greek Orthodox Church at Jerusalem's Easter celebration associated with the reappearance of light—a late-winter celebration which, is the occasion for scandalous demonstrations of a piety which frequently degenerates into orgies worthy of pagan rites. The Journal of the Marquis de Nointel, in the seventeenth century, relates scenes which cannot be transcribed and which take place periodically.

7. Following the mid-winter fertility festival the beginning of February subtended the season between the winter solstice and the spring equinox, a time the Celts revered as *Imbolc*, observed in anticipation of the birth of farm animals and the planting of crops.

In Celtic Ireland the year consisted of two six-month periods marked by the feasts of Beltine (the "Fire of Bel," also called Cetsamain, "First Samhain") celebrated on 1 May as the festival initiating summer (when druids drove cattle between two fires as a protection against disease) and Samhain (also "Samain") that originally launched the summer season, but eventually marked summer's end on 1 November. These semi-annual periods were further divided by the quarterly feasts of Lughnasadh (the god Lugh's jubilee) on 1 August, and Imbolc, on 1 February.

Imbolc, a feast of purification for the farmers (also called oímelc "sheep/ewe milk"), referred to the lambing season. This date survived on the ritual calendar when Christianity commandeered the Celtic goddess Brigit for St. Brigit, who retained her strong pastoral associations. By remarkable coincidence, the Imbolc celebration became St. Brigid's Feast Day on 1 February, and in Ireland—where she stands second in reverence only to St. Patrick—she is celebrated as "The Mother of the Gael." St. Brigit's great foundation at Kildare, Ireland, was probably instituted atop a pagan sanctuary dedicated to her Celtic forbear, and in modern Scottish folk tradition Brigit served as the midwife of the Virgin Mary. Also called Brigantia (Celtic: High One) in Celtic religion Brigit was goddess of poetry, crafts, prophecy, and divination: the equivalent of the Roman goddess Minerva (Greek Athena) her day was a major holiday. Brigit's feast day—the pagan festival of Imbolc, when ewes came into milk—marks the eve of Candlemas known as Groundhog Day.

8. Fernández-Armesto (2002) 86.
9. Camille (1998) 87.
10. Camille (1998) 250.
11. William Tyndale was educated at Oxford and, while an instructor at

# Notes—Chapter 12

Cambridge in 1521 he became convinced that scripture should govern the Church and that Christians should be able to read the Bible in the local vernacular, a possibility that, for the first time, grew feasible with printing.

In 1523 Tyndale began translating the Christian Scriptures from the Greek but the next year he had to escape England because of political and Church opposition. Nevertheless, financial support from London merchants reached him on the continent. His translation was printed in Cologne beginning in 1525, but Catholic authorities suppressed it. The first copies reached England in 1526 and were immediately outlawed before Tyndale started to translate the Hebrew Scriptures, that were issued in Marburg in 1530. Before finishing his translation he was captured in Antwerp and executed at Vilvoorde in 1536.

Initially printed in Zürich or in Cologne, Miles Coverdale's was the first complete English Bible. Issued on 4 October 1535, it quickly sold out and a second impression was issued the same year and a third in 1536, followed by another edition published in England by James Nycholson in Southwark in 1537; then, achieving official endorsement, a new edition of the same year was licensed by the king, the King James Version.

## Chapter 12

1. The note, written in his capacity as Bishop of Milan, was addressed to the staunchly Christian Emperor Valentinian II (375–392) in reply to the Memorial of Symmachus. Ambrose (334/340–397) countered and mocked his rival's representation of Rome by suggesting that the discontinuation of pagan rites, cited by Symmachus, had not caused a famine. Ambrose's taunt also appears in the work of his contemporary, St. Augustine, who tells the tale this way:

> Rome was taken and burnt by the Gauls? Perhaps [the gods] were present, but asleep? For at that time the whole city fell into the hands of the enemy, with the single exception of the Capitoline hill; and this too would have been taken, had not the watchful geese aroused the sleeping gods! And this gave occasion to the festival of the goose, in which Rome sank nearly to the superstition of the Egyptians, who worship beasts and birds (*The City of God,* Book II, chapter 22).

2. Without a distinctive modifier, the name refers to the familiar tame goose, descended from the wild grey or greylag goose. Any qualifier would suggest that we consider something other than the barnyard bird because other species are differentiated by appending words for color (black, blue, blue-winged, pink-footed, white-fronted) or another attribute or habits (laughing, fen, marsh-goose, snow) or native region (wild American, Canada, Chinese goose).

3. The "fair ladies" of Southwark appear in the refrain of the ditty "London Bridge Is Falling Down," because if the bridge collapsed—as it perennially threatened after the 13th century, which occasioned numerous repairs over several centuries—how would London's customers for theater, bear-baiting, and whoring get to the pleasures of Southwark? Since the song is addressed to "My fair lady," the vocalist must already be in Southwark offering a laggard's excuse for not returning to London: the bridge is impassable. This was not far-fetched. "[I]n 1212, when London Bridge caught fire at either end, trapping those in the middle ... three thousand dead were said to have been pulled out of the Thames" (Girouard 1985:74). This song enshrined recollections of the place's danger and the illicit entertainments to be had at Bankside. Even the Medieval bridge's stone replacement did not fare well. Sold at auction, and its masonry moved piece by piece, the bridge was re-erected ... in Arizona.

4. No ascetic himself, in 1546 Henry VIII closed the Southwark stews and shut down the bishop's sex operation. His geese migrated, some north across the Thames. Their whereabouts settled them in suitably named locations associated with a trade: Cokke Lane, Petticoat

## Notes—Chapter 12

Lane, three different Love Lanes, and Gropecunte Lane in Cheapside; London enjoyed no monopoly on the vocation and Oxford also had its Grope Cunt Lane. (From the 13th through the 17th century Oxford's current Magpie Lane was Gropcunt Lane, or Grope Lane. This narrow thoroughfare runs south, across from University Church of St. Mary the Virgin on the High Street to Merton Street, with Oriel College's Rhodes Building to its west. Propriety changed other towns' Gropecunt roads to become Grape Lane or Grove Street.) London's seamy locations—like Southwark, a district beyond London's municipal jurisdiction—flirted with the city walls that circumscribed their trade's legal limits.

5. Not only was the Bishop's palace and income derived from taxing the miserable stews and whores of Southwark but when the prostitutes' wretched lives ended the Church would not bury them in a hallowed cemetery. In his 1598 Survey of London, the Tudor historian and topographer John Stow recorded an unconsecrated "plot of ground called the singlewoman's churchyard." This parcel of un-hallowed land offered a burying ground for the destitute, homeless, and the strumpets whom the Church pretended to ignore, except for their income. Stow recounted how "these single woman were forbidden the rites of the Church, so long as they continued that sinful life"—that very livelihood that richly furnished a Church whose final succor they were denied. In the 1990s the Museum of London partially excavated the plot, today found under the name "Crossbones Garden" at Redcross Way, London, SE1.

6. That is, whoring. Despite his age and our modern conception of age-appropriate youthful experiences, Romeo is already a well-practiced brothel client. When making their calls—with that kinsman to the Prince, his buddy Mercutio—aside from patronizing the girls, they probably also drank, and sang naughty songs with the prostitutes. Such visits did not compromise Romeo's marriageability, but should condition our notion of his sexual innocence and his friends' escapades.

7. Cheveril (often spelled, cheverel) is full kid-skin leather known for its pliancy and flexibility. A glover's son, Shakespeare knew the properties of different leathers.

8. Shakespeare, *1 Henry VI*:

BISHOP OF WINCHESTER: Gloucester, thou wilt answer this before the pope.

GLOUCESTER: Winchester goose, I cry, a rope! a rope! Now beat them hence; why do you let them stay? Thee I'll chase hence, thou wolf in sheep's array. Out, tawny coats! out, scarlet hypocrite! (I:3).

9. Smith (1980) 168.

10. Most of the early references to "lay" as a sexual term date only from the 1930s:

1934—John O'Hara *Appointment in Samarra* "You're wrong about one thing," said Julian... "I didn't lay that girl" (vii. 212).

1936—John Dos Passos *Big Money* "Gosh," he was saying at the back of his head, "maybe I could lay Elsie Finnegan" (305).

1938—Graham Greene *Brighton Rock* "I'm marrying her for your sake, but I'm laying her for my own" (V.v.214).

There is one prominent, early if ambiguous, appearance of the word. Describing the different classes of women—all of whom act the same and should be morally levelled and equated—in Geoffrey Chaucer's "Manciple's Tale" (212–22) he used "lay" [leyn] as part of a sexual pejorative:

Ther nys no diference, trewely,
Bitwixe a wyf that is of heigh degree,
If of hir body dishonest she bee,
And a povre wenche, oother than this

And, God it woot, myn owene deere brother,
Men leyn that oon as lowe as lith that oother.

～

There is no difference truly,
Between a wife that is of high degree,
If of her body dishonest she be,
And a poor wench, other than this

## Notes—Chapter 12

....
And, God knows, my own dear brother,
Men lay the one as low as lies the other

11. The temptation to find earlier, even medieval, sexual meanings in slang—in so-called canty or canting—would place words like "laid" in the patois spoken by members of the English criminal underworld. Their speech, then as now, represented a coded defensive "antilanguage." Such vernacular is characteristic of an "antisociety" trying to guard its meaning from casual or unauthorized eavesdropping, since its speakers' activities were mainly illegal and abhorred by the rest of British society. Likewise, the celebrants of old-time Christmas represented a shrinking minority often persecuted by otherwise mutually warring Christian factions.

12. A Catholic convert, T. S. Eliot (the grandson of the distinguished Unitarian minister, William Greenleaf Eliot) plodded into the same poetic territory. After Ezra Pound's crucial editorial guidance excised over a full introductory page of Eliot's throat-clearing meanderings, we arrive at his opening line of *The Waste Land* (1922). "April is the cruelest month, breeding/ Lilacs out of the dead land" (lilacs being indigenous to New England and rampant in springtime). With increasing retrospect, this seems a clumsily contrarian riff on the vivacious opening lines of Geoffrey Chaucer's *Canterbury Tales* (c.1387): "Whan that Aprill with his shoures soote/ The droghte of March hath perced to the roote/ And bathed every veyne in swich licour." Not bitterness but joy, the perfect rebuttal to Eliot's proto-Catholicism.

13. Greene (1962) 18.

14. Even lacking a document that proves this assertion (a report that "On Christmas Day farmer so-and-so and Yeoman Jones sat with their friends in such-and-such a tavern/brothel carousing and drunkenly bellowed out that disgusting song *The Twelve Days of Christmas*") the tone of the stanzas unroll one plausible obscenity after another. An imagined vocal accompaniment to hard drinking and whoring presents the most reasonable situation for the carol's rowdy performance ... once its content reemerges, exposed after long dormancy like the blinking groundhog.

15. To entrench elite power by demonstrating terror, surviving antimodern societies cultivate a taste for brutality. Their public's enjoyment of such amusements, usefully (for the ruling class) inures non-elites to others' suffering. The connoisseurship of sadism formerly appeared part of the everyday occidental world, and not just in England:

> The Roman carnival that took place in February 1510 was even more jubilant and unruly than usual. All of the familiar entertainments were on show. Bulls were released into the streets and slain by men on horseback armed with lances. Convicted criminals were executed in the Piazza del Popolo by a hangman dressed as a harlequin. South of the piazza, races along the Via della Corso included a competition between prostitutes. An even more popular attraction was the "racing of the Jews," a contest in which Jews of all ages were forced to don bizarre costumes and then sprint down the street to insults from the crowd and sharp prods from the spears of the soldiers galloping behind. Cruelty and bad taste knew no bounds. There were races between hunchbacks and cripples [King 2003:188].

16. Didier (1901) BR 2.

17. A work published in London, as late as 1785, features testimony to good times shared with friends frolicking at Goose Riding: "a goose whose neck is greased being suspended by the legs to a cord tied to two trees or high posts, a number of men on horseback riding full speed attempt to pull off the head, which if they effect, the goose is their prize. This has been practiced in Derbyshire within the memory of persons now living" according to Capt. Francis Grose (1785:74).

Isaac Newton (1642–1727) copied down advice that might strike us as oddball, except that titan of science recorded as earnest counsel things which,

## Notes—Chapter 13

presumably, people wished to learn, as how:

> To make birds drunk.
> Take such meat as they love as wheat, barley &c. steepe it in lees of wine or in ye juice of Hemlock, & sprincle it wher birds use to haunt. Sodden Garlick sprinkled amongst corne sowne.
> To make pigeons, partriges dicks & other birds drunk. Set black wine for y{m} to drink where they come.

Learning how to make birds drunk seems so alien a notion as to thoroughly separate that world from ours (Isaac Newton, *personal notebook,* 1659). As an outlier, ortolans (now threatened with extinction) are drowned in cognac/armagnac before being eaten, but that anachronistic bit of cuisine hardly represents mainstream cooking and is now outlawed in France.

## Chapter 13

1. Austin's 1909 transcription of the carol settles no questions of authenticity, however much we crave an authoritative version. We don't, and really can't, know how Austin selected variant verses to include, and in what order he sorted them. His musicianship dictated some choices, like adding the Rings' extra rhythmic beat (if he did add it, rather than record an extant version). In choosing and arranging the verses, in many cases sequence-switching would make no difference. Because Austin published his version of the carol (which might seem to award it the status of a touchstone of accuracy) does not take priority in ruling about what the song may have been before. Yet, there remains a deep numerical logic in some of the verses that precludes their re-arrangement. The number of Maids Milking, Swans Swimming, Geese Laying, or Lords Leaping, etc. have no bearing on the song. The remaining verses, that provide the song's spine, support and give meaning to the whole. Many of the verses reveal a genuine correlation between numbers and connotation; such insinuations cumulatively color the entirety, regardless of Austin's alterations in transcription.

2. Whicher (1949) 3.

3. Francis Grose's 1785 *Classical Dictionary of the Vulgar Tongue* defines "Patrico" or "Pater Cove" as any minister or parson but especially those "strolling priests that marry people under a hedge without gospel or common prayer book, the couple standing on each side of a dead beast, are bid to live together till death do them part; so shaking hands, the wedding is ended." To perform this sham of temporary expedience the parties were unmarried—to each other.

4. Although the learned, pious, and much-married, Henry VIII famously broke with Rome, the high-water mark of English Catholicism had passed centuries earlier when, for the first and only time, an Englishman was elected pope. Born in Herfordshire, Nicholas Breakspeare (c.1100–1159) as pope Adrian IV wrestled with titanic clashing forces of the Byzantine and Holy Roman empires while he tried to repair papal finances. Yet, as a lasting memorial of this otherwise forgotten pope, Adrian also decreed that obtaining access to the sacraments trumped feudal prerogatives and serfs could be free to marry without obtaining their lord's consent. His pronouncement unconditionally established marriage as a sacrament.

5. Old-style Christmas and the marriage ceremony were closely associated, almost equivalent. In England and America Puritans denounced both institutions. But ridding the golden rings of their Yuletide sexuality was no easy chore for Puritans; the ring's history is ancient and deeply embedded in culture. The wearing of the ring dates back, at least in Anglo-Saxon ceremony, to the laws of King Ethelbert (ruled from 860).

After a legally binding engagement, the *handfasting*—arranged by the fathers of the sometimes juvenile bride and groom—presents were exchanged. "It was the *handfasting,* not the marriage ceremony which produced the exchange of vows which are now part of the Anglican wedding service ... And it was the *handfasting* which produced the word

## Notes—Chapter 13

'wed'. This originally meant to pledge, the sum of money handed over to the girl's father. Later it also came to mean the ring which was given at the same time, and which was worn on the bride-to-be's right hand until the marriage. During the ceremony, the groom transferred the 'wed' to the bride's left hand" (Monsarrat 1973:6–7). The word wed is related to wages, make of that what you will.

Since Puritans eschewed the use of wedding rings, as redolent of the former Roman Church, the song's reference to gold rings pre-dates ascendant Puritan influence.

6. Monsarrat (1973) 45.
7. Monsarrat (1973) 45.
8. Smith (1980) 168.
9. The rings' donor, perhaps sexually satisfied in unsanctified circumstance, appears in the *Comedy of Errors* (V:1) when the Courtesan demands "Sir, I must have that diamond [ring] from you." This was a gift given when the donor, locked from his house, spent the time carousing with the whore to whom he warmly responds: "There, take it; and much thanks for my good cheer." The ring, a memento for shared pleasure, did not celebrate sexual fidelity.
10. Affections purchased with gold sustain Benjamin Franklin's 1733 caustic humor in *Poor Richard's Almanack*. For modern readers his wit depends on recognizing that "proof" means to test.

The proof of gold is fire;
The proof of a woman, gold;
The proof of a man, a woman.

Hence 90 proof whiskey has been tested to 45% alcohol.

The usually misunderstood quip that "It's the exception that proves the rule" decidedly does *not* mean that irregular occurrences certify an otherwise established theory. Such oddities push the borders of a system (aviation's "envelope") and strain a precept's application. The adage means that seeming exceptions stress-test a rule.

11. Karras (1996) 94.
12. The song might refer to groups of friends or (in common canty, by the early eighteenth century) the word meant a conclave of people in league for a collective purpose: the Watergate Ring, or a ring of thieves—and something else. As a verb, to ring means to surround, encompass, encircle, to position round about. The round of people suggests a "circle of friends," or a group of like-minded people forming a closed circuit, a conspiracy or an orgy, or a salacious circle dance.

13. A ring, as shorthand for an orgy, compared chains of simultaneously linked homosexuals. Defining the extremely lewd and inherently demeaning terms derived from the Latin *spinter* (the upper left-arm bracelet worn by Roman women), Friedrich Karl Forberg remarked that "Spintries ... are those who, *linked like the rings of a bracelet,* thus accomplish the pleasures of Venus" [emphasis added] (1884/1966:181). Talvacchia's masterful commentary and translation of the *I Modi*, fully discussed this passage (Talvacchia, 1999:Chapter 3). The carol might invoke this image of linked sexual participants, one version of which, mutual masturbation, is still called a "circle jerk."

The rings might also refer to "rimming," which is the act of licking someone's anus. This form of stimulation, like all sex, was not recently invented, and a song as bawdy as *The Twelve Days* might include rimming in its catalogue of pleasures, an inventory no less complete or richly investigated than the orgiastic explorations of Hieronymous Bosch, whose paintings rest securely within high art's canon.

14. This usage can be found in *Romeo and Juliet:* "Twould anger him to raise a spirit in his mistress' circle (II:1)," used interchangeably with ring. Partridge (1947/1968:79,175) discussed this equivalence where the ring is simply equated with "The escry."

15. The heroine's name in this play derives from the Greek myth of a priestess named Hero. It's an odd name for a sweet girl. In the myth her lover (Leander) dies when swimming to their nightly tryst; Hero seems bad luck. Shakespeare conjured no reference to her original myth; the play bears neither structural resemblance to the ancient story nor

includes any content references. We might wonder why Shakespeare chose the name. To further the joke of the play's double-entendre title, the name Hero might be pronounced, her-O: cunt.

This makes sense of an otherwise slight line. When Don John insults her he says (III:2:93), seemingly redundantly, "Even she: Leonato's Hero, your Hero, every man's Hero." That odd repetition makes sense if an Elizabethan actor, knowing full well the word's twin meanings, increasing stretched out her name's pronunciation in deep sarcasm so that it sounded: "Even she: Leonato's Hero ... your HER-o.... every man's her-O," meaning that she was available to anyone.

16. Restad (1995) 19.

17. The emotional and physical release, the rank obscenity, of ancient festivals survived into post-industrial life. A sometimes raunchy Anglo-Spanish conceptual artist—who does not shy from using her own nudity—Ursula Martinez (in comments about her play the *Office Party Xmas 2007,* directed in London by Cal McCrystal for the Barbican Pit) remarked:

> Until the age of 18, I spent every summer holiday in Spain in my mum's village ... The whole summer was a long build-up to the local fiesta ... The entire village would participate in five days of dancing, drinking and eating. There was bullfighting, street bands, processions and fireworks. And the fiesta never really felt complete unless you "got off" with someone. Festivals, celebrations and fiestas have existed around the world since the earliest civilisations ... They exist because they play an important part in society and community life. They offer a sense of belonging and unity. They allow us respite from the normal rhythms of everyday life. They provide a chance to celebrate and let one's hair down and, in many festivals, finding a partner is an important part of the ritual.... I'm no anthropologist, but in some ways the office party is our contemporary replacement for the local festival. It's a pretty poor alternative—it doesn't serve the whole community and it only lasts a few hours—but it's what we've got. It's our chance to celebrate, to indulge, to be naughty and, above all, it's a chance to come together (Martinez 2007:1).

18. Nissenbaum (1996) 6.

19. While the effect would be the same with or without the extra word, in his printed version Frederic Austin apparently introduced another modification when he published the song, inserting the initial "On" at the beginning of each verse.

## *Chapter 14*

1. Precisely to regulate their performance, and coopt the celebration, in recent centuries "Carols would be sung by groups of singers called the town waits, who were appointed by the civic authorities to provide music for ceremonial occasions, often out of doors. The waits ... tramped the night streets ... hoping to be given food and money in exchange," for their performance (Weir and Clarke 2018:95). That is, in place of universal uproar, the government assigned well-behaved specialists to impersonate and professionalize a version of the old-time gaiety. (Just as, centuries before, to control capitalist excesses towns ran their own brothels staffed by municipally regulated professionals.) Authoritarians—or totalitarians hoping to supply a diverting enemy for an otherwise victimized population—continue to feed pacifying and ersatz folklore back to the consumerist-satisfied folk.

2. Partridge (1947/1968) 66.

3. Some, reluctant to acknowledge lewdness, suppose that *calling birds* simply "don't exist" and suggest instead "that 'calling' was a variant on 'colley', which itself was slang for birds colored coal black, or blackbirds" (Decker 1994:58). Despite an anonymous 1774 broadside of the song (Angus, Newcastle) the printed version of 1780 uses the regional English expression "four colly birds," colly

meaning "coal-black." We also find that "'Colly' is recorded as a verb meaning to turn the head from side to side, as some birds do" (Smith 1980:167). If you believe the audience was only partially served by the carol, the singers will introduce alterations so that, "colley becomes coaly becomes calling becomes Cornish ... by the whim of the singer" (Palmer 1991:5), but in his 1909 version of the song, Frederic Austin replaced "colly birds" for "calling birds" which became the standard, but he may have been recording an old usage and not inventing his own interpolation.

Substitutions beckon endlessly and if calling can become colley there is no reason why the process of extrapolation cannot continue indefinitely until we arrive at cully.

A Flogging Cully was "a debilitated lecher (commonly an old one), whose torpid powers require stimulating with a rod. One who hires a girl to flog him on his posteriors, in order to procure an erection." Or, there is the phrase Dark Cully, meaning "a married man that keeps a mistress, whom he visits only at night, for fear of discovery"—either case noted by Capt. Francis Grose in 1785. In many similar usages the cully was a kept mistress, masochist, or a short-term sex worker—none as innocent as Decker's hopeful direction.

Whimsical interpreters cannot substitute convenient words of partial resemblance but should address the actual song's likely vocabulary. That a word sounds like another offers scant basis for robbing a word of its identity. Dismissing oral tradition disrespectfully demotes the subject. Why shouldn't there be "calling birds"? There are *bird calls*. "Calling birds" does not corrupt some pristine earlier and more authentic, but unknown, version unless we distrust that the oral heritage can endure long and through much travail. The heirs of Homer grasped with ever-diminishing historical accuracy the world heescryibed yet each new generation sang the *Iliad*'s words about long-gone Bronze-age warriors and their smoldering city otherwise forgotten.

4. As Jacques Rossiaud, noted about the Medieval livelihood's lack of social isolation: "During ... family gatherings prostitutes ate, drank, danced and talked with the men, their mothers and their wives just like the assembled kin. They were not simply invited along to exercise their profession. Whatever resulted from the merrymaking took place within the family and festive space" (1988:69).

5. Karras (1996) 95.

## *Chapter 15*

1. Smith (1980) 167.

2. Regional speech, barely comprehensible beyond each home British district, obstructed vernacular speakers' exchanges (and still does). That fragmentation retarded the ascendancy of regional literatures to national prominence and, eventually, international recognition. An occupying force kept the splintered local parties skirmishing for crumbs of power until, at last, the overlords' linguistic and political loyalties merged with the natives. An old colonialist story, sadly repeated endlessly around the world.

3. Like Fauconbridge, English-speakers still think they can traverse the world speaking only their native tongue. How did Shakespeare know this would be the case? Otherwise he wouldn't have parodied the mono-lingual English traveler. Another mystery about that mysterious author.

4. "Frenchified" meant "clapped, poxed," as recorded in the influential work of the anonymous "E. B.," known only as a learned antiquarian gentlemen, whose c.1690–98 *A New Dictionary of the Terms Ancient and Modern of the Canting Crew,* was published to explain the talk of the underclass "In its Several Tribes of Gypsies, Beggars, Thieves, Cheats, &c. With an Addition of Some Proverbs, Phrases, Figurative Speeches, &c. Useful for all sorts of people, (especially foreigners) to secure their money and preserve their lives; besides very diverting and entertaining, being wholly new."

## Notes—Chapter 15

Capt. Francis Grose (*Classical Dictionary of the Vulgar Tongue*, 1785) mentioned the definition of the "French Disease" as, "the venereal disease, said to have been imported from France; French gout, the same. He suffered by a blow over the snout, with a French faggot stick, i.e. he lost his nose by the pox [syphilis]."

5. For these archaic meanings, see: Farmer Henley (1890). Other vernacular expressions include: French vice, a euphemism for all sexual malpractice; and curiously, a French pigeon, "A pheasant killed by mistake in the partridge season." French meant nothing good.

6. While the English blamed the French for delivering the Great Pox (as opposed to smallpox) every country preferred its own infectious villain.

Initially, it was called the "disease of Naples," but rapidly became the "French Pox" ... the Spanish disease in Holland, the Polish disease in Russia, the Russian disease in Siberia, the Christian disease in Turkey and the Portuguese disease in India and Japan ... [while] the Portuguese called it the Castillian disease, and a couple of centuries later ... the Tahitians call[ed] the venereal disease *Apa no Britannia*—the British disease (Porter 1997: 166).

7. Though we may now conceive "French" deportment as refined, in Shakespeare's time quite the opposite view prevailed. In *Romeo and Juliet* Mercutio taunts his lovesick best friend for inconstancy as they meet in a street (II:4):

MERCUTIO: ...Signior
 Romeo, bon jour! there's a French
  salutation
 to your French slop. You gave us
  the counterfeit
 fairly last night.
ROMEO: Good morrow to you both.
 What counterfeit did I give you?
MERCUTIO: The ship, sir, the slip; can
 you not conceive?
ROMEO: Pardon, good Mercutio, my
 business was great; and in
 such a case as mine a man may
  strain courtesy.

Today "the slip" may mean going AWOL as "French leave" represents a severe military infraction. More informally, the term refers to taking an abrupt and unceremonious departure without bidding the host or hostess a good-bye. And such a hasty exit was actually a French custom, whether or not fleeing creditors or, in Romeo's case, an old girlfriend. On the other hand, the French accuse some of English departure/leave, exactly the same hasty social offense.

8. Science's self-correcting method organizes information to arrive at truths subject to dis-proof. These scientific truths are neither moral nor religious truths but data-sets subject to a process of revision that ever-more-closely approaches some ultimate understanding of states-of-affairs. In this, too, we have externalized our own bodies as "the human can be rather crudely defined as a large mass of self-regulating cells" (Black 2018:34). Numerous bodily systems engage in feedback that regulates information to maximize function and keep us alive. Science tries to make sense of that juncture of our bodies and the world—something the carol singers attempted without science and its method but in a sensual self-confirmation that proved they were yet alive through mid-winter. To deny this, it seems to me, is to deny life.

9. Moderns are surprised at how similar are undomesticated 'animals' to humans, as if we were not, all along, creatures in nature. There's an interesting continuity here. All technology externalizes and amplifies our biological selves. A hammer (among the earliest technologies) amplifies a hand made stronger and indestructible. A microscope intensifies our vision. A telephone carries our voice over the next hill and shouts across continents to an intended hearer.

10. When used to defame, the word never refers back to a small furry feline. Pussy meant something dear and cherished, not an animal. Hence, not a redundancy, a "pussy cat" meant a darling kitten.

11. Farmer & Henley (1890).

## Chapter 16

1. The Bible maintains this differentiation throughout scripture, beginning when Noah "sent forth a dove to see if the waters were abated" (*Genesis* 8:8). Further along, *Genesis* specifically commanded: "Take me a heifer of three years old, and a she-goat of three years old, and a ram of three years old, and a turtledove, and a young pigeon" (15:9). Being named separately, a pigeon and turtledove are different creatures.

*Leviticus* contrasts an "offering of turtledoves, or of young pigeons" (1:14), the two being distinct, a specificity preserved throughout that book and into *Numbers,* as well as into Christian Scripture, where *Luke* repeats the details of Temple practices: "a sacrifice according to that which is said in the law of the Lord, A pair of turtledoves, or two young pigeons" (2:24).

The birds are invoked as part of the erotic scenery in an amorous poem that insinuated passionate sexual love into the Biblical canon, the *Song of Songs:* "The flowers appear on the earth; the season of the singing of birds is come, and the cooing [turtle]dove is heard in our land" (2:12). The ancient *The Song of Songs* likely pre-dates much of the Bible, becoming a sensual anomaly in the canon as *The Twelve Days of Christmas* survived to become the hedonistic aberration, bringing libertine possibilities into the scrubbed modern family-centered Christmas. Probably the same mechanisms of misprision operated in both cases.

2. In 1771, Samuel Foote's Prologue to his *Maid of Bath* cautions that "The gaming fools are doves, the knaves are rooks [strident crows]." According to cynics, there's one born every minute—a dove, that is. This connotation of guilelessness continued unabated into the nineteenth century and beyond, witnessed by Tennyson's 1850 *In Memorium* vi, "O somewhere, meek unconscious dove, Poor child, that waitest for thy love!"

3. The reverberations of his flinty Puritan up-bringing echo in Benjamin Franklin's 1757 quip "God helps them that helps themselves" (in *Maxims prefixed to Poor Richard's Almanac).* His remark echoes Sophocles (496–406 BCE) observation that "Heaven never helps the men who will not act" [Unknown Dramatic Fragment 228] a line that itself recognizes Aeschylus's (525–456 BCE) "God loves to help him who strives to help himself." [Fragment 223]

Contradicting Christian aesthetics, even before Nietzsche the feckless were neither everywhere admired nor seen as godly. The guileless are not always and in all places *a priori* regarded as faultless. Hindu or Protestant gauges of fate (destiny, Providence, karma) posit such folks the ready instruments of evil impulses otherwise to be thwarted by, apparently unearned, superior knowledge (Grace).

4. Smith (1980) 166.

5. Each Gospel presents a similar image: *Mark* (1:10), *Luke* (3:22), and *John* (1:32). For example, "And Jesus, when he was baptized, went up straightway out of the water: and, lo, the heavens were opened to him, and he saw the Spirit of God descending like a dove, and lighting upon him" (*Matthew* 3:16). Importantly the bird is *not* the incarnation of the holy spirit and does not contain, vessel-like, the Holy Spirit but is used as a metaphor, that the spirit descends "like" a bird, in a bird's gently fluttering manner that alighted, not like an arrow, thunderbolt, or a falling rock. Over the centuries, Christian artists created innumerable doves to illustrate this analogy.

Doves may represent messengers of peace and deliverance from anxiety, like Noah's dove (*Genesis* 8:8–12), but extra-biblically the dove is also a fallguy.

6. The absence of the Trinity, or any other Christian symbolism, from this "Christmas" song, has repeatedly irked certain observers. The Church's agents have tried to capture the song, from whose grasp, Thank God! it has repeatedly escaped.

Ace Collins claimed the carol as "one of the most important teaching tools of the Catholic Church" (2001:169). His claim is as utterly unsupported as sightings of the Loch Ness monster. Claiming victimhood, spokesmen for the Roman Catholic Church have attempted to commandeer this song, alleging it was an underground and subversive tutoring aid for catechism and other purposes. Nothing historical upholds this fanciful assertion. Protestants venerated the same symbols as the Catholics (symbols supposedly hidden within these verses to avoid Catholic martyrdom). This song was never property of any Church.

The most sacred pagan shrines had churches dropped on top of them—eliminating the possibility of heathen worship and, simultaneously, reaping the residual spiritual benefits of whatever cultic mysteries adhered to the memory of those places; and this song was treated similarly. (Christianity is not alone in this technique; Mosques were dropped on top of Hindu shrines and churches, notably the Hagia Sophia, and became Mosques, as did the Jews' tomb of Abraham in Hebron.) Pagan gods were renamed or—essentially unchanged in their attributes and names—absorbed whole into the roster of saints; pagan holidays, like Christmas, were added to the annual Christian cycle, their observance controlled by the Church when the celebrants refused to abandon their dearest traditions. Attempting, mostly successfully, to expunge the memory of a pre-Christian Europe, wherever possible a Christian coating varnished the landscape to commandeer pagan holy spots, wells and springs, mountains and caves, festivals, and songs.

7. Many doves wear a stripe around their neck that resembles a torque (or torc): a thin collar of twisted, often precious metal that encircles the throat in a single piece, unlike a necklace of chain, or loops that hangs limply from the neck. Torques were worn in antiquity among the Greco-Roman mediterranean cultures but especially by ancient Gauls and Britons. Some antique statues portray these highly significant body adornments that solemnly avouched the wearer's clan and tribal self-identification. The turtledove, and more vividly, the larger collared dove, wear a Celtic torque, the sign of unconverted pagan clan loyalty. These, like the golden rings, marked a distinctly non-Christian social order.

## Chapter 17

1. Palmer (1991: 5). Palmer also noted that the verse, about a partridge in a pear tree is varied to be sung as, "all in the bareley" (IBID). This reading obviates the need to construe the first day's gift as having a significant cost. It is also highly improbable. Or was sung by people who had already lost the carol's overall sense.

2. The history of the Christmas tree can be sketched briefly.

Hebrew Scriptures railed against astrology that invested meaning in the seasons ruled by the sky's whirling Zodiac, thereby attributing good or bad fortune to the stars' influence. Scripture denounces what can only be described as the making and keeping of proto-Christmas-trees:

The Lord says, Learn not heathenish ways, and be not dismayed at the signs of heaven, for the heathens are dismayed at them. For the customs of the people are vain: for one cuts a tree out of the forest, the work of the hands of the workman, with the ax. They deck it with silver and with gold; they fasten it with nails and with hammers, that it move not (*Jeremiah* 10:2–4).

These perduring fertility customs—linking the seasons, plants, winter death, and spring re-birth—caused Gervase of Tilbury (1150–1228) to remark that in England grain was exposed on Christmas night to acquire fertility from the falling dew. The tradition that trees and flowers blossomed on this night is first quoted from an Arab geographer of the tenth century. In a thirteenth-century French epic, candles are seen on the flowering tree, a visionary premonition of the Christmas tree. In England Joseph of Arimathea's rod was said to flower at Glastonbury—that "Vatican" of Celtic Britain. (When 3 September became 14 September, in the revised calendar of 1752, 2000 people watched to see if the Quainton thorn would bloom on

## Notes—Chapter 17

Christmas New Style, and when it did not, they refused to keep the New Style festival.) From this belief of the calends practice of greenery decorations (forbidden by Archbishop Martin of Braga, c. 575, because Druids venerated mistletoe) the Christmas tree developed. It was first definitely mentioned in 1605 at Strasburg, and introduced into France and England only in 1840 by Princess Helena of Mecklenburg and Albert, the Prince Consort, at which point other witnesses supply fresh testimony.

A luminary among English intellectuals, Harriet Martineau (1802–1876)—a novelist and an important Victorian economic and historical writer who comfortably read the most difficult scholarly German—bridged Germanic and British culture. Her 1838 *Retrospect* tried to make German culture appealing for her educated peers, and that book offered unimpeachable testimony to her recollection that, "I was present at the introduction into the new country [England] of ... the German Christmas-tree ... The tree was the top of a young fir, planted in a tub" (III. 182).

3. Heinrich Heine's easily dated work (conveniently titled, "Im Oktober 1849" as one of his suite of *Lazarus Poems*) pinpoints Teutonic feelings toward one of the holiday's most prominent ornaments:

> Germania, das große Kind,
> Erfreut sich wieder seiner
>   Weihnachtsbäume.
>
> (Germany, that big child
> Once again delighted with its Christmas tree).

4. Epstein (2000) 145.

5. The comparison of a person to a tree was established earlier in the play when Queen Elizabeth bemoans:

...an act of tragic violence:

> Edward, my lord, your son, our king, is dead.
> Why grow the branches now the root is wither'd?
> Why wither not the leaves the sap being gone?
>
> (*Richard III* II:2)

At Richard's London residence in Baynard's Castle (III:8) Buckingham's entreaty contains the description of: "the corruption of a blemished stock" and a "royal stock graft with ignoble plants." In Shakespeare's late, and zany, *Pericles, Prince of Tyre*, Pericles bemoans:

> You gods that made me man, and sway in love,
> That have inflamed desire in my breast
> To taste the fruit of yon celestial tree, (I:1)

The comparison is extended when Antiochus, whose daughter Pericles compared to a tree, likens Pericles to "so fair a tree/ As your fair self."

This metaphor continued down to 1807 and Wordsworth's *Force of Prayer:* "He was a tree that stood alone, And proudly did its branches wave" (xiii). The ultimate source for such comparisons may be *Isaiah* (11:1): "And there shall come forth a rod [branch] out of the stem [trunk] of Jesse, and a Branch shall grow out of his roots."

6. Those were the last days of their reign: the rumbling double-decked Routemasters yielded to sleeker (Borisbus) models, banishing their spiral staircases opening at the back. Twenty years before I nearly died when, to the wide-eyed amazement of the helpless conductor, I jumped aboard an already moving bus and barely held on to the rear platform standee's pole as forward momentum forced me backward, hanging out over the street and unable to pull myself upright with my left hand which was holding a stack of LP records freshly purchased from an Indian emporium at Marble Arch, whose proprietor checking out my purchases a few moments earlier had looked up and said "Ah, I see you like classical music," meaning Vilayet Khan and Bismilah Khan, as opposed to Bollywood soundtracks. Odd last words to have heard had I not been able to scramble back onto the moving platform. The buses' perfume, low-octane diesel fumes' memory-jogging soot: formerly the smell of London. All—the aromas, sights, cool damp air, textures of stone and wet asphalt sidewalks—compound a place and moment, with carolers.

## Notes—Chapter 17

7. Smith (1980:165). This seems a better theory than proposing that, "The first gift, a partridge in a pear tree, may have been inspired by an old drinking song and nursery rhyme, 'A Pie Sat on a Pear Tree'. There is also a French Canadian version called Une Perdriole" (Leach 1950, vol. II:1134). A perdreau is a young partridge.

8. Wong (2002) 14.

9. Even a French source has been suggested, since the Red Leg Partridge perches in trees more frequently than the common partridge, which was not successfully introduced into England until about 1770. This reading is only sustainable if the song is no older than the late eighteenth-century—an impossibility (Opie 1977: No. 100).

10. The only remotely pertinent citation (*Jeremiah* 17:11) offers a moral injunction that "As the partridge sits on its eggs, and hatches them not; so he that gets riches, and not by right, shall leave them in the midst of his days, and at his end shall be a fool." Meaning, that if a partridge stole the nest of another bird its eggs would be sterile—not a very good match for our song. The Bible also cites this bird, warning: "let not my blood fall to the earth before the face of the Lord: for the king of Israel is come out to seek a flea, as when one hunts a partridge in the mountains" (*1 Samuel* 26:20).

Along these lines, Decker noted that "Partridges may be a sly, chastening emblem signifying a lack of faith (it was said to be a partridge that betrayed the Holy Family's location to Herod) or fickleness (the bird abandons it young)" (1994:61). An unreliable or treacherous bird only makes sense if this verse is supposed to be morally allegorical, which contradicts the song's sly remainder that delivers description without a concluding moral.

11. Since the carol form virtually disappeared with the Reformation, being largely supplanted by the metrical psalm, if the song pre-dates the Reformation, some believe a "partridge in a pear tree" might have been a garbled version of a Latin phrase read in churches, *parturivit in apertis* ("gave birth in the open"). Such *soto vocce* substitutions delight schoolboys to this day. ("Peas and Potatoes Filias Fosdick" for "Pator et Filius Spiritus Sanctus" was a favorite replacement in the 1950s, which, and who knows? may still be sung in church choir by wily but cherubic-faced choristers—such adolescent humor never dies.) As part of the seasonal hijinx a naughty sleight-of-hand that replaced silly English for Church Latin seems wholly credible. Indeed, part of this verse's appeal may have been to satirize the Church, but why sing the verse twelve times? With a bit of metrical adjustment, such a puny joke could have been relegated to a later verse that repeated only a few times.

12. Smith (1980) 166.

13. Farmer (1897) iv, 247.

14. With words and music by Boudleaux Bryant, as performed by the Everly Brothers, in 1958 *Bird Dog* reached a peak Billboard position of #1. The lyrics can be readily found online.

15. That idiomatic language's ingeniousness appears in its mirror-image crowned with an equally sumptuous vocabulary: "Jewish folklore and Yiddish folk speech ... in its diversity, inventiveness, and range may be compared to the multilayered richness of Elizabethan English" (Leviant 2021:xii). An odd comparison at first glance but with further examination the correlation makes ever greater sense.

16. It's not as if folk-culture collectively lost its olfactory sense. Perhaps the first person to play music that could be called jazz, the cornetist Charles Joseph "Buddy" Bolden (1877–1931) composed a blues song called "Funky Butt." In the past and now, those living on society's fringes effortlessly trespass propriety's constraints, with the extra enjoyment of smashing such curbs.

17. This same root produced the variants of *perd,* such as the Latin *pēdare* and Petard, or petar, that early bell-shaped ordinance to breach a wall or gate upon which one is apt to be blown up (hoist) if careless—with its attendant sound as *Hamlet* jokes: "the engineer Hoist with his own petar" (III:4).

The explosive device suggested an

## Notes—Chapter 17

obsolete metaphor in the visual arts. The French used *pétard* to mean "fireworks" and referred to an outrageously wild or extravagantly colored painting purposefully designed to attract attention. The word went out of fashion after twentieth-century painting rendered the term outmoded: seeking more emphatic hues, painting loosed its tether to descriptive naturalism and intensified color ran wild.

18. Another fart-root borrowed from the French: *pétillant* refers to slightly sparkling wine. English oenophiles savor the delightful term "petillance" that describes the fine crackling of a fizzy wine upon the tongue when it is lightly carbonated but not so full of bubbles as Champagne or seltzer water.

19. Smith (1980) 166.

20. Decker (1994:58). Yet, there is no reason to introduce magical emblems when the song's other images carry distinctly non-supernatural identifications; that is, things in the song represent the world as it is, rather than serve as substitute emblems or magical utensils to transform the world. Symbols may indicate nothing in themselves (be abstract signs) and are arbitrarily assigned meaning (as in Morse code, the colors of traffic lights, etc.). But the images in the *Twelve Days* mean what they say they mean; we must figure out their original references, though long-gone and contextual. Rarely symbols, the verses mostly offer coded portrayals.

21. This comparison has never gone out of fashion. Gerald Murphy's 1929 oil painting *Wasp and Pear* (Museum of Modern Art, NY) playfully exaggerated the fruit's "hips" to mimic a woman. At the pear's bottom twinkles a star-shaped blossoming vulva-surrogate that makes semantic sense adjacent to the wasp that mounts (leaps) the pear. The wasp, after all, is a creature known for stinging, although bees and wasps also pollinate.

That wealthy and highly sophisticated friend of Cole Porter and Picasso, Murphy (1888–1964) likely riffed on Shakespeare's delightfully salacious line from *The Tempest* (V:1), when Aerial sings, "Where the bee sucks, there suck I," concluding "Merrily, merrily shall I live now/ Under the blossom that hangs on the bough." What flower? what tree? In an earlier play, Romeo had already specified.

22. Barnette (1997) 27.

23. Shakespeare invoked the same imagery in a less rhapsodizing love-struck tone when, akin to today's cursing street slang, in *Measure for Measure*, Lucio recalls being dragged before the presiding justice in a paternity claim:

I was once before him [the Duke] for getting a wench with child.
DUKE VINCENTIO: Did you such a thing?
LUCIO: Yes, marry, did I but I was fain to forswear it;/ they would else have married me to the rotten medlar (IV:3).

Spat out in disgust his word-choice could be translated into modern patois as that 'contemptible pussy'. In fairness to semantics and the play's indelicate context, the comparison to rancid fruit would more properly be rendered as 'that stinking cunt'. The twentieth-century's best translator of Provençal, Paul Blackburn absolved this word's usage and rendered *con* as cunt. Blackburn pointed out the word "derived from the same source as our word cuneiform" and that major Provençal poets "did not boggle at using it and other words at a similar level of the vocabulary. If it was good enough for the 9th Duke of Aquitaine, it's good enough for you. I figure these people 800 years ago were having a good time ... and why shouldn't you know about it?" (1978:274–5). And, also the mid-winter carol singers enjoyed their boisterous revels.

24. As recently as the 1950s, in Giuseppe di Lampedusa's posthumously published masterpiece, *The Leopard,* the medlar played a sly sexual reference. Having excused himself from his wife and children after dinner, the Prince, on his way to visit his mistress—accompanied in his coach by his worried confessor—finds: "The last medlar had scarcely been eaten when the carriage wheels were heard crunching under the porch" (di Lampedusa 1960:30). Eating an overripe medlar visually foretold

## Notes—Chapter 17

the evening's erotic adventure when visiting (making a call on) his compliant mistress.

25. Noticing and using such resemblances is hardly as primitive as it sounds. The outlook presages biological classification (phylogenic nomenclature) by cladistics. That taxonomic tool arranges species by retained anatomical features, inherited by shared descent. In this system animals (and subsequently studies of human artifacts subjected to such analysis) are categorized and sorted by whether or not they have one or more shared unique characteristics. Such shared features might indicate a common history and close relationship. These affiliations are graphically expressed as cladograms, a tree-shaped diagram.

26. When a women sits astride a reclining man while accomplishing intromission she takes a position now called the Cowgirl, because she rides him. When she faces her partner's feet a Reverse Cowgirl results, and the male views the pear-tree.

27. Blending the relevant images, Shakespeare set a brothel scene that invokes both the tree-as-person and prostitute-as-goose. The bordello's madame, the "Bawd" tries to coax the virginal princess into her new trade:

> Marry, whip thee, gosling: I think I shall have
> something to do with you. Come, you're a young
> foolish sapling, and must be bowed as I would have
> you (*Pericles, Prince of Tyre* IV:2).

28. Halliwell (1924). Presumably garbling a misheard "partridge in a pear tree," some version use "juniper tree" or "June apple tree." Or some dainty hearers, knowing the intended reference, bowdlerized the verse.

29. This was a pavilion in the *Hameau de la Reine*, the Queen's Hamlet, a recreational fantasy village built by Marie Antoinette near the Petit Trianon between 1783–1786 as a plaything and refuge from the court. Of the hamlet's twelve rustic cottages five were reserved for the queen. The remaining seven served functional agricultural purposes where she played at being a milkmaid, donning appropriately regal versions of rustic attire. While the queen often visited the mill and the dairy, the nearby Petit Trianon (built in 1768 by King Louis XV for his mistress Madame de Pompadour) was given to Marie Antoinette by her sexually dysfunctional husband Louis XVI. Here the queen maintained her private bedroom and boudoir, a small symmetrical room with a special feature. At her command two large and fiercely expensive Venetian mirrors raised from below the floor, elevated by counter-weighted cords drawn through hidden pulleys; the mirrors covered the window panes, sealing the room from the outside world but exposing all within it to multiple views.

30. Lynne Lawner (1988) heroically reconstructed the book, the *I Modi*. Lawner especially noted the volume's suppression as each generation winnowed what it inherited from previously unabashed collectors, until not a copy of the book remained. A more richly annotated version (and a forthright translation) appears in Talvacchia (1999). Intended for the aristocracy and intelligentsia, Aretino and Raimondi's deluxe volume of libidinous visual feasts, like Marie Antoinette's mirrored private bedroom, cost a lot, was carefully planned and, in its refinements, utterly differed from peasant's grubby and hasty sexual celebrations.

31. Something very close to this image appears in a drawing by Jackson Pollock, c.1939–40. In the course of eighteen months of therapeutic psychoanalysis, Pollock illustrated the male view of intercourse. The image appears in an untitled "psychoanalytic drawing," a sketch by which the often inarticulate and alcoholic artist supplemented his verbal sessions with Dr. Joseph Henderson. (Reproduced in Thaw and O'Connor 1978, Vol. III p. 117, cat # 555; also illustrated as Wysuph 1970: plate 57.) This crayon and colored pencil drawing on grey paper, 12¼ × 18¾ inches, is neither dated nor signed, although its approximate date, c.1937, was

determined from context: the period of his treatment.

32. Each denomination grapples with the mystery of a god who creates creatures to desire their own sex. Some sects welcome all who approach, appreciate the diversity of cosmic creation; some Churches tolerate and try to coax the deviant; others just stone to death degenerates; none of this range of erotic expression and recreation was even a problem raised by *The Twelve Days of Christmas*.

33. A slightly up-dated version of the exclamation, "God's wounds" would be the mild oath, "Gadzooks!", a contraction of God's hooks, being the nails of the Cross.

34. Wood (2003) 37.

35. Anal sex was a widespread practice among medieval English prostitutes, and presumably amateur women. Such is witnessed by the case of one John Rykener who was picked up as a transvestite streetwalker whose clientele was ignorant of his sex. In his testimony, "Rykener did not indicate that his performance 'as a woman' was in any way unusual." (Trial transcript quoted by Karras 1996:82.) Unlike denizens of brothels or bath houses, medieval streetwalkers resembled nonprofessional practitioners of casual sex or riotous holiday merrymakers, in that they did not take their clothes off but were, like the King of Misrule and his Christmas consort, opportunistic couplers in public spaces.

36. Shakespeare's Laertes may have wittily cautioned his sister Ophelia not to open her "chaste treasure" to Hamlet but, instead to play "in the rear of your affection, Out of the shot and danger of desire," thereby likening sex (and birth control, the "danger of desire") to a battle whose foremost target may be substituted by one rearward. Because Hamlet has not learned to prolong sex and master his ejaculations, he poses the "danger" of becoming pregnant, "his unmaster'd importunity." (Laertes's battle-of-the-sexes metaphor refers not just to jostling egos; the shot of cannon and muskets conjures spurting penises.)

> LAERTES: If with too credent ear you list his songs,
> Or lose your heart, or your chaste treasure open
> To his unmaster'd importunity.
> Fear it, Ophelia, fear it, my dear sister,
> And keep you in the rear of your affection,
> Out of the shot and danger of desire (*Hamlet* I:3).

In *Much Ado About Nothing*, Leonato is convinced that his daughter Hero has dishonored him, herself and her future husband. He rails at his insensate daughter, fainted upon the ground. Hero's betrayal is so terrible that even if she had saved her chastity by "only" engaging in anal sex, "the rearward of reproaches," that transgression would suffice to condemn her; rearward may not only mean "least."

> Wherefore! Why, doth not every earthly thing
> Cry shame upon her? Could she here deny
> The story that is printed in her blood?
> Do not live, Hero; do not ope thine eyes:
> For, did I think thou wouldst not quickly die,
> Thought I thy spirits were stronger than thy shames,
> Myself would, on the rearward of reproaches,
> Strike at thy life (IV:1).

Then, around 1594–5 when he wrote *Loves Labors Lost* (first performed and first published in 1598, in the Quarto edition, though perhaps the play was printed at an unknown earlier date), Shakespeare puts these words into the mouth of Adriano De Armado:

> Cupid's butt-shaft is too hard for Hercules' club;
> and therefore too much odds for a Spaniard's rapier.
> The first and second cause will not serve my turn;
> the passado he respects not, the duello he regards
> not: his disgrace is to be called boy; but his

## Notes—Chapter 18

glory is to subdue men. Adieu, valour! rust rapier! be still, drum! (I:2) "Cupid's butt-shaft is too hard for Hercules' club;" acknowledges that anal sex requires a firmer erection than vaginal, while "too much odds for a Spaniard's rapier" probably reflects Queen Elizabeth's rejection of a royal Spanish suitor such as had brought down her sister, Mary. The phrase "his/ glory is to subdue men" excludes women as sexual partners, and "rust rapier!/ be still, drum!" contrasts the penetrating sword/penis with the drum as vulva/vagina, a comparison used in verse 10 of *The Twelve Days* to contrast the drummers' matrix with the pipers' instrument.

Eric Partridge, notes that Shakespeare often uses the darkness (today we might say 'Where the sun doesn't shine') of the vagina in a "pun: that the semen-bullet shall hit her pudend, a difficult shot in the dark. Shakespeare often employs the metaphor of the penis-pudend archery or fencing." (See: entry on "darkness" 1947/1968:67.) In addition to archery or fencing, add Laertes' artillery assault.

37. The partridge might not even refer to a vaginal fart but the real article. The partridge in a pear tree could describe a sexual position today called the "reverse anal cowgirl."

In matters carnal, today's kinkiest sex was known and enjoyed long ago, beginning on the first day of Christmas. In an otherwise merry recitation of mainstream, "plain vanilla," pleasures, anal sex was, and remains, widely practiced by virtuous girls (Christian and otherwise) as a means of birth control. Its practice retains virginity while sampling recreational and pre-marital sex. Today in Catholic South America, heterosexual anal sex is reportedly more widely practiced than in Protestant lands precisely so that sexually active young ladies preserve their commodity-virginity until marriage.

38. For a good survey of Renaissance's social and theological objections to the woman-on-top positions see: Talvacchia (1999:120–124). Her notes on the classical and Church discussions of this "unnatural" situation are especially enlightening.

39. Rossiaud (1988:109 n. 9). Rossiaud further observes: "When François Villon speaks of fat Margaret astride him it is, he clarifies, 'so she would not spoil her fruit'. The position of the woman on top was quite possibly used with greater frequency by adulterous lovers or by concubines than by prostitutes and their clients." The "fruit" reference would certainly have been understood by singers of *The Twelve Days*'s first verse.

This verse perhaps refers back to, or reenforces, a reference to the Maids-a-Milking that can describe something now partially lost to us. Milking may describe repeated stroking; the *Kama Sutra* features a position called the "Milkmaid" in which an unmoving woman sitting atop a supine man "milks" the erect penis by adroitly contracting the vagina (with so-called Kegel contractions). If such a reference were intended, it was a desire cited twice in the song in different ways and in separate verses.

40. Early accounts include the phrase "my true love sent" me the gifts. In a 19th-century version "my mother" gave the gifts. By the twentieth century, and especially in America, the line appears as "my true love gave to me." Or the most popular version never changed and the recorded variants represent outliers.

## Chapter 18

1. The great American poet, Gilbert Sorrentino (1968:29) summed the situation's literary hazard: "Something plus something is not one thing." He warns of inorganic combinations. Yet, true to Sorrentino's admonition, this verse does not combine two things but muses on an event's two essential aspects.

2. The identical sum is found in a standard pack of modern playing cards and if the Joker is assigned the value of 1.234 the total equals the solar year. Each suit could represent a season of 13 weeks, and the 52 cards the weeks. But our song has no obvious suits and is not divided into fourths. Perhaps prehistoric

## Notes—Chapter 19

numerologists noticed that the calendar could be arithmetically compressed into a twelve day period judiciously placed astride the mid-winter solstice (facing backwards and forward like the double-faced Roman god Janus, namesake of the month, January). With this song's numerology, twelve days could stand for the whole year.

3. This is not an exclusively Latin gesture; an eighteenth-century English dictionary defines *Cunny Thumb'd* as "to double one's fist with the thumb inwards, like a woman," that is, not only as a woman would effeminately make fist but to create an image like the *figa* that mimics a woman's primary sexual characteristics, hence "cunny," cunt (see: Francis Grose, 1785).

In *Henry V*, while the English are encamped in Picardy, tensions rise in the beleaguered army's ranks; drenched, weary, ill with fevers, one of their number is to be executed for looting (III:6) and when Pistol's attempt to pardon him fails he curses an officer:

PISTOL: Die and be damn'd! and figo for thy friendship!
FLUELLLEN: It is well.
PISTOL: The fig of Spain!

"Figo" means "fuck you!", a curse that Pistol later snarls at the face of the disguised King who prowls the pre-dawn English campfires before the battle of Agincourt. Shakespeare's audience would have savored the highly derogatory references to Queen Elizabeth's erstwhile royal Spanish suitors: "The fig of Spain!"

4. Partridge (1947/1968) 156.

## Chapter 19

1. Carol singing, suppressed as pagan or Popish, survived only in remote English country districts and "not until the time of Dickens was it rediscovered by antiquarians and revived in English cities" (Lomax 1960:238). Door-to-door carol singers, or street corner carolers as I encountered, enact a nostalgic fixture of modern urban culture that yearns for a past that was long ago expunged in its original and vital form.

2. Greene (1935/1977) clvii.
3. Wardroper (1995) 10.
4. The lusty meaning of the late Medieval song *Greensleeves* has been mislaid, like the carol of the 12 gifts. Yet Greensleeves' antiquity, so deeply woven into tradition, grew patinated with venerably harmless old age—entirely at odds with its original racy context. Today Greensleeves prettily associates with sad sweet goodness.

Although the Stationers' Register had only begun recording printers' publications in 1557, by 1580 an 'up-dated' version was licensed to be printed in London as "A New Northern Dittye of a Lady Green-Sleeves." The song's authorship has been spuriously attributed to Henry VIII's infatuation with Anne Boleyn, while the tune was not written down until 1652.

It seems a lament sung by a "lover" flung aside by an ambitious courtesan. The wearer's green sleeves may once have functioned as the same sort of notice now indicated by the words "Red Light District." Today few of us wear uniforms that announce our trade (even when a first name is sewn on a shirt pocket) but the past was different. Vestimentary obligations to wear clothes that signaled rank or profession were common when Greensleeves was new and "Ordinances requiring prostitutes to wear some sort of visible sign can be found everywhere and were renewed frequently (in 1441 and 1458 in Avignon, 1468 and 1475 in Lyons, and so forth)," noted Rossiaud (1988:8 n.10).

Born just as Chaucer was dying, Rogier van der Weyden (1399–1464) painted a supposed prostitute *The Magdalene Reading*, 1438, (The National Gallery, London) wearing a green over-dress, greensleeves. Green robes in medieval art blare an alert and cautioned beholders, a little like a Hell's Angels outfit today. There's a famous example, and then some.

Originally, Robin Hood was a yeoman, not a maltreated vassal of Richard I, but Robin's story changed as folk-mythology modified, conforming to evolving ideas of honor, order,

## Notes—Chapter 19

and justice. He moved from Barnsdale Forest to Sherwood Forest; as a minor figure in *Ivanhoe,* Sir Walter Scott contrived to make him a Saxon-Englishman resisting the Norman overloads however, throughout his many other transformations, this forest-dwelling outlaw wore Lincoln Green. Green was probably a disreputable color. In *Henry IV part 1,* when Falstaff tries to impress the Prince of Wales with his courage in the face of adversity, he claims to have been set upon by ruffians who robbed him:

But, as the devil would have it,
three misbegotten
knaves in Kendal green came at my back (II:4).

Aside from its camouflage value, perhaps Kendal Green or Lincoln Green associated with outlawry or the disreputable: the male version of wearing greensleeves.

5. Decker (1994) 58. Frederic Austin's 1909 version differs slightly from the present form; he arranged the personnel of verses 9 through 12 in a different order.

6. When it was completed London Bridge had only a chapel at its center but squatters' houses quickly appeared, replaced by substantial buildings. By the sixteenth century massive houses piled five stories high on the wooden bridge. The threat of its collapse was real.

7. John Locke, *Two Treatises of Government,* 1690, Chapter V Section 27.

8. The creed of economic independence molds today's young Conservatives (political heirs of Thatcher and Reagan), who scorn mutuality as 'socialism'. Transatlantic versions of Tea Party zombies would hardly believe themselves Scrooge's moral legatees because they annually wrap themselves in modern Christmas and sanctimoniously hold aloft the bitter Cross instead of compassion's beacon.

9. Dickens artfully resurrects just such an un-named song of Ebenezer's youth. When the Ghost of Christmas Present takes him to a miner's hut Ebenezer listens as, with his impoverished family gathered round, "an old man, in a voice that seldom rose above the howling of the wind upon the barren waste, was singing them a Christmas song; it had been a very old song when he was a boy; and from time to time they all joined in the chorus."

10. Dickens buried hints about Scrooge's age throughout the story, in recollections that were period-specific. His readers would have recognized Scrooge's manners and customs as obsolete. So, when "Scrooge looked fixedly at" the door knocker that suddenly resembled his dead partner Marley, Scrooge, though startled, resolutely "walked in, and lighted his candle ... and he did look cautiously behind [the door], as if he half expected to be terrified with the sight of Marley's pigtail sticking out into the hall." Late eighteenth-century style decreed that men wear pigtails—a fashion long-gone for Dickens' audience who might recall grandfather's hairstyle. The Pigtail was a "Plait or queue of hair hanging down from the back of the head or the back of a wig [attested from] 1688" but, by 1804 the military pigtail was shortened and finally was "cut off in 1808" (Cox: 1966:113). That last date—forty years before the story takes place—supplies a terminus for fashionably wearing this hairstyle.

11. The situation developed pretty much the same on the North Atlantic's western shore. American clergy and business leaders influenced the early nineteenth-century press to help amend the holiday, to reform its naughty ways. American Christmas—gradually reconfigured as a family-centered festival to nurture the growing Victorian middle-class—minimized the holiday's drinking, begging, fornicating, feasting, mumming, gambling, and fighting. Most importantly, the holiday provided a lengthy respite from work, as Scrooge begrudged his employee Bob. The crusade was guided by the reconfigured patron saint of consumerism, Santa Claus, a large elf unrecognizable to elders who had known his earlier incarnations. Only in 1856 Massachusetts made Christmas Day a state holiday, which undoubtedly vexed Puritan ghosts of Christmas Past who, by repeatedly trying to assassinate the holiday, had worked assiduously to expel its infection from the pure New World.

# Works Cited

Arcangeli, Alesandro. "Dance and Health: The Renaissance Physician's View," *Dance Research*, April 2000 vol. 18, No. 1.
Baggini, Julian. *A Short History of Truth: Consolations for a Post-Truth World* (London: Quercus), 2017.
Baines, Anthony. *Bagpipes*, Occasional Papers in Technology 9 (Oxford: Oxford University Press), 1973.
Barnette, Martha. *Ladyfingers and Nun's Tummies* (New York: Random House), 1997.
B.E. *A New Dictionary of the Terms Ancient and Modern of the Canting Crew* (London: W. Hawes, P. Gilbourne, and W. Davis) c.1690–98; Reprinted, London: Smith, Kay, 1899.
Best, Henry. Reprinted in *Being the Farming Account Books of H. Best 1641*, Surtees Society, 1857.
Black, Sue. *All that Remains: A Life in Death* (UK: Black Swan), 2018.
Blackburn, Paul. *Proensa: An Anthology of Troubadour Poetry*, ed. George Economu (Berkeley: University of California Press), 1978.
Bourreau, Alain. *The Lord's First Night* (Chicago: University of Chicago Press), 1995/1998.
Bunting, Basil. "Lecture on 'Realism,'" in *Basil Bunting on Poetry* (Baltimore: Johns Hopkins University Press), 1999.
Camille, Michael. *Mirror in Parchment: The Luttrell Psalter and the Making of Medieval England* (Chicago: University of Chicago Press), 1998.
Cipolla, Carol M. *Clocks and Culture: 1300–1700* (New York: W.W. Norton), 1977.
Collins, Ace. *Stories Behind the Best-Loved Songs of Christmas* (Grand Rapids, MI: Zondervan), 2001.
Cox, J. Stevens. *An Illustrated Dictionary of Hairdressing and Wigmaking* (London: Hairdressers' Technical Council), 1966.
Croft-Coke, Rupert. *Sherry* (New York: Knopf), 1956.
Decker, Andrew. "Traditions: The Twelve Days of Christmas," *Traditional Home Holiday* 1994.
Dekker, Thomas. *The Wonderfull Yeare 1603, wherein is shewed the picture of London lying sick of the plague*, 1603.
Dickens, Charles. *A Christmas Carol* (New York: Atheneum), 1940/1966.
Didier, Eugene L. "Christmas," *New York Times*, 14 December 1901.
di Lampedusa, Giuseppe, trans. Archibald Coquhoun, *The Leopard* (New York: Pantheon), 1960.
Epstein, Alan. *As the Romans Do: The Delights, Dramas, and Daily Diversions of Life in the Eternal City* (New York: William Morrow/HarperCollins), 2000.
Fallows, David. *Introduction and Inventory: Oxford, Bodleian Library Ms. Canon, Misc. 213* (Chicago: University of Chicago Press), 1995.
Farmer, John S. *Merry Songs and Ballads* (privately printed), 1897.

# Works Cited

Farmer, John S., and W.E. Henley. *Slang and Its Analogues: Past and Present* (London: Harrison and Sons), 1890.
Fernández-Armesto, Felipe. *Near A Thousand Tables: A History of Food* (New York: Free Press), 2002.
Forberg, Friedrich Karl. *Manual of Classical Erotology* (New York: Grove Press), 1966, facsimile of 1884.
Galambush, Julie. *The Reluctant Parting* (San Francisco: Harper), 2005.
Girouard, Mark. *Cities and People* (New Haven, CT: Yale University Press), 1985.
Gomme, Alice Bertha. *The Traditional Games of England, Scotland, and Ireland* (London: David Nutt), 1894.
Graves, Robert. *The White Goddess* (New York: Farrar Straus, and Giroux), 1948/66.
Greene, Richard Leighton, ed. *The Early English Carol* (Oxford: Clarendon Press), 1935/1977.
Greene, Richard Leighton. *A Selection of English Carols* (Oxford: Clarendon Press) 1962.
Greer, Germaine. *Shakespeare's Wife* (New York: HarperCollins), 2007.
Grose, Francis. *Classical Dictionary of the Vulgar Tongue* (London: Printed for S. Hopper), 1785.
Halliwell, James Orchard. *Dictionary of Archaisms and Provincialisms* (London: Routledge), 1924.
Harrison, William. *Description of England* ed. Georges Edelen (Washington/New York: Dover & the Folger Library), 1587; 1969/1994.
Hollander, Lee M., trans. *Heimskringla: History of the Kings of Norway* (Austin: University of Texas Press), 2007.
Husk, William Henry. *Songs of the Nativity: Being Christmas Carols, Ancient and Modern* (London: John Camden Hotten), 1868.
*Isaac Newton's personal notebook* (Holograph in the Pierpont Morgan Library, New York) in Newton's own hand, with an annotation in an unknown hand: "Isacus Newton hunc librum/ possidet test: Edvardo Secker pret: 2d 0f." 1659.
Karras, Ruth Mazo. *Common Women: Prostitution and Sexuality in Medieval England* (New York: Oxford University Press), 1996.
Kazmierczak Manzione, Carol. "Sex in Tudor London," quoting Guildhall Library record of the Bridewell Hospital [MF511/II] in *Desire and Discipline: Sex and Sexuality in the Premodern World*, ed. Jacqueline Murray and Konrad Eisenbichler (Toronto: University of Toronto Press), 1996.
King, Ross. *Michelangelo and the Pope's Ceiling* (New York: Penguin), 2003.
Lawner, Lynne. *I Modi: The Sixteen Pleasures* (Evanston, IL: Northwestern University Press), 1988.
Leach, Maria, ed., The *Standard Dictionary of Folklore, Mythology and Legend* (New York: Funk and Wagnalls), 1950.
Leviant, Curt. "Introduction to Sholem Aleichem," in *Moshkeleh the Thief*, trans. Leviant (Philadelphia: Jewish Publication Society), 2021.
Lomax, Alan. *The Folk Songs of North America* (New York: Doubleday & Company), 1960.
Maines, Rachel P. *The Technology of Orgasm* (Baltimore: The Johns Hopkins University Press), 1999.
Martinez, Ursula, and Christopher Green. "A Bit of a Do: On Office Christmas Parties," *The Guardian*, Work news & features section, Saturday 1 December 2007.
McCarntey, George. "The Reel Christmas," *The Weekly Standard*, 27 December 1999.
McDowell, Edwin. "Some Say Meese Report Rates an 'X,'" *New York Times*, 21 October 1986.
McGee, Harold. *On Food and Cooking* (New York: Charles Scribner), 1984.
Monsarrat, Ann. *And the Bride Wore...: The Story of the White Wedding* (New York: Dodd, Mead & Company), 1973.

## Works Cited

Morris, Desmond. *Manwatching: A Field Guide to Human Behavior* (New York: Harry Abrams), 1977.
Nissenbaum, Stephen. *The Battle for Christmas* (New York: Alfred Knopf), 1996.
Olson, Elizabeth. "Twelve Days of Christmas, 364 Gifts and 1% Inflation," *New York Times*, 25 December 2014.
Opie, Iona, and Peter. *The Oxford Dictionary of Nursery Rhymes* (Oxford: Oxford University Press), 1977.
Palmer, Roy. "Twelve Ways with Twelve Days," *English Dance and Song* vol. 53, No. 4, 1991.
Partridge, Eric. *Shakespeare's Bawdy: A Literary & Psychological Essay and a Comprehensive Glossary* (London: Routledge), 1947, revised 1968.
Porter, Roy. *The Greatest Benefit to Mankind: A Medical History of Humanity* (New York: W.W. Norton), 1997.
Rand, Harry. "It's February in the Early Fifteenth Century: What's For Dinner?" in *The Primacy of the Image* (Leiden, Netherlands: Brill), 2017.
Rand, Harry. *Rumpelstiltskin's Secret: What Women Didn't Tell The Grimms* (London: Routledge), 2020.
Rand, Harry. "What the Kitchen Maid Made: Vermeer's Kitchen Maid," *Bulletin van Het Rijksmuseum*, Amsterdam, Autumn 1999.
Restad, Penne L. *Christmas in America* (New York/Oxford: Oxford University Press), 1995.
Rossiaud, Jacques. *Medieval Prostitution*. Trans., Lydia G. Cochrane (Oxford: Basil Blackwell), 1988.
Russett, Cynthia Eagle. *Sexual Science: The Victorian Construction of Womanhood* (Cambridge: Harvard University Press), 1989.
Smith, Gordon Ross. "Lyrical Indecencies in The Twelve Days of Christmas," *University of Hartford Studies in Literature* vol. 12, No. 3, 1980.
Sorrentino, Gilbert. *The Perfect Fiction* (New York: W. W. Norton), 1968.
Talvacchia, Bette. *Taking Positions: On the Erotic in Renaissance Culture* (Princeton, NJ: Princeton University Press), 1999.
Thaw, Eugene Victor, and Francis Valentine O'Connor, eds. *Jackson Pollock: Catalogue Raisonné* (New Haven: Yale University Press), 1978.
Wardroper, John. *Lovers, Rakes and Rogues: Amatory, Merry and Bawdy Verse from 1580 to 1830* (London: Shelfmark Books), 1995.
Weir, Alison, and Siobhan Clarke. *A Tudor Christmas* (London: Jonathan Cape), 2018.
Weiss, Peter, trans., and Geoffrey Skelton. *The Persecution and Assassination of John-Paul Marat as Performed by the Inmates of the Asylum at Charenton Under the Direction of the Marquis de Sade* (New York: Atheneum), 1966.
Whicher, George F. *The Golliard Poets: Medieval Latin Songs and Satires* (New York: New Directions), 1949.
Wong, Kate. "Taking Wing," *Scientific American*, January 2002.
Wood, Michael. *Shakespeare* (New York: Basic Books), 2003.
Wysuph, C. L. *Jackson Pollock: Psychoanalytic Drawings* (New York: Hudson Press), 1970.
Young, Michael. *The Metronomic Society* (London: Thames and Hudson), 1988.

# Index

Numbers in ***bold italics*** indicate pages with illustrations

abstinence 185; from drinking 39
adultery 127, 173, 213*n*39; outlawing of 173; *see also* infidelity
Aesop 101
Agas, Ralph ***115***
*Agas Map of London* ***115***
agricultural economy and worldview 95, 96
agriculture: animal husbandry and 4, 153; calendar 197*n*6; Christian interventions in 190*n*13; *Museum Rusticum et commerciale* 196*n*5; peasants 59, 133; rhythms of rural life according to cycles of 37–38, 104–105, 119, 153; Roman god of 30; serfs 82; Versailles, Marie Antoinette's play vers 211*n*29; workers 95, 104
Albert (Prince Consort of Mecklenburg) 208*n*2
Albert (Prince of England) 155
"all fall down" *see* falling down
Ambrose 198*n*1; *see also* St. Ambrose
the Amish 190*n*9
Anabaptists 190*n*9
anachronisms 15, 72, 147; culinary 201*n*17; language 103; manners 157
Anacreontic Society 194*n*2
anal sex 212*n*35, 212*n*36, 213*n*37; *see also* anus; oral sex; sex
animal husbandry 4, 153
animal imagery: as symbols of human desire 101; *see also* bird imagery
animal kingdom 112
animals: Aesop's representation of 101; baiting of 39; dressing or costuming as 33, 38, 41, ***63***, 133; exotic ***83***; farm or farmyard 61, 101, 171, 192*n*2; fecundity of 98; milk and 97; milking of 94, 95, 99, 104; people as ensouled versions of 107; possessed by Satan 23; post-partum 104; sex with 10; yoked 104; *see also* farms; livestock; milk
Anouilh, Jean 79–80
*Anthony & Cleopatra* (Shakespeare) 123
anti-authoritarianism 107
anti-clericalism 13
anti-language 11
anti-pornography associations 195*n*12; *see also* pornography
Antiochus 208*n*5; *see also Pericles, Prince of Tyre* (Shakespeare)
anus 164, 194, 202*n*14; *see also* oral sex; vulva
"apple tree" as euphemism for sex 162–163; "June apple tree" 211*n*28; *see also* fruit trees
apples, games involving 124
archaic: beliefs 188; expressions 205*n*5; slang 2; usage of verbs 191
Aretino, Pietro 55, 167
arse: Elizabethan understandings of 168; farts emanating from 168; *open arse* as slang for medlar fruit 162–163; *see also* anal sex; ass; farts
arsehole: "Hen's Arsehole" as slang for the mouth 149
Ashton, John 133
ass 168; sex and 164; *see also* anal sex; arse; farts
Austin, Frederic 215*n*5
"Away in a Manger" (carol) 15
Ayto, John: *Dictionary of Rhyming Slang* 187*n*4

babies, delivering of 123
baby formula 95

221

# Index

baby goats 137
bagpipes 73; dancing to sound of 87; as penis/scrotum 75, 76, **78**, 194*n*3; sexual connotations of 76; *see also* blowjob; penis
bandorla 69
banjar 69
banjo 68–69; skin-headed 193*n*1
bastards 124, 128, 129
bathhouse 192*n*7
Bavarian Märzen (March Beer) 189*n*2
bear baiting 123
The Beatles 196*n*2
*Becket* (play) (Anouilh) 79
Becket, Thomas à 79
Bede (monk) 28
Beltine, feast of 197*n*7
Berlin, Irving 190–191*n*3; *I'm Dreaming of a White Christmas* 191*n*3
Berry, Duc de **58**
Best, Henry 73
bird imagery and slang 12, 102–103; "to bird" as reference to "calling," i.e. hunting for girls 139–140; "birds" as British reference to girls 12, 102; bird's nest reference to pubic hair 138; as bryd(e) or bride 138; "chicks" as reference to young women or girls 12, 102, 138, 143; "cock" as penis 103, 138; doves and turtledoves as symbols of chaste/unchaste love 151–152; "fledglings" as reference to human infants 137; "flipping the bird" as slang for "Fuck You!" 173; as girl or woman 138; "goose" as reference to foolhardy, foolish, or rash females 112, 115; "goose" as reference to prostitute 12, 113–115, 118; "goose" as reference to simpleton 112; "goose" as reference to venereal disease 10, 12; "partridge" as slang for prostitute 159–160; "quail" as slang for prostitute or promiscuous woman 160; salacious references connected to male birds 103; sexual jargon and 102; "turkey" as reference to moron 112; "Winchester goose" as reference to Southwark prostitutes 12–13, 187*n*6; woman-as-bird 138; *see also* birds; fowling
bird, vulva, fruit as symbolic trio 173
birds (general category of): Christmas season and 101; female 102, 149; fiery nature of 102; game 159; as juvenile of any feathered animal 137; making them get drunk (forced inebriation) 201*n*17; male 103; as mentioned in a general fashion in *Twelve Days of Christmas* 101, 125, 137–138, 149; in Old English usage 137; *see also* blackbirds; calling birds; chickens; cock; doves; eagle; fowl; geese; grouse; hens; partridge; peacocks; pigeons; quail; sparrows; swans; turkey
"bird's nest" (slang for pubic hair) 138, 165; *see also* pubic hair
birth of a child: Kindsfuß given on the occasion of 29; Messiah 39, 40; sex as necessary component of 95; virgin 32, 81
Bishop of Milan 198*n*1
Bishop of Winchester 13, **77**, 113, 187*n*6, 198*n*4, 199*n*5
bishops **78**
*The Black Arrow* (Stevenson) 103
black bird 198*n*2
black clothing as fashion uniform 113
black color: bird 198*n*2; coal-black 203*n*3; *see also* colley
Black communities, US 24
Black Death 178, 188*n*2
black wine 201*n*17
blackbirds 203*n*3; *see also* birds
Blackburn, Paul 210*n*23
blackening of the face 133
Blackfriars 190*n*8
blow job (slang for fellatio) 76, 194*n*1; *see also* fellatio; oral sex
blown over the snout (slang for catching the pox) 205*n*4
blown up (slang for hoisted) 209*n*17
Bocskay, Georg **164**
Bolden, Charles Joseph "Buddy" 209*n*16
*Book of Common Prayer* 129, 133
Borcht, Pieter (or Peter) van der **84, 85, 86, 87**, 88, 117
bordellos 20, 61; private 18; Southwark 188*n*6; state-run 17; *see also* brothels; leaping-house; whorehouse
Bosch, Hieronymus **78**, 202*n*13
Boston, Massachusetts 15, 43
bottle feeding 95; *see also* baby formula; lactation
Bourne, the Rev. Henry 34, 189*n*9
bowdlerization: of carols 163; of Christmas 15; of *Greensleeves* (song) 177; of *Twelve Days of Christmas* 211*n*28
Boxing Day 189*n*4
Bradford, William 41

# Index

breasts (human female mammary glands) 96–100, 196n7; *see also* lactation; milk
bride 131, 201–202n5; *see also* groom; marriage
Bridewell Hospital, London 18, 89
Brigantia *see* Brigit
Brigit (goddess) 197n7
Brooks, Phillips 16
brothels 14; community-run (Medieval) 17; *Holland's Leaguer* (Southwark Brothel) *77*; *see also* bordellos; leaping house; whorehouse
Brown, Rita Mae 174
Brueghel, Pieter (or Peter) (the Elder) 87, 117, 141; Borcht's works after *84*, 88; *Kermis at Hoboken* 87–88; *Peasant Dance 74*
bryd(e) or bride: as bird 138; *see also* bride
Bunting, Basil 145
Burns, George 130

"call": "call girl 140; called to the bar" 141; paying or receiving, in sense of a visit 140; as reference to a decoy bird or lure 139; "tapsters" responding to 140
"calling": as answering to a charge or career 141; "to bird" as implicit reference to 139; as responding to a summons 139
"calling birds": as reference to a summons to a party 153; as reference to pimping 139; as reference to working girls 141as referencing plans for a social or flirtatious visit 140; *see also colley*; "four calling birds"
Candlemas Day 197n6, 197n7
candles 30, 72, 182, 184; on Christmas tree 207n2; *see also* Candlemas Day
cannibalism 195; "Cannibals" (illuminated manuscript) *83*
cant, canty, canting 12; class-specific nature of 157; common 118, 202n12; criminal 11; medieval 200n11; *New Dictionary of Terms… of Canting Crew* ("E.B.") 217n4; *see also* jargon
carnality 4, 57, 153; dancing and 23; as sins of the flesh 98; *see also* lust
carol singers/carolers 7, 9, 14, 121; bawdy references made by 3; "chambering" (fornication), whoring, and generalized misbehavior linked to 34–36;

jailing of 17–26; Robin Hood as natural ally of *38*; *see also* minstrels
carols and caroling: American 16; amnesia regarding history of 26–27; beer-drinking and 38; *carol* and *carole*, origin of word 21; *carolle* (dance) 22, 61, 154; Catholic and Puritan opposition to 25, 45, 136; "chambering" associated with 34; as childrens' song 24; Church's opposition to 22–23, 25–26, 56; courtly love rebutted by genre of 59; cultural amnesia regarding 26, 16–27; as "dance-song" 24; definition of 15; "dirty" 18, 21; disreputability or indecency of 21, 22–25; drumming in 69; earthiness of 24; Easter 20; erotic associations of 25; as "filthy heathen songs" 26; gifts and gift-giving associated with 29; harsh realities reflected in 14; history and definition of 15–16; human nature reflected in 4; Husk as first collector of 47; jail as punishment for singing 17–26; laundering of filthy history of 25; lewdness of 21, 37; magic and witchcraft, associations with 44; modern 15–16; nature-cults and 44; old-time 16–17, 24–25, 37; original form and intent of 2, 15, 26; as pagan dance song 21, 23; paganism and 32; Passiontide 20; as popular religious songs 19; pre–Christian 21; religious 23; as religious songs 19; as remnant of Papistry 25; as ring-dance 25; as rowdy secular songs 20; salaciousness of 69; as "song in general" 24; Victorian 190n1; whoring associated with 35, 56; wickedness of 34; *see also* Christmas carols; *Twelve Days of Christmas*
Carrier, Donald 9
Carter, William 197n6
*Catholic Encyclopedia* 197n6
Catholics and Catholicism: Anabaptists oppressed by 190n9; anal sex and 213n37; carol falsely claimed to be teaching tool of 206n6; caroling perceived as Catholic practice by Protestants 26; English 25, 201n4; marriage sacraments 130; prohibitions against caroling issued by 17, 25, 45; Roman Catholic Church 13, 130; Roman celebrations around January 1 condemned by 31; suppression of "lusty" versions of Christmas by 178–179; T.S. Eliot as

223

# Index

convert to 200$n$12; Yule celebrations, attempts to suppress 39
Cave, Edward 65
celibacy **58**, 98; *see also* abstinence
Celtic feasting and fertility rites 32, 108, 182; Bridgit as goddess of 197$n$7; Brigantia as goddess of 197$n$7; Glastonbury as center of 207$n$2; Matres as goddesses of 32, 105; Mother Earth as earth-goddess of 32
Celtic-speaking regions of United Kingdom 145; Ireland 197$n$7
Celtic torque 207$n$7
Celts 197$n$7
chain-number song 46, 47, 49, 67
chains (jewelry, as euphemism for orgy) 202$n$13
"chambering" (euphemism for fornication) 34, 37, 55, 62, 90, 92, 167; caroling associated with 35; "to indulge in lewdness" 35; *see also* fornication; leaping; screwing; sex
chaste Christmas, new invention of 177
chaste female 59, 117
chaste love, turtledoves mistaken as symbols of 151–152
chastity 5, 11, 60, 212$n$36
Chaucer, Geoffrey 151; *Canterbury Tales* 200$n$12; death of 214$n$4; "Manciple's Tale" 199$n$10
cheveril (kid-skin leather) 114, 199$n$7
chickens 96; as generic "birds" (as opposed to "fowls") 137; *see also* cock; hen
"chicks": as reference to sexually available women or girls 12, 102, 138, 143; *see also* bird imagery and slang
Child, Francis J. 38
Christianity: Brigit changed to St. Brigit by 197$n$7; caroling remade by 47; dove as symbol of Jesus in 152; hatred of caroling and Yule songs 25, 33; "the lady" in 54; Lent and 195$n$8; Lithuania's conversion to 188$n$6; old and new 25; partridge as being outside of 159; Puritans and 43; usurpation of Christmas 44; worldview of 23; *see also* Catholicism; Protestantism Puritanism
Christians 1, 20; authority of the Bible according to 39; devout 30, 34; dread of pagan Christmas season 29–32, 34; "Leap-Christians" 64; modern 167; pious 16; pre–Christians 21

Christianizing 192$n$9, 197$n$6; of Europe 32; of Yule 28
Christmas: blossoming of trees and flowers on eve of 207$n$2; bowdlerizing of 15; carol-singing currently linked to concepts of 46, 90; chaste version of 177; clergy opposition to carol-singing on 23; Father Christmas **183**, **185**, **186**; global celebration of holiday 136; licentious celebrations of 52; "misrule" of 37; old carols associated with 20; as pagan festival 29–32; pre–Christian versus theological 136; in Puritan America (early 18th-century) 43; repeal of 1681 law banning Christmas festivities 133; as season of drinking, obscene caroling, fighting, and whoring 189$n$10; suppression of "lusty" versions by Catholics and Puritans 178–179; turkey as holiday luxury food of 40, 111; Victorian 154, 177; Victorian reinvention of 16, 37; war on 4; *see also* Saturnalia; Yuletide
"Christmas boxes" 189$n$4
*Christmas Carol see* Dickens
Christmas carols/songs 1–2, 8; bawdy 42; Catholic Church's condemnation of 17; hidden indecency of 10, 14, 17; old 20; origins as pagan round dances 17; pagan rituals linked to 31; pagan round dances as origin of 17
Christmas festivals 57, 80, 90; repeal of 1681 law banning Christmas festivities 133
Christmas Fool 39
Christmas goose 111; *see also* geese and goose
Christmas tree: as German cultural practice 155, 208$n$2, 208$n$3; history and origins of 207–208$n$2
circle (as reference to the vulva) 131, 163; *see also* vulva
circle dance 54, 74, **85**, **117**, 130, 188$n$12, 202$n$12
"circle jerk" as euphemism for mutual masturbation 202$n$13; *see also* masturbation
"circle of friends" 202$n$12
the Clink (London prison) *13*
Clink Street, London *13*
clitoris 99
Clovis, conversion of 188$n$6
coal-black 203$n$3; *see also* colley
cob (male swan) 103; *see also* swans

224

# Index

Cock(e) Street, London **115**
cockles: "hot cockles" (game) 124; *see also* games
cock (male poultry bird, including chicken and pheasant) 138, 148, 149; *see also* cock (slang for penis); peacock
cock pits (cock fight) 123
cock (slang for penis) 103, 138
cock-sure (slang for social climber) 193$n$9
Cokke Lane, London 198$n$4
Cold War 98
Coleridge, Samuel Taylor 72, 189$n$8
Collared Dove of England 152, 207$n$7; *see also* doves
*colley* (slang for blackbirds) 203–204$n$3
Collins, Ace 206$n$6
"colorful" language 3; *see also* cant; jargon
*Comedy of Errors* (Shakespeare) 202$n$9
common canty 118, 202$n$12; *see also* cant
common folk 26, 30; Church and 104; marriage as celebrated by 130; verbal pranks of 132
Common Prayer: *Book of Common Prayer* 129, 133
common speech 10
"common woman" (slang for streetwalker) 187$n$6; *see also* harlot; prostitute; whore
commoners 59, 63, 79, 82, 83; courtroom and 146
Commonwealth 62, 65; preacher of 130
consumerism 108; Christmas and 185, **185**; industrial modernization and 95; Santa Claus as patron saint of 215$n$11; Scrooge and 184
consummation (sexual) 72, **87**, 99, 108, 132
copulation 10; Christmas 76; Weiss on 192$n$9; *see also* fornication; fucking; leaping; sex
courtesan 214$n$4; in *Comedy of Errors* (Shakespeare) 202$n$9; as "gold digger" 99; "Lady of pleasure" as 55; *see also* dancing ladies
courtly love 168; carol as rebuttal of 59
courtly woman 117
Coverdale, Miles 198$n$11
Cromwell, Oliver 129
Crossbones Garden 199$n$5
crows *see* rooks
cuckoldry 173

cuckoo's egg (referring to something innocent looking but lethal) 27
Cumean Sybil 172–173; *see also* Michelangelo
*cunny see* cunt
*Cunny Thumb'd* (slang) 214
cunt: *cunny* as slang for 214$n$3; fig imagery and 173, 214$n$3; Grope Cunt Lane, Oxford 199$n$4; Grope Cunt Street, London **115**; Gropecunt Lane, Cheapside 199$n$4; Gropecunt roads (assorted) 199$n$4; Shakespeare's Hero pronounced as "her-O" as slang for 203$n$15; stinking 210$n$23; worthlessness of 173; *see also* pussy; vagina; vulva
Cupid's bow 152
Cupid's butt-shaft 212$n$36, 213$n$36; *see also* anal sex
cygnet 103; *see also* swans

dairy at Versailles 211$n$29
dairy farming 94
dairy maids 171; *see also* maids
dance and dancing: Brueghel's depiction of 87; *carol* and *carole* as reference to pagan dance song 21–24, 61, **117**; "dirty dancing" 22, 24, 192$n$1; fornication and submission tied to 55; health and wellbeing linked to 188$n$12; lavolta 53, **53**; pagan 42; pagan round dances, Christmas carols and 17; ringdance (carol) 23, 25, 130; sexual activity invoked by 52, 53; street 50; wild 85; *see also* circle dance
"dancing ladies" 29, 55, 138; obsolete and ribald associations tied to 61; as sexually active 55, 56, 59; *see also* "twelve ladies dancing" in *Twelve Days of Christmas*
"dancing with her heels" (slang for energetic sex) 54, 76, 88
Dante Alighieri: *Divine Comedy* 171
Decius (Emperor) **58**
"Deck the Halls" (drinking song; carol) 16, 46; "gay apparel" of 16
Decker, Andrew 191$n$9, 204$n$3, 209$n$10
defloration, lordly privilege of 62; *see also* virginity
Dickens, Charles 190$n$3, 214$n$1; *A Christmas Carol* 48–49, 179–184, 215$n$9; "Christmas Festivities" (short story) 45–46; "A Christmas Tree" (short story) 155; Scrooge (character

225

# Index

of) 48, 179–184, 215$n$8, 215$n$11; sympathies for the indigent *185*; turkey-eating promoted by 111
*Divine Comedy* (Dante) 171
double-entendres 14, 54, 68, 99, 159, 163, 187$n$2, 203$n$15
double-meanings 131, 139, 149, 187$n$2
doublespeak 3
dove as simile or metaphor: in Chaucer 151; as fall guy 206$n$5; as fidelity and love 152; as gaming fool 206$n$2; as guileless patsy 151; in *Hamlet* (Shakespeare) 151; as Holy Spirit 152, 206$n$5; as innocent or simpleton 151; "lovey-dovey" 160; meaning of two (a pair) 153; as messengers of peace 206$n$5; Noachian 206$n$1; as symbols of fidelity 152; as symbols of pagan fecundity 152; in *Taming of the Shrew* (Shakespeare) 151
doves 111, 138, 150–153; in Bible (*Genesis*) 206$n$1, 206$n$5; as birds of Venus 103; Collared Dove of England 152, 207$n$7; Noah and 206$n$1, 206$n$5; Ringdoves 150; Rock-dove 150; Rock pigeon also known as 150; striped neck of 207$n$7; *see also* pigeons; turtle doves
drinking and drunkenness 35, 37, 39, 62; bellowing of obscenities and 92; caroling and 110, 200$n$14; "drunk as a lord" (slang for complete intoxication) 65–66; kermis-day 87; making birds drunk (forced inebriation of birds) 201$n$17; moderate or in moderation 65; by peasants 79–80
*droit du seigneur, droit de cuissage* 192$n$3
Druids 208$n$2
drum and fife 73, *85*
drumming: clitoral 99; drum as vulva/vagina 213$n$36; eroticism of 67–70; *see also* masturbation; "ten drummers drumming"
drunkards 57, 59, 62, 148; Borcht's depiction of 88; Breughel's depiction of *75*
drunken women: "geese-a-laying" as reference to 120, 121
Dudley, Robert *53*
Dylan, Bob 5

eagle 137
ecclesiastics 21, 128; Christmas as season of 195$n$9
effeminacy 103
"eight maids-a-milking" in *Twelve Days of Christmas* 91–100; as innocence 104; tamed nature evoked by 101, 102
ejaculation: female 196$n$13; Hamlet's lack of mastery over 212$n$36; male 99
"eleven lords a-leaping" in *Twelve Days of Christmas* 8, 191$n$13, 62–66; "leaping" as intensifier of "lord" 102, 109; peculiarity of line 29–30; as reference to sexually mounting 9, 11; sexual depravity of 66; socio-sexual connotations of 59; six prostitutes (geese a-laying) mirrored by 118; vulgarity of phrase 109; *see also* leaping; Leaping Lords
elf *see* Santa Claus
Eliot, T.S. 200$n$12
Eliot, William Greenleaf 200$n$12
Elizabeth I (Queen of England) 25, 52; beer for breakfast consumed by 88; rejection of royal Spanish suitor by 213$n$36, 214$n$3; in *Richard III* (Shakespeare) 208$n$5; *La Volta* dance, fondness for 52, *53*
Elizabethan age: carol's loss of popularity during 24–25; fart, types of 168; ribaldry in Shakespearean productions of 10
Elizabethan English 160, 209$n$15
Elizabethan prostitute: "goose" as slang for 12, 118; "quail" as slang for 160; *see also* bird imagery and slang; prostitute; whore
Elizabethanism 42
the Epiphany 47, 191$n$9
erotic, erotica, eroticism: aristocracy and 157; carols as 25; drumming as 67, 68; fig tree as 162; homoeroticism 89; medlar tree as 163; milkmaids 95; pan-eroticism 93; same-sex erotic preferences 72; six geese a-laying as being "obviously" erotic 118–119; women as erotic equals of men 70; *see also* pornography
erotic poems 5
eucharist 22
Evelyn, John 65
excommunication (religious) 22

the Fall (biblical) 69
"falling down" as expression referring to mass death 178
Fallows, David 19

# Index

Falstaff, John (Sir) (fictional character) 62, 76, 131
farm girls 99; *see also* milk maids
farmers 59, 59–60, 92, 96, 104, 120, 153; farmer's daughter 95; farmer's wife 171; *see also* agriculture; animal husbandry; *Imbolc*
farms 4, 94, 171, 192; farmstead 95, 101, 153, 171
fart: bagpipe/buttocks 194*n*3; *fartan* or *feortan* (Old English) 161; *fertan* (German) 160; partridge-farts (partridge birds as sources of) 160–162, 168, 213*n*37; *perd* as rootword of 160; *pétillant* (sparking) wine as fart-rooted French word 210*n*18; types of 168; vaginal 168, 174, 213*n*37
Father Christmas **183, 185, 186**
Fauconbridge 146, 204*n*3
"Feast of Fools" **63**, 189*n*5
feasts and feast days 9, 20; Beltine 197*n*7; Celtic 182; Christmas 43, 80, 189*n*4, 195*n*1, 215*n*11; Fooltide 41; harvest-related 37; Imbolc 197*n*7; Lughnasadh 197*n*7; meat consumed in 28, 29, 37, 81; Presentation of Christ in the Temple 191*n*9; religious 39; St. Bridgit 197*n*7; St. George **74**; Scrooge's memories of 180; village 80; wedding 130; wintertime or mid-winter 81, 91, 153
fellatio 76; *see also* blow job; oral sex
Fellini, Federico 190*n*14
Ferdinand I **164**
*Fertan see* fart
*fica* (Italian; slang for vulva) 171; *see also* vulva
fig: as cunt 173; *faire la figue* (obsene gesture) 171; "Fig of Spain" 214*n*3; *see also* cunt
fig tree 162; *see also* fruit trees
*figa* 171, 214*n*3; *Cumean Sybil* putto giving the **173**
Fire of Bel 197*n*7
"The First Nowell" (carol) 190*n*1
"five golden rings" in *Twelve Days of Christmas* 101, 125, **127**, 127–135; fornication and 133–134; infidelity symbolized by 129; Puritan rejection of wearing of 129; Yuletide sexuality associated with 201*n*5; Yuletide singing about marriage and 129, 132
Fleiss, Heidi 140; *see also* madam(es); whoremasters

"flipping the bird" (slang for "Fuck You!") 173; *see also* fuck and fucking
flora and fauna 159
flowers 116; erotic symbolism of 206*n*1, 210*n*21; sexual innuendo of 116–117
Fool: asses and 41, 189*n*6; Christmas Fool 41; *see also* "Feast of Fools"
Foolishness 112, 115
Fool's Tide, Fooltide 41, 62; *see also* Yuletide
Foote, Samuel 206*n*2
Forberg, Friedrich Karl 202*n*13
foreplay: dancing as 192*n*1; female 99; male 72; romantic 52; sexual 69
forfeits (game of) 124, 154, 175, 177, 182, 191*n*8, 191*n*9; memory feats of gibberish lists associated with 110; playing and singing 47–49; as reward-song akin to beer pong 38
fornication 11; "chambering" as euphemism for 34; Christmas festivities associated with 43, 137, 169, 215*n*11; criminalization of 173; "dance" as euphemism for 55; open-air **86, 87**; unconcealed 133; *see also* "chambering"; foreplay; fucking; leaping; screwing; sex
four calling birds 137–153; *see also* "calling birds"
"fowl": as Christmas food 102; eating of 102; as specifically referencing hawks and herons 137
fowling (bird catching) 139; as euphemism for looking for girls 139
France, Jean de **58**
Franklin, Benjamin 202*n*10, 206*n*3
the French 145
French aristocracy 52
the French Disease (reference to venereal disease) 205*n*4
French gout (slang for venereal disease) 147, 205*n*4
"French" hens 112; *see also* three French hens
French language: Anglo-Norman 145; *carole* 21; old French 103; spoken in England 144; *la volte* 53
"French leave" (slang for going AWOL) 205*n*7
French pig (slang for venereal bubo) 147
French pigeon (reference to pheasant killed by mistake during partridge season) 205*n*5
French pox (venereal disease) 147, 205*n*6

227

# Index

French vice (euphemism for sexual vices of all kinds) 205*n*5
"Frenchified" (slang for venereal disease) 147, 204*n*4
the Frenchman (slang for venereal disease) 147
Freud, Sigmund 194*n*3
fruit, imagery of: "apple-shaped" woman 162; *Ruby-fruit Jungle* (Brown), sexual association of; "unripe" as reference to not-yet-jaded whore/goose 122; *see also* fig; medlar, pear
fruit trees, imagery of: "juniper tree/June apple tree" 211*n*28; as reference to sexualized female anatomy 164; as slang for female pelvic region 174; *see also* apple tree; fig tree; pear tree
fruitfulness 105; dove as symbol of 152
fuck and fucking: by dancing ladies of *Twelve Days* 59; euphemisms in *Twelve Days* 122; fertility rites and 134; "figo" as Italian slang for "fuck you!" 214*n*3; "flipping the bird" as slang for "Fuck You!" 173; "fucked up" as SNAFU 193*n*8; lordly, in *Twelve Days* 62, 118; "partridge in a pear tree" as euphemism for the results of good athletic fucking 168; quest for 81; by the "six geese/prostitutes" in *Twelve Days* 118; in as vulgar expletive 66; Webster's *Duchess of Malfi* 10; *see also* copulation; fornication; leaping; screwing; sex

"Gadzooks!" (slang) 212*n*33
Galileo 107
galliard 53, 192*n*2
game birds 159, 161
games: chess 64; dicing or shooting craps 55; drinking 38, 182; erotic word games 119; festivals and 90; hide and seek 91; "hot cockles" 124; tavern 48; *see also* forfeits
gander (male goose) 103, 112; *see also* geese and goose
Gauls 112, 198*n*1
geese and goose: anthropomorphic attributes of 122; barnyard guarding behavior of 112; Christmas goose 111; edibility of 111; festival of the goose 198*n*1; gander (male goose) 103, 112; as general name for webbed-footed bird 111; gosling 112, 211*n*27; in urban settings 96

geese and goose in figures of speech: "a-laying" (as erotic or sexual acts) 118–119; "a-laying" (figurative, as in singing) 18, 121, 124; "a laying" (as girls of loose morals) 120, 121; "a-laying" (literal, as in laying eggs) 123–124; as boisterous or loose women 120, 124, 130; "green goose" as reference to a goddess 12, 122; "green goose" as reference to fresh young whore 12; as reference to foolhardy, foolish, or rash females 112, 115; as reference to prostitute or whore 12, 113–115, 118, 120, 122, 211*n*27; as reference to simpleton 112; as reference to venereal disease 10, 12; as term of endearment 12; "Winchester goose" as reference to Southwark prostitutes 12–13, 116, 185, 187*n*6, 198*n*4; *see also* prostitute; six geese a-laying in *Twelve Days of Christmas*
gelid (jelly) 28
*gelu* (frost or cold) 28
*Genesis*, book of 61, 192*n*1, 194*n*1, 206*n*1, 206*n*5
*The Gentleman's Magazine* 65
George V 44
German and Germanic cultural practices: Christmas tree associated with 208*n*2, 208*n*3; Kindsfuß 29; language 28; Martineau's work in 208*n*2; midwinter festival 189*n*5
Gervaise of Tilbury 207*n*2
getting laid *see* laying, to lay, meanings of
Globe theatre 118
"God's wounds" 212*n*33
golden rings *see* five golden rings
Gomme, Alice Bertha 191*n*8
Gomme, Sir George Laurence E. 191*n*8
goose *see* geese and goose
Goose of Winchester *see* Winchester Goose
Goose Riding (activity) 200*n*17
gosling 112, 211*n*27; *see also* geese and goose
graves: "to lay" as reference to burial in 126; rituals and practices of 126
Graves, Robert 41, 189*n*6
Great Fire of 1666 **115**
the Great Pox 205*n*6
Greek Orthodox Church 197*n*6
Greene, Graham 199*n*10
greenery decorations, forbidding of 208*n*2

## Index

greenery in nature 105
greenhorn 122
*Greensleeves* (Medieval song) 177, 214–215*n*4
Greer, Germaine 93
Grey-Hen 148; *see also* birds; hen
Grise, Jehan de **63**
groom (male betrothed) 201–202*n*5
Grope Cunt Street **115**
Grose, Francis 200*n*17
Groundhog Day 197*n*6, 197*n*7
grouse: Ruffled Grouse 159
Guinea hen 149; *see also* birds; hen

Hamilton (Archbishop) 34
*Hamlet* (Shakespeare) 116–117, 151
handfasting 201*n*5; *see also* marriage
harlot 66; common 18; *see also* common woman; streetwalker; whore
Harrison, William 189*n*10
Heath-cock 149; *see also* birds; hen
Heath-Hen 149; *see also* birds; hen
heels: "cooling their heels" (redoubled efforts in dancing) 99; "dancing with one's heels" (energetic sex) 54, 76; "kicking one's heels" (waiting in attendance for someone) 55
Hefner, Hugh 143
Heine, Heinrich 208*n*3
Helena (Princess of Mecklenburg) 208*n*2
Hen 111, 138; as female chicken 102; "French" 112; as slang for bed-partner 143; *see also* chicks; cock; three French hens
hen-pecked 149
Henderson, Joseph 211*n*31
*Henry* (plays) *see* Shakespeare
Henry II 187*n*6
Henry VII 188*n*6
Henry VIII 188*n*6, 198*n*4, 201*n*4
hermits *see* St. Paul the Hermit
Hoefnagel, Joris **164**
Holland 205*n*6
*Holland's Leaguer* **77**
Holy Scripture 9
Holy Trinity 152
homoeroticism 89
homosexuality: in Antiquity 195*n*11; "ring" imagery suggestive of 202*n*13
hookers 118, 122, 123, 160; *see also* harlots; streetwalkers; whores
Hopkins, John Henry, Jr. 15
humors, bodily 188*n*12

hunters and hunting 159, 160, 161; hunter-gathering 159
Husk, William Henry 47, 49
hustler 122
Hutterites 190*n*9

"I Heard the Bells on Christmas Day" (carol) 16
Imbolc (feast of purification) 197*n*7
inalienable rights 180
indecency 14; of carols 10, 14; of dancing 55; old time 124; of pastimes catalogued in *Twelve Days of Christmas* 44, 134, 160, 187*n*1; of pipers piping 76; *see also* lewdness; obscene, obscenities; smut, smuttiness
infidelity 36, 129, 163, 173; *see also* bastard; cuckold
innuendo *see* sexual innuendo
*I've Been Working on the Railroad* (song) 68–69; history and origins of 193–194*n*1

*Jack Juggler* (children's music) 197*n*5
Janus 214*n*2
jargon: archaic or antiquated 3, 54; as means to conceal 11; sexual 102; of *Twelve Days of Christmas* 3–4, 12, 91, 109, 136; *see also* cant
Jeremiah, book of 207*n*2
"Jingle Bells" (carol) 15
Joan of Arc 98
Joanna I of Castile (Joanna the Mad) **78**
John (King) *see* *King John* (Shakespeare)
John, Gospel of 11, 206*n*5
"Johns" (slang for clients of prostitutes) 140
Johnson, Samuel: *Dictionary of the English Language* 112
Jones, Inigo 195*n*9
Jonson, Ben 10, 190*n*9; *The Alchemist* 42, 99, 189*n*8
Joseph of Arimathea 207*n*2

Kahn, Michael 9
karma 206*n*3
Kerk-mass (Scottish) 85
kermis (Flemish) 85, 87–88
Key, Francis Scott 194*n*2
kid-skin leather *see* cheveril
kids (i.e., a juvenile goat, as slang for children) 137
Kindsfuß (gift) 29
King James Bible 9, 198*n*11

# Index

*King John* (Shakespeare) 139
kink 79, 213*n*27

lactation 95, 96, 99, 104
"ladies' dancing," meaning of 55–56; *see also* "dancing with her heels"; "twelve ladies dancing"
"Ladies' fever" (slang for syphilis) 55
lady: as courtesan or mistress 55; Lady as female member of Royal family 56; as lady luck 55; lewd imagery of 56; as mistress of the house 56; screwing by or of 56
"Lady-feats" (slang for "bout of venery") 55
"lady-love" 59
"lady of pleasure" (slang for courtesan or mistress) 55; *see also* courtesan; harlot; whore
"Lady of the Lake" (slang for kept mistress) 55
laid *see* laying, to lay, meanings of
lamb (as reference to a human female) 151
lambing season 104, 197*n*7
Lampedusa, Giuseppe di 210*n*24
*Larousse Gastronomique* 164
lavolta (dance) 52, 53, **53**, 192*n*1, 192*n*3
Lawner, Lynne 211*n*30
lay (a lyric poem intended to be sung) 121
lay (a song) 18; as *lied* (German song) 121
lay or lay person (as person contradistinguished from clergy) 119, 120
laying, to lay, meanings of: as "bringing to bed" or giving birth 123; as burying in the grave 123; as "getting laid" 119; as laying eggs 123; as laying in wait (for customers, for food) 122; as loudly singing 121; as resting 123; as sexual pejorative 199*n*10; as sexual term 199*n*10; as taking to bed in the sense of having sex 199*n*10; word games involving 121; *see also* six geese a-laying
"Leap-Christians" 64; *see also* Christians
leap day 63
leap-ore 64
"leaping" (as reference to a male in the act of sexually mounting or screwing) 9–11, 128, 143, 175; 192*n*1, 193*n*8; by husbands 62; Shakespeare's use of 187*n*1, 187*n*2; *see also* chambering; fornication; fucking; sex

leaping house (brothel) 62, **64**; *see also* brothel; whorehouse
Leaping Lords 9–12; English national identity and 145; peasantry's misery on account of 65; sexual access of 62; sexual depravity of 62–66; sexual prerogatives of 62; *see also* eleven lords a-leaping
Leda (mythological) 103
Lesbos, Island of 147
*Leviticus* 206*n*1
levity 129, 195*n*8
lewdness 10–11, 57; of carols 14, 18, 21, 37; "chambering" associated with 35; of Christmas holiday 17, 43–44, 133; forfeit songs and 48; of mid-winter festivals 39; of *Modranicht* 32; peasant culture and 80; purple orchids as signifier of 117; of *Twelve Days of Christmas* 50, 56–57, 59, 70, 76–80, 118, 149, 163, 170, 174, 176–177; *see also* indecency; obscene, obscenities; smut, smuttiness
lied *see* lay (a song)
livestock 94, 171, 192*n*2, 195*n*7
Locke, John 181
Lomax, Alan 191*n*5
London: Agas Map 115, **115**, **116**; coffee houses in 88; edicts of 1334 prohibiting wearing of false beards 33; English Renaissance 17; forfeits game played in 47; modern 7–9; plague in 1660s 190*n*8; *Remonstrance Against Christmas*, shopkeeper protests against 41; repeal of 1681 law banning Christmas festivities 133; stews (brothels) 98; Victorian 40–41
London Bridge **114**
"London Bridge Is Falling Down" 178, 198*n*3
London Brothel, a leaping house, interior **64**
London dialect 145
London Eye 113
Longfellow, Henry Wadsworth 16
Louis XV 211*n*29
Louis XVI 211*n*29
Love Lane Street, London **115**
*Loves Labors Lost* (Shakespeare) 12, 122, 212*n*36
lovesick 163m 205*n*6
Lugh (god) 197*n*7
Lughnasadh, feast of 197*n*7; *see also* feasts and feast days

## Index

lust 57, 107, 188, 127; lusty women 12; *see also* leaping lords
lute 69

Madame de Pompadour 211*n*29
madam(es) 52, 140, 147, 211*n*27; *see also* whoremasters
magic: carols' relationship to 22, 44; emblems of 210*n*20; religion and 190*n*13; reverse 54; *see also* witches and witchcraft
*The Magic Mountain* (Mann) 179
magic password: "Open Sesame" 9
magician 26, 88, 178
maid, maidens: barmaids **85**; "cold" (as sexual duds) 116, 117; dairy 171; "dilettante" as 141; as female attendant 99; maid-servant 99; maiden aunt 98; as man who abstains from intercourse 97; medlars imagined as 163; nursemaids 95; "old maid" as spinster 97; as reference to unmarried woman 97; springtime 51; "virgin" as 98; "young birds or animals" as 138; *see also* eight maids a-milking; milkmaids
Maid Marian 98, 196*n*10
*Maid of Bath* (Foote) 206*n*2
Maid of Orleans (Joan of Arc) 98
maiden name 97
maidenhead 66, 98; "pole" tax on 192*n*3; *see also* droit du seigneur
maidenhood (spinsterhood) 98, 196*n*9
maids-a-milking *see* eight maids-a-milking in *Twelve Days of Christmas*; milk
Malthus, Thomas 180–181
mammals 94, 96
mammary glands 97; *see also* breasts
Mann, Thomas 179
March Beer *see* Bavarian Märzen (March Beer)
Mardi Gras, New Orleans 120
Marie Antoinette 211*n*29, 211*n*30
marriage: Christian 127; Church's overseeing of 126, 128, 134; forbidden to be performed during Christmas seasons 129; gold rings and 126; mid-winter 132; Puritan 130, 133; Roman Catholic 130; seasonal associations of 132; temporary 128; Yuletide 128, 132; Yuletide singing about 129; *see also* handfasting; the wed; wedlock
Martin of Braga (Archbishop) 208*n*2
Martineau, Harriet 208*n*2

Martinez, Ursula 203*n*17
Mary mother of Christ *see* Virgin Mary
Mary queen of Scots 213*n*36
Mass (Catholic) 22; Christmas 22
mass death 178; *see also* Black Plague
mass media 17
Massachusetts: Christmas as state holiday in 215*n*11
Massachusetts Bay Colony 41, 133
massage 68
Massinger, Philip 139
masturbation: female 68, 69; mutual 202*n*13; "stretching the pipe" as euphemism for 76
Mather, Cotton 43, **43**
Mather, Increase 43
Matres (Celtic goddesses of fertility) 32, 105
Maximus of Turin 31
Mayne, Jasper 10
McCartney, Paul *see* The Beatles
McCrystal, Cal 203*n*17
McGillis, Kelly 9
medlar fruit **164**; edibility of 164, 210*n*24; *open arse* as slang for 162; sexual imagery associated with 162–164, 210*n*24; as slang for vulva or vagina 163
medlar tree 163, 164
Meese Report 89
Memorial of Symmachus 198*n*1
Mennonites 190*n*9
*Merchant of Venice* (Shakespeare) 131
Michelangelo di Ludovico Buonarroti 172; *Cumean Sybil* and detail **172, 173**
*Midsummer Night's Dream* (Shakespeare) 152
milk: as noun or transitive verb 94; split milk 93; symbolic possibilities of maids and 196*n*10; *see also* breasts; dairy; lactation
"milk the ram" (slang for "doomed to failure) 94
milkmaids: dairy farming and 93–95; implied innocence of 104; Marie Antoinette's playing at 211*n*29; pastoralism of 101, 102; as potential erotic playmates 95; sexual availability of 96
Minerva (goddess) 197*n*7
minstrels 59, 74, 121
*Mira calligraphiae monumenta* **164**
miracle cures 190*n*13
miracle plays 39, 85

# Index

mirror-images 55, 72, 106, 107, 135, 209*n*15
mirror-world 119
mirrored rooms 166; bedroom of Marie Antoinette 211*n*29, 211*n*30; Hall of Mirrors, Versailles 166
mirrors 166, 211*n*29; use in sex games 165
misrule 31, 84, 147, 182; Christmas 37; King of Misrule 212*n*35; Lord of Misrule 62, 169; Master of Misrule 133, 134; Yuletide 127
moderation *see* drinking
*Modranicht* ("Mother Night") 32
monolingualism 204*n*3
Moor-Hen 149; *see also* birds; chicken; hen
*Moor of Venice (Othello)* 61, 187*n*2
Mother Earth (as earth-goddess) 32, 105
motherhood 95, 98, 104
Mozart, Wolfgang Amadeus 15
*Much Ado About Nothing* (Shakespeare) 73, 187*n*1
mugging 42
mummery 42
mumming 32, 33, 215*n*11
Murphy, Gerald 210*n*21
mushrooms and mushrooming 159

Naples canker (slang for venereal disease) 47, 205*n*6; *see also* venereal disease
the nativity 31, 40, 132; *Songs of the Nativity* (Husk) 47
Newton, Isaac 107, 200–201*n*17
"nine pipers piping" in *Twelve Days of Christmas* 30, 74, 114; drinking songs connected to 113–114; "drummers" (of "ten drummers drumming") sexually contrasted to 213*n*36; lewdness implied by 76; *see also* pipes and piping
Nissenbaum, Stephen 1, 189*n*9
Noah 206*n*1, 206*n*5
Nowell [Noel] *see* "The First Nowell" (carol)
Nurse *see* Romeo and Juliet
nursery rhyme: "A Pie Sat on a Pear Tree" 209*n*7; 'Une Peridriole' 209*n*7; *see also* "Ring Around a Rosy"
nursing 95–96; wet-nursing 95
Nycholson, James 198*n*11

"O Little Town of Bethlehem" (carol) 16

obscene, obscenities 3, 4, 42; of ancient festivals 203*n*17; caroling as 55, 92, 167, 189*n*10; class-specific 157; gestures 171; "Lady-feats" 55; ring-dancer's performance of obscene songs 130; Shakespearean 10; of *Twelve Days of Christmas* 14, 175, 176, 200*n*14; *see also* indecency; lewdness; smut, smuttiness
Odin 182, 189*n*5
Ophelia (fictional character) 121, 212*n*36; *see also* Hamlet
oral sex 76, 77, 79; *see also* blow job; fellatio; pipes and piping
orgasm 72, 92, 108
orgy: drunken 39; mid-winter 80; 'ring' as euphemism for 131, 171n 202*n*12; 202*n*13
*Othello (Moor of Venice)* (Shakespeare) 61, 187*n*2, 194*n*3

pagan and paganism: afterlife, versions of 36; calendar 32; carol (English) and *carol* (French and Anglo-Norman) associated with 17, 21–23, 25; Christmas understood as assimilated pagan holiday 39–40; clan loyalty 207*n*6; customs attached to Christmas 31; dancing 42; in England 188*n*6; fecundity of 152, 197*n*6; fertilization festivals of 105; folkways 4; generosity 184; gift-giving associated with 33; gods 207*n*6; holidays 128; holly leaves 16; Imbolc festival 197*n*7; joy of 34, 197*n*6; Plough Monday of 105; rites 198*n*1; Rome and 29; round dances associated with 16; Saturnalia 30; sexual rites of 83; shrines 207*n*6; Virgin Mary as banisher of 54; "wed" of 127; yule (noun) or juul (noun) associated with 28; Yuletide associated with 28, 41
Palmer, Roy 207*n*1
Papistry 25 39
Parliament: Act of 1644 40; adultery outlawed in 1650 by 173; Boxing Day created in 1871 by 189*n*4; *Remonstrance Against Christmas* 1652 presented to 41; repeal in 1656 of Cromwell's strictures regarding quiet marriages 129
*Parliament of Love* (Massinger) 139
Parliamentarians 136
parson *see* "Patrico"
Pasteur, Louis 148

# Index

"Patrico" or "Pater Cove" (slang for minister or parson) 201$n$3
Partridge, Eric 3, 213$n$36
partridge imagery and slang: as reference to "reverse anal cowgirl" sexual position 213$n$37; as reference to vaginal fart 168, 213$n$37; as slang for prostitute 159–160; as symbol of lack of faith 209$n$10
"partridge in a pear tree" in *Twelve Days of Christmas* 30, 125, 153–169, 209$n$7, 211$n$28; bowdlerization of phrase as "juniper tree/June apple tree" 211$n$28; deciphering of meaning of 154, 155; as euphemism for results of a good athletic fucking 168; as garbled version of *parturivit in apertis* ("gave birth in the open") 209$n$11
partridges: partridge (*perdrix*)-farts 160–162, 168, 213$n$37; perdreau (young partridge) 209$n$7; Red Leg Partridge 209$n$9; roosting capabilities of 159; stealing of eggs by 209$n$10; verse to be sung as "all in the bareley" 207$n$1
"Patapan" (French carol) 190$n$1
peacock 149; peacock's tail 196$n$7
peahen 149
pear: as surrogate for vagina 210$n$21; as symbol of fertility 162; *Wasp and Pear* (Murphy) 210n
"pear-colored" (as the color red) 166
pear-shaped: musical instruments as analogies for women's bodies 69; women's bodies as being 156, 162
pear tree: as erotic feminine symbol 162; as female 162; as person 156; as sexual reference 157; *see also* partridge in a pear tree
peasant dances 24; Breughel's depiction of *74–75, 87*–88
peasants 37–38, 40, 42, 57, 65–66; agricultural 59; lustiness of 79–80; pipes as common property of 73; politics of 60; St. Paul the Hermit 58
pecker (slang for penis) 138; *see also* penis
pederasts 90
peepshows 166
Pelham, Peter 43
penis: bagpipe-as-penis *78*, 194$n$3; as "cock" 103, 138; double-entendres terms for 163; "flipping the bird" as surrogate 173; "milking" of 213$n$39; pear tree (of *Twelve Days of Christmas*) as 157, 165; as pecker 138; pipes as penis 89; prick as slang for 76; "priest's penis" as slang for purple orchid 117; slang words for 163; "stretching his pipe" (slang for male masturbation) 76, 114; sucking of 76; as tree trunk 157, 165

Pepin the Short *127*
*Pericles, Prince of Tyre* (Shakespeare) 147, 208$n$5, 211$n$27
phallic: fruit 164; imagery 187$n$2; play 76
phallus: linga-phallus of Shiva *78*
Picasso, Pablo 210$n$21
Pierpont, the Rev. John 15
pigeons: as distinct from dove 151; "dove" as reference to English pigeons of all varieties 150; "French," as reference to a pheasant mistakenly killed during partridge season 205$n$5; in *Genesis* 206$n$1; in *Leviticus* as sacrifice 206$n$1; in *Luke* (Gospel of) 206$n$1; making pigeons drunk 201$n$17; passenger 46; Rock Pigeon 150
pimps 18, 115; in *Parliament of Love* (Massinger) 139
pipers 82, 84, 90; in *Peasant Dance* (Breughel) *75*; piping pipers 76; as soloists 171; as strolling musicians 73
pipes and piping (instrument playing) 71–76, 78; ardent associations of sound of 72; bagpipe-as-penis *78*, 194$n$3; bagpipes 75, *78*, *87*; in *Circle Dance* (Borcht) *85, 86*; circle dancing to sound of *117*; clay tobacco 88; feasting and 81–90; food associations of 81; homoerotic suggestiveness of 89; martial connections to sound of 73; penis as 89, 213$n$36; pipes of pan 73; "Pistol" as reference to 76; sexual symbolism of 76, *78*; Shakespeare's mention of 73; "stretching his pipe" (slang for masturbation) 76, 114
"piping hot," food and sexual references of 90
Plough Monday 105
point-of-view (POV) style videos 166
Pollock, Jackson 211$n$31
pornocopia 92
pornography (porn), pornographic 5, 34, 145; carols' use of imagery 76, 83; collectors of 167; early 60; folk- 177; Meese Report 89; modern 157; monotony of 139; movie loops 166
*pornos* 34

# Index

Porter, Cole 22, 210n21
prick (slang for penis) 76
priest and priesthood: hedge-priests 128; lay-priest 120; loathing of carols 25, 119; pagan songs, attempts to extirpate 22–23
"priests' penis" 117
promiscuity 43, 160; *see also* wanton, wantonness
prostitutes: Southwark 12–13, 113; streetwalkers 122; "Winchester Goose" as slang for 12–13, 187n6; *see also* "geese a laying"; harlots; quail
Protestants and Protestantism 129, 136, 207; Church of England 104; English 25; gauges of fate 206n 3; objections to caroling 25–26, 104; veneration of symbols shared with Catholicism 207n6; views of Christmas 39–40
psychoanalytic drawing *see* Pollock, Jackson
pubic hair 138; "bird's nest" as slang for 138, 165
public torture *see* torture as entertainment
pudenda 138
Punxsutawney, Philadelphia 197n6; *see also* Groundhog Day
Purification of the Blessed Virgin festival 191n9
Puritans 10, 41, 133–134, 136, 215n11
pussy (as insult directed at a man) 149, 205n10, 210n23
"pussy cat" (as darling kitten) 205n10

quail 159; partridge-like 160; as slang for prostitute 160
Quainton Thorn 207n2
Queer Theory 195n11
quiet marriages 129

Radical Reformation 190n9
"railroad song" *see* I've Been Working on the Railroad (song)
Raimondi, Marcantonio 5, 167
Ravel, Maurice 67
Reagan, Ronald 215n8
red *see* "pear-colored"
*Remonstrance Against Christmas* 1652 41
Restoration of 1660 41
rhyming slang 187n4; *see also* cant
ribaldry: of Christmas (Old Christmas) 34, 41, 70, 111; criminalization of singing ribald songs 18, 89; "French" associated with 143; rhyming slang and 187n4; Shakespearean 10, 163; social-class specific 157
ring (as euphemism for vulva) 131, 163
ring (as shorthand for orgy) 131, 202n12, 202n13
"Ring Around a Rosie" (dittie) 178
ring-dance, ring dancers 23, 25, 130; *see also* circle dance
ring doves 152
rings *see* five golden rings
Robin Hood 98, 214n4
"Robin Hood's Birth, Breeding, Valor, and Marriage" (penalty song) 38
Robinson, Jane 18, 19–20, 89
Roman Catholicism 25
*Romance of Alexander* **63**
*Romeo and Juliet* (Shakespeare) 113–115, 138, 158, 167n2, 202n13, 202n14; Mercutio 113–115, 163–164, 199n6, 205n7; Nurse 138; Romeo and whoring 199n6
rooks (crows) 206n2
Rossiaud, Jacques 188n7, 204n4, 213n39, 214n4
Rudolph II **164**
the Runes 189n4
Rykener, John 212n35

St. Ambrose 111–112
St. Augustine 198n1
St. Brigit 197n7
St. George **74**; flag associated with **75**
St. Paul, conversion of 182
St. Paul the Hermit **58**
St. Patrick 188n6, 197n7
St. Patrick's Day 85
Saint Paul *see* St. Paul the Hermit
Santa Claus (Santa) 1, 32, 173, **183**, 215n11; *see also* Father Christmas
Saturnalia 30–33, 41, 178; Boxing Day boxes reminiscent of 188n4; candles associated with 182; fertility rites associated with 134; gift-giving during 32; influence on *Twelve Days of Christmas* 67; pre–Christian and Christian opposition to 39, 136; raunchy atmosphere of 33
Scot or Scott, Sir John 193n9
Scott, Charles 196n5
Scott, Sir Walter 112, 215n4
Scottish folk tradition 197n7
screwing (slang for having sex) 11, 54,

234

# Index

57, 141, 150; *see also* chambering; fornication; fucking; leaping; sex
Scrooge *see* Dickens, Charles
Sears, Edward Hamilton 15
Secker, the Rev. William 130
Senones *see* Gauls
Sermon on the Mount 190$n$9
Sessions, Kirk 18
"seven swans a-swimming" in *Twelve Days of Christmas* 104, 108–109, 125–126, 138; implying women faint with pleasure 108; *see also* swans
sex and sexuality: dancing connected to/denotatively identical to 52, 53, 54; drinking and 37; extra-marital 130; folk-hero's search for 81; folklore and 80–81; gratified lust 80; heterosexual intercourse 57; marriage-authorized 130; music and music-making associated with 69; pagan mid-winter rites and 83; pan-sexual release 90; social breakdown and 60; survival and 44; unwise 60; *see also* anal sex; carnality; chambering; copulation; foreplay; fornication; fucking; homosexuality; oral sex; orgasm; screwing; wanton, wantonness
sex trade 185; *see also* common woman; John; madam(es) pimp; prostitute; whore; whoremaster; Winchester Goose
sexual consummation 72, **87**, 99, 108, 132; *see also* fucking; screwing; sex
sexual debauchery: chambering and caroling associated with 35; *see also* kink; pederasts
sexual depravity *see* Leaping Lords
sexual deprivation 38, 80
sexual identity 36
sexual innuendo 24, 68; birds and 109
sexual misbehavior 25
sexual molestation 3
sexually available girls *see* bird imagery and slang; chicks; dancing ladies
sexually mounting *see* leaping
Shakespeare, William 3, 4; *Anthony & Cleopatra* 123; bawdy public for plays of 11; "bird's nest" as euphemism for pubic hair 165; Bunting on 145; *Comedy of Errors* 202$n$9; Elizabethanism of 42; "French" as joke in 147, 205$n$7; Globe Theatre 113; "goose" as reference to prostitute 113–114; *Hamlet* 116–117, 151; 1 *Henry IV* 82, 196$n$10;

*Henry IV part* 1 215$n$4; *Henry IV part* 2 **76**, 79; *Henry V* 10, 52, 157; 1 *Henry VI* 115, 147, 199$n$8; 2 *Henry VI* 192$n$3; *Henry VI part* **3 137**; *Henry VIII* 55, 142; *King John* 139; "leaping" as references to sex 187$n$1, 187$n$2; *Loves Labors Lost* 12, 122, 212$n$36; *Merchant of Venice* 131; *Midsummer Night's Dream* 152; modern English's debt to 106; mono-lingual English traveler parodied by 204$n$3; *Much Ado About Nothing* 73, 187$n$1; *Othello (Moor of Venice)* 61, 187$n$2, 194$n$3; parodies before 145; *Pericles, Prince of Tyre* 147, 208$n$5, 211$n$27; "Pistol" character, jokes regarding 89; plays as popular entertainment 53; ribaldry of 10; *Richard III* 56, 156; *Romeo and Juliet* 113–115, 138, 158, 163–164, 167$n$2, 199$n$6, 202$n$14, 205$n$7; smutty jokes made by 91; *Taming of the Shrew* 151; *The Tempest* 210$n$21; *Troilus & Cressida* 115; *Twelfth Night* 97; *Venus and Adonis* 140; vernacular language of his plays as clues to decode *Twelve Days of Christmas* 54, 176; Wheeler (Elizabeth) as family friend of 168
Sharia law 196$n$6
sheep: "wolf in sheep's array [clothing]" 199$n$8
sheep milk 196$n$5, 197$n$7
sheep-shearers 73
"Silent Night" (carol) 16
Silver, Larry 85, 88
sin: deadly 80; old word 41; *Twelve Days of Christmas* as catalog of 80
sinfulness 89, 147; single women and 199$n$5
singlewoman's churchyard 199$n$5; *see also* strumpets
sins of the flesh 98
Sistine Chapel, the Vatican *see* Michelangelo
six geese a-laying in *Twelve Days of Christmas* 110, 125, 126, 170; erotic overtones of imagery of 118–119; femaleness of 103, 112; as representing six foolhardy females 112
Skelton, John 55–56
smut, smuttiness 5, 26, 84; of Christmas carols 14; in Shakespeare 10, 91; of *Twelve Days of Christmas* 150
sociolect 11
sodomites 90

**235**

# Index

solstice *see* Winter Solstice
Sorrentino, Gilbert 213*n*1
Southwark prostitutes 12–13, 113
sparrows 103, 148
spinster 97, 98; *see also* maid
*spinter* (Latin, referring to bracelet worn by Roman women) 202*n*13
Spintries (slang for sexual acts akin to "circle jerk") 202*n*13
stews or stewhouse (slang for brothel) 57, 192*n*7; legal or illegal 92; London 98; Southwark 187*n*6, 198*n*4, 199*n*5; *see also* brothel; whorehouse
Stow, John 199*n*5
streetwalker 17, 122, 187, 212*n*6; transvestite 212*n*35; *see also* prostitute
strumpets 18, 121, 199*n*5; *see also* harlots
subcultures 11–12, 141, 187n*n*4
supernatural 190*n*9; light around infant Christ 158; *see also* magic
swans: as birds of Venus 103; cob (male swan) 103, 148; cygnet (baby swan) 103; swimming by 104, 105, 108–109, 126
swimming *see* swans
swimming-as-sex 103, 105
sybil *see* Cumean Sybil
Symmachus *see* Memorial of Symmachus
syphilis: "goose" as slang for 12; Henry VII's fear of 188*n*6; "Ladies fever" as slang for 55; "Naples canker" as slang for 147; pox as reference to 205*n*4

*Tabulæ Fortunæ* (offering of food and drink) 32
Talvacchia, Bette 211*n*30
*Taming of the Shrew* (Shakespeare) 151
Tchaikovsky, *Nutcracker* ballet 51
Tea Party (US, 20th-century) 215*n*8
teats 94, 99, 104, 196*n*6; *see also* breasts
*The Tempest* (Shakespeare) 210*n*21
"ten drummers drumming" in *Twelve Days of Christmas* 67–70, 191*n*13
Tennyson (Lord) 206*n*2
Tertullian 31
Thatcher, Margaret 215*n*8
theoboros 69
three French hens 7, 49, 125, 143–149, 152; as parody of licentiousness and creative lust 153
torture as entertainment 123–124
Trapp, John 62, 193*n*5

Treveylan, *Life and Letters of Lord Macaulay* 103
*Troilus & Cressida* (Shakespeare) 115
trollop 123; *see also* lady; prostitute
turkey: American 111; Christmas 40, 111; as moron 112; wild 112
Turkey (country) 205*n*6
turtledoves 150; as distinct from pigeon 151, 206*n*1; in as (erroneous) symbols of chaste love 151; *Genesis* 206*n*1; in *Leviticus* as sacrifice 206*n*1; in *Luke* (Gospel of) 206*n*1; as ring dove or ringed-neck dove 152; in *Song of Songs* 206*n*1; as symbols of unchaste love 151–152
*Twelfth Night* (Shakespeare) 97
*Twelve Days of Christmas*: allusions found in 47; American singing of 49; birds of 101–102; as chain-number song 46; as cultural battlefield 136; as English cumulative carol 47; as forfeit (game of) song 48; form of 27; full lyric verses of 7, 49; 3–4, 12, 91, 109, 136; indecency of 44, 134, 160, 187*n*1; lewdness of 50, 56–57, 59, 70, 76–80, 118, 122, 149, 163, 170, 174, 176–177; non-literalness of 29–30; obscenity of 14; pattern of song broken by "five golden rings" line 134–135; popularity in American 130; as pornocopia 92, 139; religious imagery absent from 46–47; sexual saturation of imagery of 72; Shakespeare's language and vernacular as touchstone for decoding 53–54; shamelessness of 134; singers of 122; slang of 11–12; smuttiness of 14; sociolect of 11; whoring and 200*n*14; "X-rating" of 44; *see also* [individual lines]
"twelve ladies dancing" in *Twelve Days of Christmas* 7, 8, 51–60, 185; leaping lords as husbands of 62
"two turtledoves" in *Twelve Days of Christmas* 150–153; *see also* turtledoves
Tynedale, William 105–106, 197–198*n*11

Udall, Nicholas 196*n*5
underworld 3, 4, 24, 123

vagina 163, 168; sounds of 174
vaginal burp or fart 168, 174, 213*n*37; *see also* fart
Valencian II (Christian Emperor) 198*n*1

**236**

# Index

Valois School 53
van der Borcht, Pieter *see* Borcht, Pieter van der
van der Weyden, Rogier *see* Weyden, Rogier van der
venereal disease: "goose" as reference to venereal disease 10, 12; "Naples canker" as slang for 147; *see also* syphilis
venery (i.e. fornication) 55; *see also* fornication
Venice, Italy: Saint Mark's square 150
Venus: doves and turtledoves as birds of 151–152; pleasures of 202*n*13; swans as birds of 103
*Venus and Adonis* (Shakespeare) 140
Veranian, Maurice 2, 160
Versailles, Palace of 166; Hameau de la Reine (Queen's Hamlet) 211*n*29; mill and dairy 211*n*29; Petit Trianon 211*n*29
virgin birth 32, 81; *see also* Virgin Mary
Virgin Mary (the Virgin) 20, 54, **74**; *Book of Hours* of **117**; Brigit as midwife of 197*n*7; impregnation by God of 54; as "Mild Young Virgin" 158; Purification of the Blessed Virgin festival 191*n*9; *Seven Joys of Mary* (song) 46; University Church of St. Mary the Virgin 199*n*4
"A Virgin Most Pure" (broadside) 190
virginity 99, 104, 152; commodity-virginity 213*n*37; defloration 62; teenage prostitute's sale of 122
virgins: damsels who are not 95, 96; "maids of either sexe" 97–98
*la volte see* lavolta
voyeur, voyeurism 68, 99; *see also* kink
vulgar language (obscene) 195*n*12; *see also* obscenities; smut, smuttiness
vulgar tongue (Middle English) 144, 145; *Classical Dictionary of the Vulgar Tongue* (Grose) 201*n*3, 205*n*4
vulgarity 42; modern 187*n*1; sexual 193*n*8; Shakespearean 10, 117, 147; of *Twelve Days of Christmas* 143; winking at 11; *see also* fuck or fucking
vulva: drum as 213*n*36; engorged 166; *fica* as slang term for 171; massage of 68; O shape as reference to 163; "partridge in a pear tree" as reference to 168; pear as surrogate for 210*n*21; "ring" as euphemism for 131, 163; as "shrub" or "bush" 165

wanton, wantonness: caroling associated with 34–35; Christmas associated with fornication and 43; dancing 55; lavolta (dance) associated with 192*n*2; Maid Marian as 196*n*10; ring as symbol of wanton sexuality 126
water: drawing of 88; drinking of 88; holy 190*n*13; swimming in 103, 197*n*5; *see also* bathhouses
water-hen 149
watering down 88
"We Three Kings of Orient Are" (carol) 15
Webster, John 9–10
the wed: pagan 127; "to pledge a sum of money" 202*n*5
wedlock 126–127; *see also* marriage
Weiss, Peter 192*n*9
Wenceslaus of Bohemia ("Good King") 189*n*4
wench 123
wet-nursing *see* nursing
Weyden, Rogier van der 214*n*4
Whitehall Palace 195*n*9
whore 12; ancient Roman 34; arrests of 18; "Doll Tearsheet" as nickname for 76; "geese" as euphemism for 121; Jane Robinson 19; singing of lewd songs by 18–19, 75; *see also* chick; courtesan; goose; harlot; lady; prostitute; strumpet; trollop; wench
whoredom 14, 42
whorehouse 56
whoremaster 13, 140; *see also* madam(es)
whoring 56, 79; Christmas as season of 189*n*10; "London Bridge Is Falling Down" 198*n*3; Romeo's familiarity with 199*n*6; trade 4; *Twelve Days of Christmas*' associations with 200*n*14
Wills, Richard Storrs 15
"Winchester Goose" (slang for prostitute) 12–13, 113, 187*n*6; as "French pig" 147; in 1 *Henry VI* (Shakespeare)115, 147, 199*n*8; *see also* Bishop of Winchester; whore
Winter Solstice 104
witches and witchcraft 23–24; caroling associated with 44, 54, 107, 188*n*6; religion and 190*n*13; Salem Witch Trials 43
womanhood 95, 98, 196*n*10
women of loose morals *see* courtesan;

# Index

geese; harlot; lady; prostitute; strumpet; trollop; wench; whore
Wordsworth  208$n$5

*yule*:  pagan origins of 28–29
Yule day  18; songs of 33; Twelve Day's festival of 31
Yule Log  29
Yuletide  9, 14; carolers 192$n$9; carols 16, 20, 27, 124; Christianization of 28; fertility associated with 57; Fool's Day as substitute for 41; golden rings linked to sexuality at 201$n$5; misrule and social inversion of 62, 93, 133, 169; moral anxiety over 133; social shunning of 89; temporary marriages encouraged at 128, 132; transformation into modern religious Christmas 178; "troll the ancient Yuletide carol" (Dickens) 46

Zerber, Nikola  2, 139
Zeus  103

www.ingramcontent.com/pod-product-compliance
Ingram Content Group UK Ltd.
Pitfield, Milton Keynes, MK11 3LW, UK
UKHW041941140426
5217IPUK00014B/596